The Political Logic of Experience

John D. Caputo, *series editor*

PERSPECTIVES IN
CONTINENTAL
PHILOSOPHY

NEAL DeROO

The Political Logic of Experience
Expression in Phenomenology

FORDHAM UNIVERSITY PRESS
New York ▪ 2022

Fordham University Press has no responsibility for the persistence or accuracy of URLs for external or third-party Internet websites referred to in this publication and does not guarantee that any content on such websites is, or will remain, accurate or appropriate.

Fordham University Press also publishes its books in a variety of electronic formats. Some content that appears in print may not be available in electronic books.

Visit us online at www.fordhampress.com.

Library of Congress Cataloging-in-Publication Data available online at https://catalog.loc.gov.

Printed in the United States of America

24 23 22   5 4 3 2 1

First edition

Contents

Abbreviations

AE   Cressida J. Heyes. *Anaesthetics of Existence: Essays on Experience at the Edge.* Durham, NC: Duke University Press, 2020.

BaS   Alia Al-Saji. "Bodies and Sensings: On the Uses of Husserlian Phenomenology for Feminist Theory." *Continental Philosophy Review* 43, no. 1 (2010): 13–37.

BR   Michael Henry. *Barbarism.* Translated by Scott Davidson. London: Continuum, 2013.

BT   Martin Heidegger. *Being and Time.* Translated by Joan Stambaugh. Albany: State University of New York Press, 1996.

EaM   Maurice Merleau-Ponty. "Eye and Mind." In *The Primacy of Perception*, edited by James M. Edie, translated by Carleton Dallery, 159–90. Evanston, IL: Northwestern University Press, 1964.

EE   Sara Heinämaa. "Embodiment and Expressivity in Husserl's Phenomenology: From *Logical Investigations* to *Cartesian Meditations*." *SATS: Northern European Journal of Philosophy* 11 (2010): 1–15.

EiP   Gilles Deleuze. *Expressionism in Philosophy: Spinoza.* Translated by Martin Joughin. New York: Zone Books, 1992.

EJ	Edmund Husserl. *Experience and Judgement: Investigations in a Genealogy of Logic*. Translated by James Churchill and Karl Ameriks. Evanston, IL: Northwestern University Press, 1973.
EM	Michel Henry. *The Essence of Manifestation*. Translated by G. Etzkorn. Dordrecht: Springer, 1973.
FE	Johanna Oksala. *Feminist Experiences: Foucauldian and Phenomenological Investigations*. Evanston, IL: Northwestern University Press, 2016.
FI	Edmund Husserl. "Foundational Investigations of the Phenomenological Origin of the Spatiality of Nature." In *Philosophical Essays in Memory of Edmund Husserl*, translated by Frederick Kersten, edited by Marvin Farber, 307–25. Cambridge, MA: Harvard University Press, 1940.
FNV	Judith Butler. *The Force of Non-Violence: An Ethico-Political Bind*. New York: Verso, 2020.
HB	Anthony Steinbock. *Home and Beyond: Generative Phenomenology after Husserl*. Evanston, IL: Northwestern University Press, 1995.
Hua 1	Edmund Husserl. *Cartesianische Meditationen und Pariser Vorträge*. Husserliana vol. 1. Edited by S. Strasser. The Hague: Martinus Nijhoff, 1950. *Cartesian Meditations: An Introduction to Phenomenology*. Translated by Dorion Cairns. Dordrecht: Kluwer Academic, 1999.
Hua 3	Edmund Husserl. *Ideen zu einer Phänomenologie und phänomenologischen Philosophie. Erstes Buch: Allgemeine Einführung in die reine Phänomenologie*. Husserliana vol. 3. Edited by W. Biemel. The Hague: Martinus Nijhoff, 1950. *Ideas Pertaining to a Pure Phenomenology and to a Phenomenological Philosophy. Book 1: General Introduction to a Pure Phenomenology*. Translated by F. Kersten. The Hague: Martinus Nijhoff, 1983.
Hua 4	Edmund Husserl. *Ideen zu einer Phänomenologie und phänomenologischen Philosophie. Dreites Buch: Phänomenologische Untersuchungen zur Konstitution*. Ed. W. Biemel. The Hague: Martinus Nijhoff, 1952. *Ideas Pertaining to a Pure Phenomenology and to a Phenomenological Philosophy, Book 2: Studies in the Phenomenology of Constitution*. Translated by Richard Rojcewicz and André Schuwer. Dordrecht: Kluwer Academic, 1989.
Hua 6	Edmund Husserl. *Der Krisis der europäischen Wissenschaften und die transzendentale Phänomenologie: Eine Einleitung in*

die *Phänomenologische Philosophie*. Husserliana vol. 6. Edited by W. Biemel. The Hague: Martinus Nijhoff, 1954. *The Crisis of European Sciences and Transcendental Phenomenology.* Translated by David Carr. Evanston, IL: Northwestern University Press, 1970.

Hua 8   Edmund Husserl. *Erste Philosophie. Zweiter Teil: Theorie der Phänomenologischen Reduktion.* Husserliana vol. 8. The Hague: Martinus Nijhoff, 1959.

Hua 9   Edmund Husserl. *Phänomenologische Psychologie: Vorlesungen Sommersemester 1925.* Husserliana vol. 9. The Hague: Martinus Nijhoff, 1962.

Hua 10   Edmund Husserl. *Zur Phänomenologie des inneren Zeitbewusstseins (1893–1917).* Husserliana vol. 10. Edited by R. Boehm. The Hague: Martinus Nijhoff, 1966. *On the Phenomenology of the Consciousness of Internal Time.* Translated by John Barnett Brough. Dordrecht: Kluwer Academic, 1991.

Hua 11   Edmund Husserl. *Analysen zur passiven Synthesis: Aus Vorlesungs- und Forschungsmanuskripten 1918–1926.* Husserliana vol. 11. Edited by M. Fleischer. The Hague: Martinus Nijhoff, 1966. *Analyses Concerning Active and Passive Synthesis: Lectures on Transcendental Logic.* Translated by Anthony J. Steinbock. Dordrecht: Kluwer Academic, 2001.

Hua 14   Edmund Husserl. *Zur Phänomenologie der Intersubjektivität: Texte aus dem Nachlass. Zweiter Teil. 1921–28.* Husserliana vol. 14. Edited by Iso Kern. The Hague: Martinus Nijhoff, 1973.

Hua 15   Edmund Husserl. *Zur Phänomenologie der Intersubjektivität: Texte aus dem Nachlass. Dritter Teil. 1929–35.* Husserliana vol. 15. Edited by Iso Kern. The Hague: Martinus Nijhoff, 1973.

Hua 17   Edmund Husserl. *Formale und Transzendentale Logik: Versuch einer Kritik der logischen Vernunft. Mit ergänzenden Texten.* Husserliana vol. 17. Edited by P. Janssen. The Hague: Martinus Nijhoff. 1974. *Formal and Transcendental Logic.* Translated by Dorion Cairns. The Hague: Martinus Nijhoff, 1969.

Hua 27   Edmund Husserl. *Aufsätze und Vorträge. 1922–1937.* Husserliana vol. 27. Edited by T. Nenon and H. R. Sepp. The Hague: Kluwer Academic, 1998.

Hua 29   Edmund Husserl. *Die Krisis der europaischen Wissenschaften und die transzendentale Phänomenologie, Ergänzungsband: Texte aus dem Nachlass 1934–1937.* Husserliana vol. 29. Edited by Reinhold N. Smid. The Hague: Kluwer Academic, 1992.

Hua 34   Edmund Husserl. *Zur Phänomenologischen Reduktion: Texte aus dem Nachlass (1926–1935).* Husserliana vol. 34. Edited by Sebastian Luft. Dordrecht: Kluwer, 2002.

Hua 37   Edmund Husserl. *Einleitung in die Ethik: Vorlesung en Sommersemester 1920 und 1924.* Husserliana vol. 37. Edited by Henning Peucker. Dordrecht: Kluwer Academic, 2004.

Hua 39   Edmund Husserl. *Die Lebenswelt: Auslegungen der vorgegebenen Welt und ihrer Konstitution. Texte aus dem Nachlass (1916–1937).* Husserliana vol. 39. Edited by Sowa Rochus. Dordrecht: Springer, 2008.

IOG   Jacques Derrida. *Edmund Husserl's* Origin of Geometry: *An Introduction.* Translated by John P. Leavey. Lincoln: University of Nebraska Press, 1989.

IP   Maurice Merleau-Ponty. *Institution and Passivity: Course Notes from the Collège de France (1954–1955).* Translated by Leonard Lawlor and Heath Massey. Evanston, IL: Northwestern University Press, 2010.

LCF   Maurice Merleau-Ponty. "Themes from the Lectures at the College de France, 1952–1960." In *Praise of Philosophy and Other Essays.* Translated by John O'Neill. Evanston, IL: Northwestern University Press, 1988.

LE   Simo Pulkkinnen. "Lifeworld as an Embodiment of Spiritual Meaning: The Constitutive Dynamics of Activity and Passivity in Husserl." *The Phenomenology of Embodied Subjectivity* 71, edited by R. T. Jensen and Dermot Moran. Cham, Switzerland: Springer, 2013.

LI   Edmund Husserl. *Logical Investigations.* Translated by J. N. Findlay. London and New York: Routledge, 2000.

MHC   Sara Heinämaa, Mirja Hartimo, and Timo Miettinen eds., "Introduction: Methodological, Historical and Conceptual Starting Points." In *Phenomenology and the Transcendental,* 1–18. New York: Routledge, 2014.

N   Maurice Merleau-Ponty. *Nature: Course Notes from the College de France.* Translated by Robert Vallier, edited by Dominique Seglard. Evanston, IL: Northwestern University Press, 2003.

OTU   Sara Heinämaa. "On the Transcendental Undercurrents of Phenomenology: The Case of the Living Body." *Continental Philosophy Review* 54, no. 2 (2021): 237–57.

PE   Remigius Kwant. *Phenomenology of Expression.* Translated by Henry J. Koren. Pittsburgh: Duquesne University Press, 1969.

PhP   Maurice Merleau-Ponty. *Phenomenology of Perception.* Translated by Colin Smith. New York: Humanities Press, 1974.

PT   Martina Ferrari. "Poietic Transpatiality: Merleau-Ponty and the Sense of Nature." *Chiasmi International* 20 (2018): 385–401.

SWWE   Maurice Merleau-Ponty. *The Sensible World and the World of Expression: Course Notes from the Collège de France, 1953.* Translated by Bryan Smyth. Evanston, IL: Northwestern University Press, 2020.

TSO   Timo Miettinen. "Transcendental Social Ontology." In *Phenomenology and the Phenomenology and the Transcendental,* edited by Sara Heinämaa, Mirja Hartimo, and Timo Miettinen, 147–71. New York: Routledge, 2014.

VP   Jacques Derrida. *Voice and Phenomenon: Introduction to the Problem of the Sign in Husserl's Phenomenology.* Translated by Leonard Lawlor. Evanston, IL: Northwestern University Press, 2010.

The Political Logic of Experience

Introduction
Experience and the Problem of Expression

My project in this book is simple: to show how expression is central to experience and why phenomenology is necessary for us to understand that. In exploring this, we will see that the subject, rather than being the driving or sovereign force constituting experience, is itself constituted by a political force within experience. This is not simply an empirical claim—that individual subjects have some of their individual experiences constituted within the context of their particular political communities—but a transcendental claim: subjectivity itself is an expression of the political community in which it emerges. Hence, the political nature of subjectivity is a transcendental necessity of experience itself when experience is understood as operating according to a logic of expression.

Here at the beginning, almost every element of the preceding claims requires further elaboration and definition: what is meant by expression (Chapter 1), the subjective (Chapters 2 and 5), the transcendental (Chapter 4), the political (Chapter 6) and the logic of experience (Conclusion) must all be carefully outlined and explained for the sense of the preceding claim to emerge clearly. Indeed, as we will see, the very notion of sense itself and of its emergence must also be clarified in and by expression (Chapter 3) if we are going to be able to speak clearly and rigorously about the nature of human experience in the world.

And that, ultimately, is the task of the present book: to elucidate expression clearly and rigorously as the logic, mechanism, or force that drives experience itself. This will also require the development and clear explanation of the philosophical and methodological tools necessary for achieving this task. As such, this book will open the question of a "phenomenological politics" that is on par with the phenomenological psychology of phenomenology's earliest days. Insofar as phenomenal experience itself will be shown to be essentially political, and insofar as phenomenology will be revealed to be the mode of philosophizing that is best able to access this political core of phenomenality, this book will show that any and every phenomenology is essentially political, and every politics rests on a phenomeno-logical foundation.

Such claims fit well with critical phenomenological work both classical (de Beauvoir,[1] Fanon, etc.) and contemporary (Sara Ahmed, Alia al-Saji, George Yancy, etc.). But I want to show here that it also fits well with the work of classical transcendental phenomenologists like Husserl and Merleau-Ponty. Arguing for the inherently political nature of phenomenology is to say something about the constitution of subjective experience itself, and it is these claims that are primarily of interest to me in this work: what is the nature of experience such that any and every subjective experience is always already expressive of a particular (political) force within a particular (political) community? What is the relationship between empirical factors and transcendental conditions such that the former can be included in the latter, while still being shaped by the latter (and, in turn, the latter be shaped by and, in a sense, included within the former)?

The book is therefore primarily a work in transcendental phenomenology, though one with strong implications for critical and political thought as well. This is not simply coincidental. The book will argue that the inherently political (and not merely intersubjective) character of human experience entails the political (and transcendental) nature of phenomenology. At least two things follow from this: first, that "political" questions can never be entirely separated from our understanding of "human experience"; and second, that phenomenology remains an essential methodological tool for understanding those "political" questions. Neither claim, perhaps, is unique on its own: the first is a common theme in critical and theoretical discourses such as oppression theory, feminism, race theory, queer theory, poststructural discourses of power, critical theories of ideology, and so on; the second is a point of method argued by several critical phenomenologists, such as Johanna Oksala in *Feminist Experiences* and Cressida Heyes in *Anaesthetics of Existence*. My contention here is that clarifying expression further supports both claims by showing that experience operates according to an expressive logic that provides constitutive power to political forces.

But in thereby showing the link between the two claims, a further claim is brought to light, namely that every phenomenological description is already politically expressive, and therefore every transcendental claim concerning human experience is never fully separable from particular empirical circumstances. The potential dangers of this claim are significant, for both phenomenology (does "transcendental phenomenology" name a meaningful philosophical project, one that can avoid charges of epistemological—and perhaps even ontological—relativism?) and politics (can we ever talk meaningfully with those with whom we do not share a political community or ideology, or is the political divisiveness of our times the necessary result of our inability to ever describe human experience beyond our own situation?). But these dangers can, I think, be avoided, if we properly understand expression and what it can teach us about the nature of both experience and our attempts to describe and understand that experience.

Expression, therefore, is the key to unraveling how experience works according to a (phenomeno-)logic that is necessarily political, and explicating expression will provide a double clarification: first, of the complicated knot of knowing, being, and doing that constitutes the (political) heart of experience; and second, of the role, purpose, and task (or promise) of phenomenology. Explicating expression so as to provide this double clarification constitutes the main task of this book.

A Provisional Clarification of Terms

Before we elaborate further the significance and potential value of this double clarification for the three claims outlined earlier, let us first take a moment to define some of our key terms. By necessity, these definitions will be somewhat provisional, given that this is the introduction and the claims and definitions outlined here have yet to be fully elaborated and defended. Nevertheless, a bit of initial clarification may prove helpful.

Expression

Let us begin by explaining what is meant by "expression." In its broadest sense, expression refers to the disclosing of something through something else (see SWWE, 11).[2] Through the linguistic expression "I'm happy you are home," I disclose my joy at my wife's return. But already ambiguity threatens, for "expression" means two different things in its two uses in the previous sentences: in the first instance, it refers to a broader structure, something like "expressivity"; in the second instance (i.e., "the linguistic expression"), it refers to one part of that broader structure, namely the expression as the part that is used to disclose something else. For clarity's sake, let us from now on refer to the broader category by the term expressivity.

And we can say that every expressive process involves express*ing* an express*ed* via an express*ion*. Broadly speaking, the "expressed" is that which is disclosed, the "expression" is the means by which it is disclosed, and "expressing" is the force or process by which the expression is able to express the expressed. It is this third element—expressing—that is easily lost when we fail to adequately distinguish the broader structure (expressivity) from one of its elements (expression), a point we will return to in greater detail in Chapter 1. For now, let us simply mark that expressivity necessarily entails a force (expressing) that enables something (the expression) to disclose something else (the expressed).

A quick example illustrates why it is necessary to distinguish these three elements of expressivity. Picture, if you will, a crucifix and the letter "t." While both things are made of perpendicularly intersecting lines, in the two cases those lines disclose very different things: the religious tradition of Christianity in the first case, and one particular semantic element in a complex linguistic system in the second case. Each of these is expressed through its expression, and expressing is the force the ties those things (expression and expressed) together such that the expression discloses the expressed.

From this brief description, we can see three things about expressivity. First, it is necessarily asymmetrical: one thing is disclosed via another, and our attention is given almost exclusively to that which is disclosed; when we see a crucifix, we all but ignore the material elements making up the concrete expression (e.g., crossed bars of timber) and focus almost exclusively on the historical tradition of Christianity.[3] Second, it is co-constitutive: the expression and the expressed are what they are only in relation to each other. The crossed boards are a crucifix only because of Christianity, and Christianity is why those boards have now been placed together in that particular perpendicular fashion; the crossed pen strokes are the letter "t" only because of particular linguistic conventions, and those conventions are why I have written those pen strokes in that particular way. And third, it is generative: there is a force (expressing) that ties the other two elements together in a particular way that is related to prior historical accidents (e.g., the historical prominence of Christianity in the development of "the West"; the development of the Latin alphabet) and shapes or is partially constitutive of future occurrences.

The overarching task of the book, then, is to clarify expressivity (and not simply some concrete expressions) and its implications for experience. Initially we might be tempted to think that expressivity comes into play only with language, or at least with semiotics. We are tempted to conflate the "in-the-place-of" (*für etwas*) structure of signs (VP, 88–89; 23) with expressivity itself. The tradition of phenomenology, however, has discovered that when it comes to human experience, expressivity is not simply a matter for the philosophy of language or of signs, but is in some important way constitutive of experience itself. Donald Landes, for example, argues that expressivity "is any enduring response to the weight of the past, the weight of the ideal, and the weight of the present situation, broadly construed."[4] In this regard, expressivity is "a 'fundamental characteristic' of human experience" (16). In this book, we will be making clear that expressivity is essential to experience itself as the force that ties the various elements of experience together into one, unified experience.

Experience

But what precisely is meant by "experience," then? In its broadest sense, experience is meaningful engagement or practical contact with the world or some element within it. As such, it includes epistemological, ontological, and practical elements: it simultaneously makes claims about how we know the world, about how we are in the world, and about what we do in the world. The question of experience is therefore philosophically complex. Cressida Heyes, for example, suggests that we must distinguish, within experience, between "the prereflective encounter with the world, and that encounter as expressed through an interpretive frame," a distinction that she maps onto the phenomenological distinction between *Erlebnis* (lived experience) and *Erfahrung* (empirical or practical experience).[5] Broadly speaking, this is the distinction between our experience as given to us "immediately" in our "first-person perspective," and experience as meaningful within a shared social, cultural, or linguistic milieu. In this sense, experience is simultaneously deeply and inherently individual in an ontologically and practically significant way (my experience is, for me, different in kind from anyone else's experience) and something epistemically shared or communal (both you and I are capable of experiencing something in similar ways).

While Heyes agrees that "all experience should be understood as always already both of these" (AE, 30), the connection between these seemingly "irreducible perspectives"[6] remains philosophically and methodologically problematic. The deeply individual nature of "lived experience" in the *Erlebnis* dimension of experience suggests, to many, that experience should be understood as some kind of direct immersion that is affective or "felt" prior to its meaning something (as, for example, in the experience of feeling pain). As such, experience comes to function methodologically "as an originary point of explanation—as a foundation on which analysis is based" precisely because it is "uncontestable evidence."[7] Who can doubt or deny me *my experience* of something?

Such experience has, at times, been taken as philosophically immune from social and historical critique for one of two potential reasons. First, it may be construed as immune from critique because it is taken to be immediate and devoid of historical/social conditioning, as, for example, in some early modern conceptions of empiricism that Husserl engages with in the *Crisis*, or, perhaps, in Alcoff's notion that some forms of experience stand outside discourse and the constitution of the subject.[8] Alternatively, it may be considered immune from critique because the seeming immediacy of our experience is construed primarily as a psychological rather than an ontological phenomenon, and as such it can be understood as a mere product of subjectivity as it operates within empirical and historical circumstances. Experience is therefore best understood philosophically simply by clarifying (via critique) those circumstances and how they have shaped the epistemic and practical conditions of the subject: the appeal to the lived nature of our experience is no longer philosophically necessary.[9]

Broadly speaking, this distinction in how experience is understood is generally thought to lead to the distinct philosophical approaches of phenomenology and poststructuralism, respectively (FE, 9): the former deals with the lived dimension of experience, but only by abandoning experience's socially and culturally situated meaning, while the latter deals with the social and cultural production of experience by abandoning (at least, as philosophically or ontologically meaningful) the lived experience of individual subjects.

Like Heyes, however, Oksala argues that "this debate has been cast in simplistically binary and philosophically problematic terms" (FE, 9) because "the phenomenological emphasis on lived experience does not imply that this experience is prediscursive or immediate" (FE, 11).[10] Instead, what is needed is an account of experience that can honor the significance of both its first-person, "felt" component (*Erlebnis*) and its shared, meaningful, and therefore discursively and socially constituted component. Such an account, I would argue, is found in the phenomenological tradition, especially in its genetic and generative components,[11] where the function of consciousness or subjectivity in making sense of the world is both accounted for philosophically (unlike some poststructuralist discourses) and situated or explained epistemically and practically (unlike some phenomenological accounts that seem to treat consciousness as a prior absolute). Acknowledging and explaining the functioning of subjectivity avoids both conflating the subjectivity of our lived experience with discourse or discursive constitution, which would reduce the individual strictly to a product of its social environment, and ontologically absolutizing the subjectivity of our lived experience, as if it is wholly separable and distinct from its empirical political situation. Such a view, then, "does not eliminate the role of the individual, but it does limit it. The web of practices in which we are embedded necessarily shapes our thought and understanding. Nothing I do can change the totality of it, but equally nothing I do is politically insignificant either" (FE, 35). That I live through an experience gives it a force or power that is philosophically and politically significant insofar as it provides the "power to motivate us to demand social change" (FE, 46), change that will alter both the empirical conditions and the subjects that operate within those conditions.

If we are to make sense of this complex account of experience in a philosophically serious way, we need a careful method whereby we can trace how subjects (and even perhaps subjectivity itself) are formed in particular social, historical—let us say, for the time being, "political"—contexts without eliminating the power and force of the lived quality of individual experience.

Sense

Such a method must account for how meaning or "sense" functions, both within and beyond the subject and its individual experiences, in ways that are not simply epistemic. Philosophically, the notion of sense comes to prominence in Frege, where it comes to stand for the "objective content"[12] of a thought, that which is neither the individual conception I have in my own particular act of thinking nor the full objectivity of the thing I am thinking about: while the referent of "two plus four" and "three times two" is the same (the number six), the sense of each statement is different, though the sense is the same even when different people think "two plus four equals six." Sense therefore is "objective, inasmuch as it can [potentially] be used by several observers," though it is not fully objective since it remains "one-sided and dependent upon the standpoint of observation."[13] Frege is explicitly not interested in exploring such sense, but Husserl is.[14] Indeed, it is probably not an exaggeration to say that the entire phenomenological project finds its founding impulse or promise in explicating sense, that is, in clearly explaining the relationship between subjective conceptions and the "objective" world.[15]

After the linguistic turn, we cannot ignore the importance of meaning/ sense for how we "make sense" of the world (FE, 29), even as we acknowledge that such meaning/sense is not necessarily strictly cognitive or linguistic (as we will return to in Chapter 3). However we understand the term (meaning/sense), the method we seek to make sense of experience must be able to explain both *how* subjects make sense of the world, and *that* they are able to bestow sense (*Sinngebung*) only because they themselves have been given the ability to do so by their own immersion in a world that is saturated with shared sense.

Carefully articulating this method is a primary task of the "phenomenological politics" this book calls for, and expressivity, we will see, is essential to its cause. For expression enables us to account for how sense is able to function as a "metaphysical schema" or transcendental guide that "constitutes the intelligibility of [our experience of the world] and its rules," without functioning simply as the "cause" of our experience (FE, 34) in a way that would reduce that experience simply to its transcendental "foundations." It does this in part by showing how those "metaphysical schemas" or transcendental guides "are embedded in practices [that] can be changed by human effort" (FE, 35). Sense therefore operates transcendentally as a constitutive factor of experience, even as it is itself generated within and co-constituted by experience. Sense, we can therefore say, is *expressed* in experience, even as experience also *expresses itself* in and as sense.

Again, we are not yet in position to fully understand such claims at this introductory stage. For now, let us simply clarify that "experience" includes both the "lived" character of experience (that which makes it *my* experience or *your* experience in a significant way) and the sense that enables it to function as "meaningful" experience (i.e., as being an experience *of* this or that). Further, we wish to clarify that sense operates potentially both as the epistemic content of an experience (that which is meant by, or disclosed in, a particular experience) and as the ontological and practical means of experiencing (the force that binds a particular sense to a particular phenomenon that discloses that sense): sense functions, in experience, both as the expressed and as the force of expressing.

Perhaps changing from the language of experience to the language of phenomenology (as we began to do in the last parentheses) is helpful here. In trying to make sense of how experience operates, we can turn to phenomenology as that discipline concerned with the logic (*logos*) of the appearing (*phainesthai*) of experience. We can distinguish, then, within experience between what is experienced (the phenomenon) and the means by which it is experienced (phenomenality or phenomenal conditions). Phenomenality, therefore, is part of experience, though it is not itself experienced as a concrete object or subject of experience (i.e., not as a phenomenon). Expressivity, we will see, is a phenomenal condition of experiencing and not simply a concrete phenomenon we experience. That is to say, expressivity is *how* we experience, and not simply *what* we experience.

Politics

The phenomenal character of expressivity will have significant implications for how we understand expressivity vis-à-vis other transcendental or "ultratranscendental" moments in phenomenology, moments referred to by names like "subjectivity," "flesh," and "differance." But before we move on to discuss those implications, one last moment of provisional clarification is required. We have discussed several times already the intrusion of politics or the political into experience: the lived component of experience was said to be politically significant, and the sense/meaningful component of experience was said to be tied to political contexts. But what is meant by "political" in these cases? In its average, everyday usage, politics refers to how a country or government is run. In a slightly broader usage, "political" refers to anything pertaining to the management of people within the *polis* or political unit, especially the explicit legislation (and means of formulating that legislation) that governs within a particular *polis*. Politics, then, is about the makeup of the *polis*.

This narrower definition is sometimes expanded to a broader definition pertaining to the way in which social communities operate. In this broader sense, we can speak of the politics at work in voluntary associations that do not have an explicitly "political" component, such as the politics at work in a particular institution or workplace. This sense of "politics" has less to do with the formal rules or laws governing that institution (as if it were a *polis*) and more to do with the internal, and largely informal, social dynamics within that institution: the "politics" of who is friends with whom, of how to build social capital, of knowing the right people to get stuff done, and so forth. This sense of politics has a kind of practical normativity: normative because things can be done better or worse, but practical in the sense that the normativity is not absolute (not "right" and "wrong" in the moral sense), but relative (to the social mores of that particular institution) and pragmatic (about getting things done).

These two senses of the political are not simply ambiguous. They both rely in a meaningful way on the internal arrangement or basic makeup of a social (cum political) body. This notion of an internal arrangement is captured in the Greek word *politeia* or in the English word "constitution" that sometimes translates it. It encompasses both what makes the thing what it is (its constituent parts, such as the citizens of the *polis*) and how those things are arranged. This "how" component is not simply formal (e.g., the laws of the *polis*) but also informal (e.g., the social relations of the *polis*). But, of course, these things are not entirely distinct from each other: what makes a person a citizen is the laws that govern citizenship, and who is (or is not) a citizen influences the informal social relations, even as those social relations also influence the formal laws (which pertain necessarily to those social relations) and the persons to whom those laws apply. When I speak of the political in this book, I mean to invoke this connection between a thing's constituent parts and the formal and informal arrangements that hold between them: the political is that which constitutes a social body in the dual sense of that which is constitutive for that body (what makes a particular community what it is) and that which is constituting that body (as a constituting force). The dual connotation of constitution—as both the internal makeup of something and as the process of giving form to something—is essential to a proper understanding of the political as it functions in this book, and the roots of the political must be traced back to *politeia* rather than simply to the *polis* if one is to understand the properly phenomenological understanding of politics.

To speak of a particular context as "political," then, is to include the phenomena that make it up (people, objects, formal and informal rules, social mores and relations, institutions, etc.) and the phenomenality that constitutes or generates it: the "political" is not merely a collection of political objects (*res publica*) but also the ongoing constitution of those objects and the relations between them. Hence, calling a community political is different from simply saying it is intersubjective, insofar as politics includes a force that precedes and constitutes (or institutes)[16] subjectivity and particular subjects. Such force (phenomenologically) precedes, insofar as it mutually generates, the distinction between homeworld (where I am situated epistemically, ontologically and practically) and alienworld (where I am not so situated) as "co-relative and co-generative in an axiological asymmetry" (HB, 124).[17] Yet such a force necessarily acts within a particular homeworld: it is generative in a kind of normative and transcendental way while remaining necessarily tied to particular empirical, which is to say "historical, geological, cultural, intersubjective and normative" (HB, 178), contexts. The political is, therefore, not simply a communal or social context that shapes particular empirical subjects but is a transcendental force of phenomenality before (and so that) it can be a communal or social context shaping particular empirical subjects. And expressivity, we will see, is the key to understanding how this political force operates in and as the very logic of experience itself.

The Phenomenological Knot(s) at the Core of Experience

Already in these provisional definitions, we gave begun to work toward the task of the book: clarifying the role that expressivity plays in *how* we experience so that we can reveal the inherently political nature of experience and of phenomenology. Experience is constituted by a transcendental force that is constitutive of particular empirical circumstances even as it is also constituted within those circumstances. In phenomenology, such a force is understood as operating "generatively," which is to say that it institutes a "continual historical becoming" that is (HB, 179) "historical" insofar as it always occurs within a history that is essential (in the eidetic sense) to what is constituted within it;[18] "becoming" insofar as the being of what is generated is constantly unfolding in relation to its constitutive elements and to the history that is essential to it; and "continual" insofar as the becoming is necessarily ongoing in a self-unfolding, autopoietic way.

Generativity combines elements that are epistemic (e.g., essences, in the eidetic sense), ontological (e.g., being and becoming), and practical (e.g., the ongoing self-unfolding through the generation of "new" things), therefore, just as experience does. And this generativity, phenomenology argues, allows empirical conditions to be transcendentally operative, that is, to be "fundamental structures, rules, or conditions for the possibility of sense-emergence" (HB, 14). That this is not *ipso facto* a contradiction suggests already the need for more nuanced accounts of both the transcendental and the empirical, for if the transcendental is necessarily *a priori*, and *a priori* necessarily means outside of experience (as with Kant), and if the empirical is tied necessarily to experience—then a transcendental function for empirical conditions is necessarily impossible.

Of course, it should be clear already from our provisional definition of experience that experience is not *simply* about empirical facts and conditions, and that the transcendental cannot be *simply* "independent of experience." Rather, we saw that experience requires certain "transcendental guides" or "metaphysical schemas" that help experience be sensible, even as the sensibility of experience cannot be divorced from the capacity of individual subjects to bestow sense. Now we can understand the further claim that sense is not simply bestowed on the world by subjects; it is also generated within the world and generative of conditions that function both empirically and transcendentally. If the nature of sense (as empirical or transcendental) is therefore complicated, so too is its mode of operation: sense functions not simply epistemologically (to help us know about objects in the world) but also ontologically (it helps bring about certain things and not others, and brings them about in this way rather than that way) and practically (things come to pass or come to be because of the operation of sense).

Generativity therefore helps us see that experience operates via a particular relationship between transcendental and empirical, as well as a particular relationship between knowing, being, and doing. Each of the three modes of operation can, in a sense, function both empirically and transcendentally: in terms of knowing, for example, concepts, ideas, and the like have empirical provenance and provide empirical assistance (I can use the concepts of various numbers and of addition to figure out how many chairs I will need for Christmas dinner), even as they also provide transcendental guides shaping our very experience of the world itself, as Heidegger's "transcendental" analyses of concepts like death, guilt, anxiety, and so on attempt to illustrate, or as Charles Taylor's analysis of the shifting understanding of religion and its impact on our understanding of the world as increasingly "disenchanted" also shows.[19] Similarly, human action has an obviously empirical importance: we do particular things in the world that have an impact in that world, such as a hug that makes a grieving friend happy or a sudden change of lanes with my car that causes anger for the driver of a nearby car. But they also take on transcendental significance: today's actions become sedimented into the horizons of expectation that transcendentally shape tomorrow's "primal" experience of the world. Being, too, is both empirical and transcendental: our mode of being directly affects our attunement to the world (Heidegger), and that mode of being itself is affected by our thrownness (Heidegger) into this particular lifeworld (Husserl) or that one.

This complex relationship between knowing-being-doing and transcendental-empirical is not distinguishable from experience itself: to experience something is to engage it epistemically, ontologically, and practically in ways that have both empirical and transcendental effect. And those effects are not simply imposed on experience from without (e.g., by a "constituting subject" or by "discursive regimes"), but thoroughly constitute experience from within. Experience is not simply a bare form that is merely fleshed out in this or that particular way, based on empirical conditions. Nor is "experience" simply a code word or another way of talking about one element of objective empirical conditions (e.g., their ability to be perceived by a subject). Rather, experience is essentially empirical, rooted always and necessarily in this or that particular community, lifeworld, and so forth, a community or lifeworld that is always "mine" for the experiencing subject, not simply accidentally, but in ways that shape the entirety of the subject's experience as normal or abnormal, as good or bad or something else, as affective and associative, and so on. That is, experience is always normative, with the same kind of practical normativity that characterized the political. But this normative quality of experience itself functions transcendentally: it is part of the conditions for the possibility of sense-emergence. Therefore, we see support for the first major claim outlined earlier, namely that political questions can never be entirely separated from our understanding of (human) experience.

Making sense of all this requires a clear elaboration, not simply of the constituent parts of experience (including sense, with its epistemological, ontological, or practical modes, and its transcendental and empirical nature; subjects, with their "lived" quality of experience; objects or things, as the empirical correlates of experience, etc.) but also of the constitutive force that generates those constituent parts and the relations between them. This is the unique contribution that a phenomenological understanding of expressivity can offer: expressivity is the means or "logic" by which the phenomenality of experience is able to phenomenalize experience as experience, which is to say, by which it is able to unite the various elements of experience together into (an) experience, rather than just being a series of contiguous parts. The type of unity it creates—experiential or phenomenal unity—is, *qua* "experiential," not simply an ontological, logical, or pragmatic unity that reduces its constituent parts to one function (e.g., the logical or mathematical unity of identity), but a unity that holds its constituent parts in a co-constitutive, generative, and asymmetrical relation. Simply put, *expressivity is how experience works*. It is the very logic by which experience operates as experience. As such, the elaboration of expressivity via phenomenological means promises to help us better understand the political nature of experience itself, thereby lending support to the second major claim discussed above, namely that phenomenology remains an essential methodological tool for understanding political questions as they pertain to experience.

This leaves us the third major claim: that every phenomenological description is already politically expressive, perhaps because every transcendental claim concerning "human experience" is never fully separable from particular empirical circumstances. To see the support for this claim, we must remember that expressivity is not simply another layer or level at work in phenomenal experience, it is the means by which the various constitutive elements are stitched together. As such, explaining expressivity helps us untangle the knot at the core of experience, not by laying out the various threads that constitute it (which much of previous phenomenological philosophy has sought to do) but by explaining how the knot is tied. This is significant for how it will help us understand experience anew, and for how it addresses certain methodological issues in phenomenology and the broader philosophy of experience pertaining to the relationship between the transcendental and the empirical.

It is not, I think, an exaggeration to say that many people have difficulty understanding how the work of transcendental phenomenologists (like Husserl, Merleau-Ponty, Derrida, etc.) help us better understand the world we live in or our experience of it. While those phenomenologists have each offered various constitutive elements of experience, various strands of the phenomenological knot at the core of experience, the lack of a clearer account of how those elements or strands are tied together means that the articulation of those strands has failed to yield a clear philosophical methodology. As such, many historical phenomenologists have been content (as I was in a previous work) to affirm a sort of "phenomenology of tension"[20] in which both elements of a seeming contradiction (e.g., *Erlebnis* and *Erfahrung*, intuition and givenness, constituting and being constituted, Justice and the law, the "bad ambiguities" of the early Merleau-Ponty, the "dialectic" of the later Merleau-Ponty, etc.), must be affirmed as necessary for experience, and so "the question for phenomenology becomes how to balance these two distinct movements—how to hold them in tension—so as to preserve the possibility of phenomena and of phenomenology."[21]

The result of this unclarified tension has been that the insights of transcendental phenomenology have failed to have widespread impact beyond transcendental phenomenology. This seems true for at least three reasons:

1. With no concrete explanation given for the nature of the difference between these seemingly contradictory elements, the contradictions in question have been taken by many other philosophers (especially in the Anglo-American tradition) as logical contradictions. And since no account is seemingly offered as for how these seemingly contradictory things can both be affirmed, their affirmation by transcendental phenomenologists is taken as proof that phenomenology (and the Continental philosophies that follow from it) are either insufficiently rigorous (people just don't realize that they are affirming logical opposites), nonserious (people are just playing around with language, and not actually trying to formulate true, logically coherent statements), or distinctly antiphilosophical (denying or ignoring rules of logical order, content to traffic in "mere" sophistry and rhetoric).[22]

2. With an insufficiently clear account of how phenomenality works to tie together the various levels of phenomenological analysis, the insights of transcendental phenomenological investigation are taken simply as proto-phenomena (e.g., being, consciousness, givenness, flesh, differance, etc.) that seem like abstractions that lack connection to our actual, empirical existence. This leaves a gap between "transcendental" and "applied" phenomenology that arises from our inability to clarify how the seemingly empirical elements that make up our lived situation—particular communi-

ties with their particular mores and traditions; various distinct languages and dialects; modes of subjective interaction and inter-subjective action; and so forth—can have a transcendental effect on our experience.[23] Without this clarification, the work of tran-scendental phenomenology is rendered unhelpful for those trying to use phenomenology to analyze and alter the conditions of the world as it currently is.[24]

3. The lack of clear explanation of the connection between phenom-enality and phenomena, and/or between insights of transcendental and applied phenomenology, has led the insights of the various transcendental phenomenologists to be taken simply as parallel spools at work in the various thinkers, rather than a knot that has been tied within experience itself in a particular way for a particu-lar reason. As isolated abstractions with complex (and unexplained) interior logics, the insights of the transcendental phenomenologists cease to be compared even to each other and are often taken simply on their own terms, such that each major figure becomes its own closed world of scholarly research (where we can speak vaguely of outside "influences," or stage "readings" that "speak to" issues raised by other figures) but the notion of an ever-deepening account of the same basic issue(s) among the various figures is rarely considered. We end up, then, with "Derrida scholars" and "Husserl scholars," "Levinasians" and "Deleuzians," where each of these becomes a world unto itself, to be understood according to its own logic or its own interrelations ("early" Merleau-Ponty v. "later" Merleau-Ponty), but with a limited ability to speak to the broader philo-sophical or phenomenological problems or issues that each figure is responding to: we evaluate, for example, what Derrida says about X or Y, but not how his saying that affects or alters our broader understanding of X or Y. This results in an increasingly figure-based, rather than problem-based, approach to transcendental phenomenology, which creates issues in engaging with the broader philosophical discipline.[25] It also has implications for the creation of a culture of veneration of the "master," a culture that opens the door for oppression and abuse, both systematically (in the proliferation of a predominantly white, male, heterosexual canon) and individually (by making so much depend on the affirmation of one's own mentor or advisor—a repetition of the "master-student" account of philosophy on the small scale—sexual harassment and other forms of exploitation are easily wreaked on graduate students and others in vulnerable employment positions).[26]

These issues arise, I suggest, because phenomenology has contented itself with articulating the various constitutive elements of human experience without adequately clarifying the nature of the connection between them. As such, its methodological basis is insufficient for its findings to be accessible to those who do not already have an implicit or intuitive understanding of phenomenology. Without clarifying that methodological basis, phenomenology is taken to be bad philosophy (the Russellian option), pure abstraction, or is fragmented into various streams of internal "scholarship" that may cease to engage the things themselves (the figure-based philosophy option). My contention in this book is that expressivity is how the various threads are knotted together at the core of experience. As such, its explication is necessary if we are to properly understand experience itself, including the ways that "empirical" factors shape or influence that experience necessarily and transcendentally, and so establish a solid methodological foundation for phenomenology that can connect its "transcendental" and its various "applied" streams. This should help address the above concerns, while also lending both clarity and support to the claim that transcendental claims concerning "human experience" are never fully separable from particular empirical circumstances.

But this does not yet get us to the claim that every phenomenological description is already politically expressive, even if we can begin to see the outlines that could support such a claim. Yet establishing this claim is important if we are to properly understand the relationship between politics and phenomenology. While feminist phenomenologies like those of Heyes, Oksala, de Beauvoir, and Heinämaa or phenomenologies of race like those of Fanon, Macey, Alcoff, and Gordon[27] have been arguing for decades that gender and race, respectively, shape a subject's very experience of the world in necessary ways, their work has often been treated, within the broader phenomenological tradition, as little more than "a faithful assistant to the phenomenological project dealing with its marginal or regional subthemes" (FE, 14). By beginning with a specific focus on women's experience or the "Black" experience, these phenomenologies have often been thought by those in the "mainstream" as yielding results that were of limited phenomenological value. It is not that they necessarily had nothing to offer overall, but what they could offer was only of value to some limited empirical people and issues: feminist phenomenology was of interest only to "women's issues," which might include things like political suffrage or sexual violence but did not have a bearing on "perennial issues in philosophy," such as the nature of subjectivity or the constitution of experience. Similarly, racial phenomenologies were of interest to "Black" or "Hispanic" issues, but not to "universal" questions of epistemology, ontology, or ethics. By beginning from a particular empirical location, these phenomenologies, it was presumed, were limited in advance to being insufficiently transcendental because they could never be universal.

But we have seen already that "transcendental" need not mean "universal," and that in fact the transcendental is necessarily conditioned by the empirical. Transcendental conditions are generated out of empirical conditions that are constitutively significant. This is a commonplace claim in classical transcendental phenomenology, from Husserl's various analyses of social phenomena (e.g., in *Ideas II*) and normativity (e.g., in Hua 11 and in the D manuscripts), to Merleau-Ponty's notion of style, Heidegger's notion of being-in-the-world, Derrida's notion of the "other in me," or Levinas's account of our being hostage to the Other. The (transcendental) impact of empirical conditions on experience, the centrality of historical, social, linguistic (ultimately, of political) forces for subjectivity, the complex relationship between transcendental and empirical in matters of genesis, sense-bestowal, and methodology: all of these are well-established themes and problematics of classical transcendental phenomenology and of critical phenomenology, both of which hold that "reality cannot be understood independent of the historical and cultural community of experiencing subjects" (FE, 5).[28] Thus, "these transcendental, constitutive conditions have to be understood as intersubjective: historical, cultural, and, not least, political" (FE, 5).

Yet there seems to be a major point of difference between these two streams within, or approaches to, phenomenology. Critical phenomenology, it is said, is purposefully political and is intended to change the world, not simply describe it.[29] Classical transcendental phenomenology, on the other hand, is traditionally taken to be apolitical and merely descriptive. Yet it is not clear how this latter description holds true, given the understanding of politics and the relationship between empirical and transcendental at work here. As Steinbock puts it: "Phenomenology cannot be merely *descriptive* or a 'reflection on' matters . . . because the phenomenologist is caught up in generativity. Phenomenology becomes a *participation* in the sense development of an intersubjective historical structure that is in the process of generation as we describe it and as we bring it about."[30] Once phenomenology reaches the level of generativity, therefore, description ceases to be merely descriptive: every description of experience is another move in the generative unfolding of the phenomena under consideration. As such, generative phenomenology "does not only describe essences, and in particular social essences, but participates in the ethical becoming of social structures or essences that the phenomenologist describes" and hence "becomes a normative project of contributing to the way in which the a priori structures of society *develop historically as they are being described*" (HB, 14–15; emphasis added). Because of the role of generativity (which itself cannot be divorced from expressivity, as we will see in Chapter 1), phenomenological description is necessarily a way of contributing to the development of societal structures, and as such is already "a material practice of 'restructuring the world'"[31] that we can take to be a movement of political expressivity.

But it is not simply generative phenomenology that functions this way, since static and genetic phenomenology are "already situated in generativity."[32] Static and genetic descriptions abstract out of the concrete sense at work in experience, sense that is, we will see, necessarily generated within the expressive logic of phenomenality itself. Therefore, all phenomenology is always already both situated politically and itself carrying out a political task insofar as it contributes to the constitution of a social body both by describing something that is constitutive of that body and by constituting that body itself through its action of description.

I am not trying here to deny the innovation or the value of critical phenomenology. Nor do I want to suggest that nothing is found in critical phenomenology that cannot be found already in Husserl, Merleau-Ponty, or other classical transcendental phenomenologists. Far from it: by situating themselves purposefully in a particular tradition/community of sense, one that deviates in some constitutively meaningful way from the (predominantly white, male) sense-communities of "classical" phenomenologists like Husserl and Merleau-Ponty, critical phenomenology is bound to generate something distinct and different from what was generated by the classical tradition in phenomenology. My point is simply that critical phenomenology's being situated in a particular political community and generatively contributing to that community's self-unfolding is *not* what makes it distinct from classical phenomenology, because classical phenomenology is also situated, by its own analyses, in a particular political community that it helps to generatively become in and through its descriptions. The difference, perhaps, is that critical phenomenology is purposeful in both the political community it is trying to take up (though it may not be as easy to distinguish those communities, as both our upcoming phenomenological analyses and any notion of intersectionality will attest) and in the fact that it is trying to change that community, not simply describe it (though one cannot read the *Crisis* without a strong sense that Husserl is not simply describing but is trying to change what is happening).[33]

What difference that purposiveness makes or how the particular political communities they were part of may have contributed to the outcomes of Husserl's or Merleau-Ponty's philosophizing—these are interesting questions, but not ones that we will pursue here. Our interest here is simply to show, clearly, that experience operates according to an expressive logic that constitutes a political force at the heart of experiencing itself. As such, both experience and the phenomenological description of it are inherently political: constituted by political forces and enacting or generating political forces in turn. In this regard, critical phenomenology ought to name, not a distinct branch within phenomenology, but a "current running through the whole body of phenomenological thinking" (FE, 14). Phenomenology, to achieve its own aims and ends and to better account for experience, must necessarily be "critical," and engaging the "political" dimension of life and of the empirical situation of phenomenologists is not something that phenomenology *can* do, if one chooses to apply it in that way—it is something that phenomenology *must* do and *is doing*, insofar as it is doing phenomenology.

Why Expressivity?

Allow me to offer one final brief explanation before we turn to the overall argument of the book. It still remains to clarify why we should think that expressivity can play the pivotal role we have outlined for it in this introduction. After all, Husserl, Merleau-Ponty and Deleuze, at least, have extended discussions and explications of expressivity as an essential element of their respective philosophies. If expressivity plays such a foundational methodological and clarifying role, why has this not been recognized sooner?

At least two factors contribute to this lack of recognition, though whether they are symptoms or causes of the problem remains unclear. First, the writings on expression/expressivity are largely underappreciated in the phenomenological literature, and when they have been engaged, they have not generally been taken as offering a distinctly phenomenological account of expressivity. While there has been a certain resurgence in attention paid to expression in Merleau-Ponty's thought,[34] for example, that attention has rarely situated it within the broader discourse of a phenomenological account of expression (by relating it to Husserl's account of expression as it grows out of his debates with Frege, for example). Indeed, it is hardly fair to say that there *is* a broader discourse of a distinctly *phenomenological* account of expression: there is work on Merleau-Ponty's theory of expression, or Deleuze's account of expression,[35] but very little on a broadly phenomenological account of expression,[36] and even less on how such an account is essential to understanding the phenomenality of experience. This, perhaps, is one area where the figure-based approach to phenomenology has been especially problematic.

Second, Derrida's critique of expression in *Voice and Phenomenon* seems to have called into question the viability or desirability of expression as a term for serious phenomenological reflection.[37] Husserl's earliest forays into expression in *Logical Investigations* left unexamined the assumption that expressing is merely the producing of expressions of a certain (linguistic) type, produced by taking a preformed or preexisting sense that is "inside" the mind of the subject, and pressing it out (ex-pressing it) into the world. This "exteriorization"[38] view of expression presumes the subject is the simple performer of the act of phenomenalization: the subject constitutes phenomena as phenomena, and is itself, therefore, the driving force of phenomenalization. Many later phenomenologists (most notably Derrida in *Voice and Phenomenon*) have found this account of phenomenalization to be phenomenologically insufficient and have therefore rejected this account of expression as also phenomenologically insufficient. This, in turn, led many phenomenological and post-phenomenological thinkers to abandon the notion of expression itself as hopelessly tied to the "metaphysics of presence," and therefore unhelpful for post-Heideggerean thinking about experience. A meaningful discourse on a "phenomenology of expressivity" was seemingly ruled out, at least from 1967 onward.

But Derrida's criticism of one understanding of expression does not mean that expression itself is insufficiently phenomenological, any more than his criticism of the traditional understanding of language meant that language could be of no phenomenological value. If Derrida himself does not explicitly revive the language of expression, he also does not argue that there is nothing like the function of expression or that such a function cannot be phenomenologically helpful in some way. His argument, rather, is that expression is essentially intertwined (*Verflechtung*) with indication (i.e., with empirical elements). But such an intertwining then needs further phenomenological elaboration—an elaboration, I am arguing, that expressivity, properly understood, is best able to provide. Indeed, *Voice and Phenomenon* ends up affirming and even transcendentalizing something that functions very similar to expressivity as we will articulate it, and differance, as an ultratranscendental conception of life,[39] cannot be wholly separated from expressivity, even if it cannot also be easily equated with Husserl's early understanding of expression.

Derrida's criticism of expression in *Voice and Phenomenon*, then, leaves open (and perhaps even calls for) the possibility that expressivity could be rescued from the exteriorization view that Husserl initially tied it to. If this could be done, expressivity may yet remain a worthwhile phenomenological and philosophical concept. And such a rescue effort is worthwhile, I maintain, because expressivity opens us to properly understand the phenomenality at the core of experience. We need not call this function "expressivity," of course—the arbitrariness of language is such that we can call it anything we like, if we wish. But maintaining (and clarifying) the language of expressivity will help us see philosophical continuities, for example, between Husserl and Merleau-Ponty, that will help us better understand the relation between the elements of the phenomenological knot that lies at the core of experience and the phenomeno-logic that is necessary to tying (and to untangling) that knot.[40]

It is this relation that gives rise to the need for the method of reduction, as well as the disagreements in how to carry out that method. It is this relation that necessitates a transcendental (but neither transcendent nor immanent, per se) element of subjectivity. It is this relation that enables *Sinngebung* to move in both directions, thus opening the dual nature of phenomenological constitution (a constituting and a constituted, the touching and the touched). It is this relationship, in other words, that opens the entire problematic (or way of thinking) that we now call "phenomenology,"[41] because it is this relationship that drives the phenomenalization of experience itself. Addressing the lacuna concerning a phenomenological account of expressivity—that is, an account of expressivity as it functions in the phenomenality of experience—is therefore crucial, not simply to phenomenology but to our understanding of experience itself. Clarifying expressivity as the mode-of-relating of the constitutive elements of experience, therefore, will provide us essential insights first and foremost into the very way in which our experience is put together. As we will see, this expressive tying together of experience is not simply performed by us as subjects but is something in which we, as subjects, are always caught up. Our very constitution—not simply as distinct individuals, but as subjects in our subjectivity—is thoroughly political, influenced in a transcendental way by empirical factors.

The Argument

Clarifying expressivity, then, will help us better understand both experience and phenomenology. This is the double task undertaken in this book. To do it, we begin by fully elaborating and justifying our understanding of expressivity as it functions in phenomenology in Chapter 1. Beginning with Husserl's work in *Logical Investigations*, we will see that expressivity is characterized by the phenomenal unity of asymmetrical elements (such that I "live through" A in order to "live in" B). Because Husserl fails to appreciate the distinction between expressing and expression, however, he fails to adequately explain both the nature of the asymmetry and the nature of the phenomenal unity. Turning to Merleau-Ponty we see that the subject is capable of expressing only because the subject is first an expression. This complicates the asymmetrical nature of expressivity, revealing it to be a relative asymmetry that has a necessarily mutual component: living through A causes me to live in B, even as living in B causes me to live in A. This mutual asymmetry can only be fully explained in light of what Deleuze will call the triad of expression: expressivity is not merely a relation between two things (an expressed and its expression) but necessarily requires an act or force (expressing) that co-constitutes both expressed and expression as relata. This force is not primarily an action performed by a subject but is an innately generative process: expressing necessarily produces an expression that does not fully contain the expressed, and so pushes toward another expression and another and another. In this way, expressing emerges as a force that generates phenomenality, and so explains the "how" of our actual (phenomenal) experience.

Chapter 2 outlines the implications expressivity has for our understanding of subjectivity. If subjectivity is an expression before it is an expressing, then sense is not primarily a product of subjective action but is rather something that subjectivity is caught up in in its primal engagement with the world. This engagement, then, cannot be primarily conscious, and even less a purposive act-intentionality. Rather, subjects are engaged primarily via sensings (*Empfindnisse*) of flesh that are equally determinative of "subject" and "world." Following Sara Heinämaa, we will see that embodied subjectivity is not therefore merely a psycho-physical unity but an expressive enfleshed whole whose meaning is both drawn from, and constitutive of, its incarnate activities. In this way, we can see that expressive subjectivity— emerging from material-spiritual flesh—has sense as constitutive of its very being in a way that establishes the inherent *intrasubjective* connection between subject and world: subjectivity is always already an expression of the sense/sensing of the world.

Such a redefinition of the role of sense clearly has epistemological ramifications that Chapter 3 makes explicit. Drawing especially on Merleau-Ponty's notion of flesh, sense is not taken to be something cognitive, cultural, or spiritual (*Geistig*) added to the material makeup of the world but as the material-spiritual expression of flesh in and as the world (and as the subject, as Chapter 2 explains). As such, sense is always already ontological, even as ontology is therefore revealed to have a necessarily meaningfull tenor that may not be adequately captured by *episteme* or epistemology. In this regard, we see a phenomenological resonance with Karen Barad's "ontoepistemology" in arguing that sense/sensing is best understood as a sort of directedness or orientation within being: engaging the world cognitively/epistemologically is not primarily a knowing-about the world, but a practical interaction (a doing) that shapes and alters the world. Knowing, being, and doing are necessarily intertwined in the autopoietic nature of expressive phenomenality.

Having articulated the key elements of expressivity as the logic of phenomenality, this book then moves to explain how phenomenology is essential to making sense of that logic, and hence to making sense of (our) experience. Chapter 4 shows that the expressive relation outlined in Chapters 1–3 is also characteristic of the relation between the transcendental and the empirical in phenomenology. As such, we can see that the transcendental conditions explored in phenomenology must necessarily be generated within empirical conditions even as they condition those conditions. This enables us to speak of four levels of phenomenological constitution: empirical, transcendental, transcendentally empirical, and ultratranscendental. The expressive relation between these levels reveals that transcendental phenomenology is a necessarily political and critical endeavor: it is both politically constituted within empirical conditions and politically constitutive of those conditions, insofar as it articulates the concepts (including race, gender, sexuality, etc.) that are transcendentally (and transcendentally empirically) generative of empirical conditions.

Chapter 5 then explores whether such a transcendental method is necessary for all phenomenology (including nonphilosophical uses of phenomenology). At stake in this question is the extent to which we must be aware of the transcendental (and transcendental empirical) conditions of our experience in order to adequately articulate that experience. The chapter begins by clarifying how subjectivity is generated within the expressive logic of phenomenality. Because the subject is an expression (of flesh) before and so that it is capable of expressing, the subject necessarily emerges from the generativity enacted within flesh, and so has access to the series of co-constitutive elements that go with that expressive generativity. This implies both that every subjective action necessarily draws on its transcendental conditions (hence signaling the importance of articulating the transcendental, even for applied phenomenology), and that reflecting on subjective experience is a legitimate way of accessing the phenomena generated within the world and the conditions of phenomenality in and by which they are generated (thereby justifying the first-person perspective as a "legitimizing source of cognition" according to the "principle of principles"). To truly clarify the role of transcendental conditions in empirical actions, we must be clear on the precise (i.e., expressive) relationship between the co-constitutive elements of generativity. The reduction is the name we give to the type of reflection that enables us to see the co-constitutive elements as distinct in the way particular to phenomena, rather than simply presume that they are wholly different kinds of things, as we do in the "natural attitude." Hence, we must suspend the natural attitude so as to come to see a different relation between subjects and objects: the primal engagement we have called sensings, which is an elaboration of the uniquely phenomenological account of intentionality (as consciousness of . . . which is precisely *not* consciousness of X). In this fashion, Chapter 6 justifies and clarifies, individually and collectively, the *epoché*, the reduction, the first-person reflective perspective and intentionality as essential elements of the phenomenological method and explains how and why this method is necessary to adequately understand our experience of "things themselves."[42] It shows that any analysis of a phenomenon necessarily presupposes some account of the transcendental conditions expressed through that phenomenon and shaped by its expression, and so a truly rigorous account of any empirical phenomenon must account for those conditions, implicitly or explicitly. Hence, transcendental phenomenology can contribute to broader uses of phenomenology in three distinct (though related) ways: through the generation of insights; as a generative *Stiftung*; and as a way of sensing or engaging the world.

Having clarified the expressive logic of phenomenality (Chapters 1–3) and how it establishes a certain relation between transcendental and empirical conditions that inexorably shapes our experience in a way that phenomenology is uniquely able to access and articulate (Chapters 4–5), we are then free in Chapter 6 to articulate a distinct understanding of politics as a transcendental force of subjective constitution. Once we factor in all the co-constituted relations outlined in the expressive logic of phenomenality (subject-object; subject-world; transcendental-empirical; ontology-epistemology; etc.), it is not sufficient to speak simply of transcendental intersubjectivity, as Husserl is wont to do. Rather, we must see that, beyond the interaction between subjects, there is political force exerted in the transcendental constitution of subjects in what Husserl calls "spiritual communities." This reveals politics to be primarily a matter of constitution (*politeia*) before it can be a matter of constituted things (e.g., the *res publica*). Since phenomenology is able to rigorously articulate the various ways that subjects are constituted politically and how subjects constitute political communities, the present moment demands the generation of a "phenomenological politics" on par with the "phenomenological psychology" generated in phenomenology's earlier days.

This book clarifies how phenomenality works and how phenomenology helps us understand that, by explicating expressivity as the logic of phenomenality. But we must be careful in how we make sense of the nature of that logic, or we risk misunderstanding both the nature of the logic at work (as a phenomenal and not merely a conceptual logic) and the understanding of the political that it has revealed. The conclusion, therefore, clarifies the nature of the logic of phenomenality as a "logic of sensing" rather than a "logic of predication," and shows how this makes sense of the particular type of differentiated unity at work in expressivity. This clarification in turn enables a further clarification of the (triple) relativization of the subject to sense and of the affective relation between subject(ivity), object(ivity), and flesh. Through these clarifications, we see the precise manner in which experience is constituted within political conditions by a political force. Therefore, we can say that experience itself is necessarily political and is necessary for politics—and so, too, is phenomenology, which is the means by which the (transcendental) political nature of experience can be both articulated and transformed.

1

A Phenomenological Account
of Expressivity

The task of this chapter is to lay out the understanding and definition of expressivity that we will be using in this work, by drawing on the functions it has played in phenomenology, from its role as the first "essential distinction" in Husserl's *Logical Investigations* through its fullest application in the late phenomenology of Merleau-Ponty and in the generative phenomenology that Steinbock develops out of Husserl's work.[1] The purpose of this chapter will be to sketch an overview of both the definition and function of expressivity, and not to provide a thorough textual analysis of the concept of expression/expressivity in the thought of Husserl or Merleau-Ponty.[2] This overview will provide the lay of the land that will help us see the development of a particular (phenomenological) account of expressivity through Husserl, Merleau-Ponty, and beyond that will help orient us for the later chapters that flesh out the details of the account outlined in this chapter and examine their various philosophical implications.

To provide this overview, we will begin with the broad definition of expressivity as "the phenomenal unity of asymmetrical elements" first laid out by Husserl. Two problems arise with this initial definition, which we will turn to Merleau-Ponty to provide an answer for: (1) clearly distinguishing the act of expressing from the product of that act (an expression), by (2) clarifying the role that the subject does (and does not) play in expressivity. Addressing these problems will help us clarify the nature of the asymmetry that exists between the two terms of an expression but will leave unanswered the problem of what precisely it is that expresses itself through expressivity. We will then argue that we must account for the process of relating and not simply for the two relata at work in the relation of expressivity, and hence some account of "expressing" is required. Steinbock's Husserlian account of generativity will be used to clarify the self-generating nature of expressivity, thereby making possible an account of expressing that does not require an appeal to some transcendent subject that "expresses itself" through expressivity. This will ultimately help us clarify the phenomenal nature of the unity that is brought about in expressivity and thereby establish the key function expressivity plays in phenomenality, while opening the question of the relation between the subject and phenomenality.

Expression: Some Essential Distinctions

Let us begin at the beginning. At the very beginning of his *Logical Investigations,* Husserl outlines the "essential distinction" between expression and indication. This is essential for Husserl because he posits expression as the mechanism that relates the subjectivity of the knower with the objectivity of what is known.[3] Expression therefore functions as his rejoinder to Frege, his initial attempt to clarify "sense" as the relation between subjective conceptions and the world of referents.[4] Expression, he claims, is a fundamental element of meaning insofar as it presents itself as a "phenomenological unity" with either meaning-intention (taking something as meaningful) or meaning-fulfillment (taking something as meaning this or that in particular) and thereby allows the mental states of a particular knower to become something "objective" (LI, I, 166), that is, to transcend the merely subjective act and "become an abiding possession of science, a documented, ever available treasure for knowledge and advancing research" (LI, I, 166).

This may seem to make expression inherently linguistic, a mere vehicle to carry meaning from one person to another. But while Husserl is clearly thinking of expression in linguistic terms here, he is at pains to point out a particular feature of such linguistic interactions that constitute the expressive heart of expression. Husserl famously distinguishes, within signs, between expressions and indications as distinct *functions* at work within the use of signs. This distinction can be broadly summarized by saying that expressions "mean" while indications "point":[5] an indication motivates belief in the reality of something else by providing a "descriptive unity" between the indicator and the thing indicated, a unity that, as "a unity of judgement," is "taken as a descriptively peculiar way of combining acts of judgement into a single act of judgement" (LI, I, 184). The indicative function, then, "amounts to just this: that certain things *may* or *must* exist, *since* other things have been given" (LI, I, 184).

This pointing-beyond-itself to a distinct meaning is different from expression. An expression is marked by being "phenomenally one with the experience made manifest in them in the consciousness of the [one] who manifests them" (LI, I, 188). This "phenomenal" unity is distinct from the "unity of judgment" characteristic of indications: in expression, I do not experience the meaning as distinct from the thing I encounter but precisely as (phenomenally) one with it. It is the difference between seeing the red maple leaf on a white background between two vertical red bars and thinking "that's the flag of Canada" (indication) and reading the word "Canada" (expression). In the former case, my experience of seeing the flag causes me to think of Canada, but these are separate acts—it is only through a judgment ("that's the flag of Canada") that the connection is made. In the latter case, I read the word "Canada" and don't even notice the word itself unless I put it in quotation marks to suggest that you should consider this as the word "Canada": I "see the meaning" rather than simply "seeing according to a meaning [that is] posed arbitrarily," as Merleau-Ponty will put it later (SWWE, 70). Or, as Husserl says, in an expression I "live through" the physical or perceptual appearance of the expression so as to "live in" the enacting of meaning contained therein (LI, I, 193; see also Hua 4, 248). Here, meaning does not merely attach to a separately existing physical substrate or vehicle; rather, in expression, the meaning is phenomenally one with the expression that expresses it. The expression can be called an expression, properly speaking, if and only if it enacts this expressive function, that is, if it constitutes a phenomenal unity with what is expressed.[6]

We see, then, that expressivity, in its most basic core, is the constitution of a phenomenal unity between asymmetrical elements: I "live through" one element so as to "live in" the other. Hence, one element is almost entirely effaced, in its significance, by the expressive function: *qua* expressive, the task of the one element is to recede into the background of our attention and focus so that the other element can come to the foreground; one element is used merely as support (LI I, 193–94) for the other. This asymmetry is not experienced as asymmetrical—as A motivating one to live in or enact B—but rather as a unity. I do not experience the two parts of the expression as two parts, but as one. That I can later, through reflection, distinguish the parts is essential to the nature of this unity—the unity I experience is precisely an "*experienced unity*" (LI, I, 193), and not an ontological unity or a unity of substance.

At this early stage of Husserl's phenomenological work, constituting this phenomenal unity is assumed to be the task of the subject, enacted via act-intentionality. This is why, early on, the work of expression is characterized by Husserl as a change in intention:

Phenomenologically speaking . . . the intuitive presentation, in which the physical appearance of the world is constituted, undergoes an essential phenomenal modification when its object begins to count as an *expression*. While what constitutes the object's appearing remains unchanged, the intentional character of the experience alters. There is constituted (without need of a fulfilling or illustrative intuition) an act of meaning which finds support in the verbal presentation's intuitive content, but which differs in essence from the intuitive intention directed upon the word itself. (LI, I, 193–94)

This shift from a perceptual intention to a meaning-intention is the effect of an expression upon the subject who encounters it as an expression: the "living in" of the more important element of the expression is, at this stage, a particular kind of living—a meaningful living, a living in sense. But this meaningful living is brought about by the expression itself: I encounter the expression, *qua* expressive, as meaning-full, which therefore prompts a meaningful engagement with it rather than merely a perceptual engagement.

But two problems emerge in Husserl's analysis of expression here. First, while the analysis suggests a distinction between the act of expressing and the unity that is produced by that act, Husserl does not seem to rigorously distinguish between these two elements at this time: "expression" can refer either to the act of forming the unity or to the "product" of that act.[7] Second, in characterizing the work of expression as a "change in intention," a particular role for the subject in expression is implicitly posited, though not argued for: the subject is the one who constitutes and utilizes expressions (both by expressing and by "reading" them), and expressions are a tool or vehicle the subject can use to direct interest toward the "sense" they mean to express (LI, I, 191).

The two problems are not entirely distinct from each other: insofar as the distinction between expressing and expressions is not clearly made, Husserl views expressivity primarily in terms of expressions. Therefore, while it is assumed that subjects encounter (and even produce) expressions, the question of the constitution of the "phenomenal unity" inherent to expression itself is never tackled head on. That is, in *Logical Investigations* at least, Husserl never seeks to explain express*ing*: he merely assumes it in order to explain express*ions*. And by tying expressivity primarily to changes in meaning-intention, Husserl ties expressivity to act-intentionality. As a result, express*ing* is (implicitly) assumed to be a particular kind of act purposefully performed by subjects, for example, the act of infusing physical phenomena (phonemes, graphemes, etc.) with meaning. Such an act may be of interest to a phenomenology or philosophy of language, but it is of no immediate consequence to logic itself or to the logic of phenomenology. Hence, there is no need to examine further either the constitution of phenomenal unities or the relation between meaning, sense, and expression in *Logical Investigations*. The former issue is ignored by Husserl moving forward (at least in *Logical Investigations* and perhaps beyond: even the *Passive Synthesis* lectures seem to presuppose the ability of the subject to, e.g., make associations, form *gegenstandlichkeit*, etc.). The latter issue, on the other hand, is presumed in such a naïve way (most notably in the infamous §8: "Expressions in solitary life") that it is not, I think, an exaggeration to say that these two problems prevented the emergence of the full significance of expressivity for phenomenology for several decades, at least. For the arguments Husserl offers in §8 are the main point of contention in Derrida's *Voice and Phenomenon*, a work that made "expression" seem like an outdated and unhelpful residue of the "metaphysics of presence," and hence consigned the term "expression" mostly to the scrapheap of phenomenological inquiry (with the notable exception of Merleau-Ponty), rather than help us see that the "metaphysics of presence" was itself a shrouding of an appreciation of expression and expressing. For in not fully recognizing the distinction between expressing and expressions, Husserl failed to see the need to account for the relationship between them. As such, he failed to adequately distinguish (at least in this case) between subjective action and the products of that action. At best, this fails to explain "sense" (insofar as it merely repeats the subject-world distinction, without explaining it). At worst, this presumes either idealism/psychologism (if we decide subjective action creates all sense) or empiricism (if we decide the mode of production of the product is not significant to the product itself), both of which fail to be adequately phenomenological, as Husserl argues in the "Prolegomena" to *Logical Investigations* and in the *Crisis*, respectively.

To properly understand expressivity in phenomenology, then, we need to thematize explicitly the role of the subject in expressing, and the role of expressing in expressivity. If we merely presume, as Husserl seems to in §8, that the subject is the source of the expressing—that is, that the subject is what expresses the expressed sense in and through the expression—then we are condemned to the "externalization" view of expressivity, whereby expressivity is understood simply as taking fully formed ideas that exist within the subject and (ex)pressing them out into the world.[8] Such a view does not allow us to fully explicate "sense," insofar as it presumes that the subject has or contains sense within itself but does not explain how. If all expressivity can explain is how sense is externalized, but not where it comes from, how it is created, what justifies its use in scientific inquiry, and so forth, then Husserl's appeal to expression as the rejoinder to Frege is doomed to fall short, insofar as it fails to answer some basic philosophical and phenomenological questions: Does sense simply exist (as a bare fact) in the solitary mental life of the subject, or is it somehow produced by the actions of the subject? If the latter, is it produced in the act of expressing or in some other act? If in the act of expressing, how does that expressing work? If in some other act, then why is expression an essential distinction to logic and to phenomeno-logic, and a necessary first step in a phenomenological investigation?

What we need is an account of expressivity that does not simply presume the subject's role (e.g., as "what expresses itself"), but instead seeks to rigorously explicate it.

The Subject as Expression: Merleau-Ponty and Mutual Asymmetry

Fortunately, Merleau-Ponty, though perhaps not only Merleau-Ponty,[9] offers us such an account. This account develops over the course of his thought, at least from *The Structure of Behavior* up through *The Visible and the Invisible*, and so it can be difficult to define or delineate precisely.[10] A tentative definition, however, is found in the lecture notes contained in *The Sensible World and the World of Expression*: "we will define expression or expressivity as the property that a phenomenon has through its internal arrangement to disclose another that is not or even never was given" (SWWE, 11).[11] Here we see a continuity with the asymmetrical element ("to disclose another") and, potentially, the phenomenal unity ("through its internal arrangement" rather than by appeal to something external) outlined in Husserl's account of expressivity. But Merleau-Ponty does not simply reproduce Husserl's analyses of expression; he greatly expands and deepens them.

Tracing the development of this notion of expression through Merleau-Ponty's thought is a worthwhile (though lengthy and complicated) endeavor. Fortunately for us, it has already been done quite superbly by Donald Landes, Véronique Fóti, Remy Kwant, Renaud Barbaras, and others.[12] Rather than rehash the textual work they have already done, let us simply draw from their work the two conclusions that we can take from Merleau-Ponty's deepening of expression that are essential for our purposes here: first, the subject is an expression before it is "what expresses itself"; and second, the asymmetry of the terms of an expression can be mutually asymmetrical: I can "live through" A so as to "live in" B, even as "living in" B can lead me inexorably to "live in" A.

To understand these two claims and their importance for our appreciation of the full role of expressivity, we must recognize the way that Merleau-

Ponty alters the understanding of the "phenomenal" nature of the unity of expression. On Husserl's early account of expression discussed earlier, the "phenomenal" unity is the unity of an appearing phenomenon, a unity accomplished by the constituting power of consciousness. Merleau-Ponty, on the other hand, in a move that is utterly essential to our broader argument, conceives of the phenomenal unity of expression as pertaining to phenomenality itself, and not merely to distinct phenomena appearing to and before a consciousness: consciousness does not simply give sense to being through its own constituting power, but rather sense and being are always already intertwined, even before the constituting acts of consciousness.[13] This intertwining is phenomenal (indeed, is the very possibility of phenomenality itself) rather than simply ontological (on the side of "fact" or existence) or epistemological (on the side of "essence" or sense), and hence opens up the possibility of conscious, phenomenal experience: we are conscious because of the phenomenal condition of the world, rather than (as the early Husserl would have claimed) the world having phenomenological reality because of consciousness. Put another way, the subject is first an express*ion* of the world as sense before it is capable of express*ing* the world of sense.[14]

In understanding this claim and its relation to expressivity, we must see that this intertwining is a "phenomenal unity" that meets the essential characteristics outlined before: it is both asymmetrical and experienced as a unity. The second essential characteristic requires little justification, I think, especially after the "hermeneutic turn" of the twentieth century: it is common for us to experience the world as comprising "meaningful things" (a point we will revisit in Chapter 3). But to what extent does this unity remain asymmetrical? Here we may run into a problem when we view this asymmetry as happening already on the level of phenomenality and not simply at the later level of phenomena. Recall that the asymmetry in question is that one element of expressivity (the expression) moves into the background of our attention and focus to allow the other element (the expressed) to move to the foreground. In thinking the intertwining of sense and being at the level of phenomenalization, Merleau-Ponty does not do away with this asymmetry, but he does suggest that it might be mutual, flowing in both directions: A motivates one to "live in" B, and B motivates one to "live in" A; A effaces itself to allow us to focus on B, but focusing on B eventually leads us to move beyond B and focus instead on A. That is, he finds a way through the dilemma of asymmetry via the notion of reversibility: insofar as the (phenomenal) unity of sense and being is taken to be constitutive of experience itself on the level of phenomenality, sense and being cannot emerge or exist primarily as distinct experiences (i.e., as an experience of sense or an experience of being) and therefore it is not necessary that the asymmetry occur only in one direction (i.e., from a distinct act, A, to a distinct act, B).[15] Rather, this notion of experience itself, as Merleau-Ponty conceives of it, introduces a certain "slippage" or passage between sense and being (conceived as phenomenal conditions and not yet as distinct phenomena): sense (as sensing) inevitably takes us toward Being, and Being inevitably takes us toward sense.[16] Therefore, being and sense—as a unity found in phenomenality itself—motivate us to move from one to the other, but without simply privileging one over the other in a way that would lose the true nature of this complex relationship. Indeed, to privilege one over the other is to slide out of phenomenology (with its ability to focus on phenomenality) and into essentialism/idealism/ psychologism (if we privilege "living in" the "subjective" realm of sense and meaning) or naïve realism/empiricism (if we privilege the "living in" the "objective" realm of "facts" and beings). The relationship between being and sense remains asymmetrical,[17] then—I pass through one into the other—even if that asymmetry flows in both directions.

In conceiving of experience itself as a phenomenal unity, then, Merleau-Ponty complicates the relationship between sense and being. Sense comes to be understood, not primarily as "essence" but as the "internal logic" that inheres in "existing thing[s]" (SWWE, 13). This notion of sense is not articulated epistemically but emerges "tacitly" as "a part of the internal framework of the landscape," where it emerges as "a typical activity," that is, as "the universal context of an action in the world" (SWWE, 13). As the non-epistemic context for action, "this sense is less possessed than it is practiced" (SWWE, 13): sense is not a matter primarily of epistemic possession or articulation but of a practical enactment, a movement out of which subjects (and the world) are constituted.[18] This movement is sometimes simply called "Nature," understood as the autoproduction of sense rather than as a collection of objects.[19] On this understanding, sense (as phenomenal condition [sensing] rather than as phenomenon) is understood primordially as a background or field that provides the foundation for distinct acts of sense: sensing is a sort of "pre-culture" (N, 176) that provides the foundation for later cultural acts, and the mode of being of such a primordial sense is *Stiftung*.[20] And if sense is a field that exists, that "is," in the mode of *Stiftung*, this is in part because the "is," that is, Being, comes to be understood as interrogation (VI, 121): "the existing world exists in the interrogative mode" (VI, 103). Being is understood here in its verbal sense (VI, 115): to be is to interrogate, that is, to operate as a type of questioning, to open something that demands an answer even as it precludes giving a final and definitive answer that would close the question down entirely, and therefore enable us to stop interrogating. Such a project of interrogating is simply called "living,"[21] and it is the fundamental mode of Being of all creatures subject to *lived* experience (*Erlebnis*) and who live out of a lifeworld (*Lebenswelt*).

To return to the problem of the role of the subject in expressivity, then, we can see that Merleau-Ponty's account of expressivity posits that every subject always exists in the tradition or institution(s) (*Stiftungen*) in which it lives precisely as an interrogation of that tradition and institution:[22] the subject always takes up the *Stiftung's* projects as its own, or alters them, or questions why it should take up these projects and not others. Regardless, the subject always takes up its living within the bounds of some *Stiftung(en)*, and its whole life is then lived in and as an interrogation of "those events which sediment in me a sense, not just as survivals or residues, but as the invitation to a sequel, the requirement of a future" (LCF, 108–9). In doing so, the subject is always driven to "live in" the sense of its *Stiftung*, even as that sense exists precisely to provide the subject an orientation that enables it to "live in" being.

This reversibility of sense and being that is essential to Merleau-Ponty's late "ontology" both circumscribes that "ontology" as phenomenal unity (that is, as phenomenality), and shows the subject to be primarily the expression of that sense, not simply as a finished product, but as an interrogating of that sense that is always already an enacting of that sense: meaning (sense), being and doing/acting come together clearly here in the phenomenal conditions of experience itself. And if expression is a pressing-out (ex-pression), then sense is the interiority out of which subjects (and world) are ex-pressed, rather than the subject being the interiority out of which sense is expressed (as was the case in Husserl's early theory, most obviously in §8 of the first *Logical Investigation*). The subject's expressive ability (i.e., its express*ing*) is therefore explained as the express*ion* of the ex-pressed.

But what, precisely, is the expressed in this situation? In trying to address the lacuna of Husserl's (early) account of expression by elaborating more precisely the role of the subject in expression and in the movement of sense, we seem to have jumped out of the frying pan and into the fire. We have established some (relative) clarity on the role of the subject, but only by suggesting that the subject is *not* primarily the subject of expression but its product: the subject can *become* "what expresses itself" in an expression, but it is not so primarily. Particular subjective acts of expressing are *not* the primary locus of expressivity, but merely a secondary effect of it. And if subjective acts of expressing are primarily themselves expressions, then who or what (if anything) is the primary subject or enactor of expressivity? This problem is especially pertinent insofar as we have said that the phenomenal unity characteristic of expressivity is not necessary simply for some individual particular acts of the subject but is constitutive of phenomenality (and therefore experience) itself. Once we consider the subject primarily as an expression, and only secondarily as express*ing*, we are left to wonder what precisely it is that expresses itself in expressivity.

The Necessity of a Threefold Account of Expressivity

But perhaps we are merely talking ourselves into knots here, caught up in our own rhetorical devices. Perhaps speaking of "what expresses itself" in expressivity is only an accident of language, or the continuation of the Husserlian presumption of the constitutive role of the subject. Perhaps such language can simply be abandoned once that presumption itself has been abandoned.

The question of whether what expresses itself is a necessary feature of expressivity, or merely something tied to a particular account of metaphysics that the phenomenological account of expressivity may not be committed to, has been broached in the work of Deleuze.[23] Sean Bowden suggests that Deleuze abandons a threefold notion of expressivity (something that expresses the expressed in and through the expression) that was operative in *Expression in Philosophy: Spinoza* in favor of a twofold notion of expression in *Difference and Repetition*. If this is so, perhaps the threefold nature of expressivity comes from a particular type of metaphysics and is not essential to an account of expressivity itself, in which case, abandoning Husserl's "metaphysical" account of the subject (especially in §8 of the first *Logical Investigation*) would enable us to also abandon the notion of expressivity as requiring (1) something that expresses (2) the expressed in and through (3) the expression.

The necessity of the triadic structure of expressivity comes from the fact that we must account also for the action of relating that happens in expressivity and cannot content ourselves simply with describing the relata. The expressed-expression dyad is not sufficient to explain the relation of expressivity for Deleuze (at least in the Spinoza book) precisely because it does not explain their *relation* but only defines their constituent parts, and therefore "the idea of expression remains unintelligible while we see only two of the terms whose relations it presents" (EiP, 27). Our everyday understanding of expressivity can perhaps be content with the dyadic relation, because we take for granted, in such an understanding, that there is a subject that expresses itself in the expression, that is, that there is a subject performing the "expressing" that unites the expressed and the expression together into a phenomenal unity. Once we get beyond this naïve account of the subject's role in expressivity (and of expressivity as a phenomenon performed by subjects), we must account for the expressing itself. We must explain how the expressed and the expression are being formed into a phenomenal unity and who or what is so forming them.

We seem to be caught in a bind, then: on the one hand, the language of "what expresses itself" in an expression seems tied to a particular metaphysical account (of God, in Spinoza, and of the subject, in Husserl)[24] that we may hope to avoid. But focusing only on the remaining two terms also assumes and relies on that same metaphysical account by presuming (rather than explaining) the existence of the relata. What we need, it seems, is to find a way of accounting for the relation between the relata of expressivity, without necessarily substantializing that relation and attributing it to a transcendent subject (divine or otherwise). We need to find a way to account for the relation (or the relating) itself, on its own terms.

We can begin to find such an account in Deleuze's claim that the expressed is becoming-itself in and through its expression,[25] combined with the fact that the expression cannot be explained without recourse to the expressed. Yet, these two on their own are not enough—we necessarily need something beyond simply the expressed-expression dyad in order to explain both the expressed and the expression. For the expressed, while a cause of the expression, is not a *sufficient* cause of the expression, and this is necessarily so: if it were, then the expressed could not be expressed in any other way than its expression, and the expressed and its expression would be one and the same. So, to maintain the distinction between the expressed and the expression, it is necessary that there be other conditions that condition the expression, beyond merely the expressed. This does not reduce the causal efficacy of the expressed vis-à-vis the expression, but clarifies it: in X conditions, Y will be expressed in an expression, Z; Z is how Y is instantiated in X. But, if there are A conditions rather than X conditions, then Y will be expressed in an expression C, rather than Z; C is how Y is instantiated in A. So something beyond both the expressed/immanent cause and the expression is necessary for the expressed to be expressed in and by the expression.

Perhaps an example will help illustrate the point here. If I pass by a colleague in the hallway (the conditions—X) and I smile, perhaps offering a little nod or a quick "Hello," this is taken as a gesture of warmth and friendship. My smile is taken to be an expression (Z) of my friendliness (the expressed, Y). But if I encounter that same colleague in a different setting—say, at the funeral of their recently deceased mother (different conditions, A)—my friendliness toward them will likely take on a different expression (C): a sympathetic gaze, a comforting pat on the arm, or an encouraging hug.

In both cases, it is my friendliness that is expressed, but the differing contexts require a change in the expression itself: my smile would be out of place in the funeral setting, and the pat on the arm or the hug might communicate something entirely different than "friendliness" if offered in a workplace setting. The contextual factors set the conditions (X or A) that determine the best means (Z or C) by which my friendliness (Y) is expressed or instantiated.

These contextual factors or conditions, then, clearly alter how Y is expressed. But do they alter Y (i.e., the expressed) itself? Here, the question of temporality and the related phenomenological issues of genesis and generativity come into play. For if the "transcendent something" beyond the expressed and its expression is static and atemporal, then Y itself would not change, given X, but merely its appearance would: my friendliness would appear as a smile (in X) or as a hug (in A), but would remain the same friendliness. However, once this transcendent beyond is temporalized, we see that Y (the expressed) itself alters, given X (the conditions of expressing), for once Y appears as Z (the expression), then X is altered into X + Z. But this changing condition will now alter Y's expression: if Y in X looks like Z, then Y in X + Z will *not* look like Z but like something else, given the change in the conditions of Y's expression: once I have offered the encouraging hug or the comforting tap at the funeral, that expression of friendliness alters my friendliness vis-à-vis that friend—our friendship forever after includes that moment of comfort in a difficult time, which then colors, in some way, our future interactions, even at work. The next time I pass them in the hallway, my smile is, perhaps, a bit more sympathetic than simply warm, or instead of a quick nod of acknowledgment, perhaps my smile is accompanied this time by a slightly raised eyebrow, wondering how my friend is doing.

Though it may seem like a small, even infinitesimal,[26] thing, there are potentially large consequences to our understanding of expression once we recognize the importance of the relating and its contextual conditions for the relata of expressed and expression. For once we posit that Y's being expressed alters the conditions of Y's expression, it then follows that Y's expressions will be ever-changing precisely because of its expressing itself: its being-expressed alters the modes of that expression, entailing that the expressing can never happen once and for all but is always ongoing, always changing, not for external reasons but precisely for reasons internal to the expressing relationship itself; the expressive relationship is never simply expressed but is always expressing, and this dynamic quality is both an essential element of the expressed-expression relationship and is of a different nature than either the expressed or the expression. Expressing marks a relation between the relata, one that codetermines or co-constitutes the relata in and through the relation itself. Like the differential equation in calculus, expressing names a function or force that determines relata, and not simply another relata.

To return to our example, my friendliness (the expressed) can take on a variety of expressions, but in doing so it establishes a particular kind of relationship (i.e., friendship) that both ties my friendliness to those expressions of it and is not the same as either my friendliness (which is also expressed to other people in other ways) or the smiles, hugs, comfort, or acknowledgment that are the concrete expressions of that friendliness. In that sense, we can say that expressing is not another relata in the relation, but it is the motivating force driving the relation, ensuring that the relation is never simply "differentiated relata" but a "relationship" in the social or ethical (and not merely the logical) sense: something that carries on through time, whose relata are affected by each other and by the relationship through that passage of time, and so something that therefore ensures the ongoing alteration of the relata and of the relationship itself. Expressing friendliness produces, even as it is motivated by, friendship, and that friendship motivates expressions of my friendliness (I assure you that I do not express "friendliness" to *all* the people that I know!) that change the friendliness, its concrete modes of expression, and the friendship.

Some type of threefold account of expressivity is therefore necessary for a rigorous account of expressivity as expressivity must, by necessity, have a third term that is not another relata, but the actuality of the relating itself. While the natural attitude may be condemned to substantialize or reify that relating into a relata, within the reduction where, strictly speaking, that attitude is bracketed, such a reification cannot occur. It might even be said that avoiding that reification—moving from "what expresses itself" to "expressing"—is precisely the purpose of the reduction and is the key to the validity and value of the phenomenological method: perhaps expressing is precisely the type of relating that can enable us to make sense of phenomenalization and not simply phenomena (a point we will return to in Chapter 5).

Indeed, since we have seen that a rigorous account of expressivity must account for the expressed, the expression, and the relating that exists between them, we can see that it must explain, in the language we were using earlier, the express*ing* of an express*ed* in and through an express*ion*. But Deleuze frames this triad in other language that points to the broader significance of expressivity for our understanding of experience itself. Deleuze states that "Being, knowing and acting are the three forms of expression" (EiP, 321). And if this is true—if expressing an expressed through an expression is simply the being, knowing, and doing of one and the same phenomenal unity—then we can start to see the enormous implications of properly articulating expressivity as the intertwining of being, knowing, and acting in the knotted core of experience (even if we might wonder whether the language of acting remains too tied to the notion of volitional act-intentionality and would perhaps be better suited to language of doing rather than acting). While we will need several chapters to explore all the implications of this statement, we can already see, *in nuce*, how explaining expressivity may prove essential to untying the phenomenological knot at the center of human experience that was discussed in the introduction.

The Generativity of Expressing

But before we move on to trace out those implications, one last step remains in our initial exploration of expressivity. We have seen the necessity of accounting for both of the relata of expression and the expressing that relates them. We have also seen that the relating cannot itself be reduced to another relata, but is of a different order or quality than the relata. While we may then quibble with how we framed the problem post Merleau-Ponty—who or what expresses itself in expression?—we can see, too, that the problem remains essential to solve, even as we have taken one small step toward solving it. By shifting from the language of "what expresses itself" to language of "expressing," we have opened the possibility of a move beyond a substantialist metaphysics (a metaphysics of "the subject," a metaphysics of "presence," etc.), but we have not yet solved the initial problem: how are the expressed and the expression related, if not in and through the constitutive power of the subject? If it is not the "I can" of the transcendental subject that initially enacts express*ing*—since, as we have said, the subject's express*ing* is always already an express*ion* of sense, of the *Stiftung* in which it finds itself—then we must still explain how expressing is enacted. If expressing is the motivating force uniting expressed and expression into a phenomenal unity, then how does a phenomenological account of expressivity explain that force?

The answer has already been mentioned in this chapter, though not yet explicated. It lies in the issue of genesis (a fundamental problem in both Husserl and Merleau-Ponty),[27] which culminates in phenomenology's account of generativity. With generativity, phenomenology fully moves past its early reliance on the force or power of constituting subjectivity and takes seriously the notion of a generative power that transcends and precedes the constitutive power of the subject. This power is found in the phenomenological notion of home (*heim*). By "home," Husserl refers to a "geo-historical horizon" (Hua 15, 411) that exists through time as a "generative unity" (Hua 15, 179f; see also 391) of historical descendants, that is, of "generations" (Hua 15, 207–9). As a generative force, home "concerns intersubjective, historical movement" (HB, 266): how the past is not simply a weight that affects the individual constitutive subject but a political (in the sense outlined in the Introduction) force that moves within, and affects, history.[28]

Home must therefore be understood, not simply as a spatiotemporal location, but as a "mode of constitution that occurs 'through' and 'beyond' the ego, and does not simply begin with egological subjectivity" (HB, 189). Home is not just "where I'm from," but *how I live*: it is the political power or force of constituting, of "making-sense," that provides me with my sphere of normality, a "sphere of validity . . . which links me not only with the present but with the past and prepares world-acceptances for the future" (HB, 198).[29] While it may be enacted in part by or through individual subjects, it is not controlled by those subjects but shapes and constitutes those subjects in their subjectivity: insofar as home feels familiar or normal, not simply affectively or sentimentally, but epistemically, ontologically, and practically, home is what enables me to *experience* the world in a characteristic and normative way. Home is not simply a static origin or starting place, but an enduring generative force "where we generationally repeat ourselves" in the sense of continuing to enact that which is typical, normal and familiar to us again and again through the way we take up our tradition: "We stand in the tradition . . . taking up in us what is personal to them, necessarily transformed in us. Generatively" (HB, 195).[30] Such a taking up of the tradition is precisely how I become myself, not strictly as a monad or possessor of my own sovereign will, but as always taking up the will, decisions, and resolutions of others as my own (Hua 15, 364), interrogating the world from this sense that is mine, not because I have created it, but because it is normative to me in the sense that "it makes a difference which way [I] take it up" (HB, 168). Hence, my "own" acts of constituting are always generated as the appropriation and unfolding of my home in its ongoing generative (and generational) unfolding.

Because of this, home takes on privileged sense as that which is "normatively relevant for us" and therefore is not "reversible or exchangeable" with that which is not my home (HB, 181): I always and necessarily make sense of everything in *this* way, I always engage the world from *my* situation (my homeworld, my normativity, etc.) (Hua 15, 220).[31] As such, generativity never leaves home, even when it encounters that which is "alien" or beyond itself, because generativity is the constant unfolding and (re)taking up of home: my experience is always a "crossing over from within" and never a "taking the perspective of the alien" (HB, 249). Hence, there is always a valuation at work, an asymmetry: home is the normativity by which I evaluate the alien, even if what I encounter in the alien causes me to change or adapt the normativity of home. This asymmetry therefore does not trap me in colonialism (imposing my standards on others) or mere repetition, but it does remain asymmetrical: home is always the "here" from which I engage everything else. The world is disclosed to me in and through my home.

But this home, as we said, is not a static location or even a static ability. It is a generative unfolding, and as such "its normal, typical structure is *modified in the repeating*" (HB, 199). This modification does not undermine the home but precisely confirms it as a phenomenologically generative structure (Hua 15, 181): every repetition of home is inevitably an alteration. Home is not just something I find myself in or find in myself, it is something I am constantly working on (both appropriating and critiquing) in and through my own actions, which shape that home even as they (partially) instantiate it. Every action generated within the home, then, necessarily alters or transforms that home, even if only infinitesimally. Indeed, "this mode of transformation itself belongs to the general type of the being of the homeworld" (Hua 15, 222).

My experiencing of the world, then, is simultaneously constituted by my home (as a political and generative force) and transformative of that home. This combination of constitutive power and a being-transformed-by-the-use-of-that-power is essential to the notion of generativity itself. Indeed, generativity is necessarily co-constitutive: in constituting my own activities within my home, the generative force of the home is also necessarily constituting itself as home, and in constituting itself as home it is necessarily also constituting both the alien (that which is not "my" home) and constituting itself (the home) as becoming-alien (i.e., as changing, transforming, etc.) (HB, 244–46.).[32] Generativity, therefore, can be understood as a historical force of differentiation that necessarily relates two things together in a mutually coordinated way that constitutes each of those things as what it is only in relation to the other. It is a constitutive force that emerges within particular geohistorical and cultural situations, co-constitutively generating its constitutive elements (e.g., those situations and the subjects at work within them), while necessarily transforming those elements (and itself) through this co-constitutive generation. As such, the constitutive elements are not simply unique and distinct elements of a larger force (generativity) but are necessarily brought together in a particular kind of unity "that does not depend on a resolution in a higher synthesis" (HB, 246),[33] but which instead places the constitutive elements in a necessary co-constitutive, co-delimiting, but nevertheless asymmetrical, relation that unfolds according to its own generative power.

But remember what we said earlier about the elements of the expressive relation: they are necessarily coordinated to each other such that an alteration to one element necessarily entails an alteration to the other; nevertheless, the relation between them is asymmetrical, insofar as one element (the expression) effaces itself in its being used to disclose the other (the expressed); yet the two elements are brought together in a kind of synthesis or unity that is not a unity of identity (the two elements can still be distinguished upon reflection), but an experienced unity in which the one element necessarily takes my attention to the other. All these characteristics—the "essential" characteristics of the expressive relation—are true also of the relation brought about by generativity: generativity brings two elements (e.g., home/alien) together in a "mutually delimited" (HB, 179), "co-generative" (HB, 179), and "asymmetrical" (HB, 185) unity that is not a synthesis (HB, 246) (i.e., it does not bring about an identity between the elements). As such, we seem justified in concluding that generativity is the force of expressing, that is, the force that puts things into an expressive relation with each other, and therefore that expressing is a generative force.

And since this generative force is not controlled by subjects (though it may, at times, work through them) but is a kind of self-unfolding (driven by its own internal force), we are free to see that the question of "what expresses itself" may indeed be the wrong question to ask, for we do not need a subject—a "doer" behind the "deed," to paraphrase Nietzsche—to explain how or why expression happens. Expressing is the "cause" of expression, even as the relationship between the expressed and its expressions is the "cause" (if that language is still helpful here) of expressing. That is, expressing is less an "act" (of an actor) than it is a process, a process that results from the interaction of the expressed and its expressions, and that *is* those interactions. And this project can be phenomenologically prior to (and partially constitutive of) subjects and subjectivity. Therefore, while the expressed and expressions remain fundamentally different from each other such that there must be some other "transcendent" X that can combine them, there is no reason to take X as a substance—a thing that remains itself while undergoing changes in its accidents—rather than as a process, an unfolding, or an event. As such, while we are conditioned to think of sense in terms of the expressed (sense is what is expressed in an expression), there is no reason we cannot think of sense also, perhaps, as being a process (a sensing). *Qua* process, sense/sensing has a certain generative role: we do not just express sense via an expression, but perhaps also sense is expressing itself through us (to get close to the Heideggerian claim that language speaks (through) us).

Expressivity, the Subject, and Phenomenalization

The problem of expressivity is not, therefore, simply the problem of identifying how sense is "carried" in an expression such that a subject's interior mental life can become an object to be thought or taken up by others. It is rather the problem of the relation of sense, genesis, and actual existents, a relation that is not simply another relata, but a process: the relating of sense, genesis, and actual existents. It is the problem of the relating of knowing, doing, and being, and to look for a subject as the primary enactor of that relating is to already presume a certain account of that relating that is verifiable (since subjects do, in fact, express things), but not necessarily primary: we must be open to the possibility, perhaps even the fact, that the subject is, in the end, an expression before, and so that, it is capable of expressing. In this way, our investigation (and perhaps phenomenology more broadly) is committed to the relativization of the subject to sense, and not, as is commonly understood with phenomenology, the relativization of sense to the subject.

To appreciate this point, we must remember that expressivity begins in phenomenology as Husserl's primary rejoinder to the problem of sense raised (but not pursued) by Frege. At that stage, Husserl defined expressivity as the phenomenal unity of asymmetrical elements. Such phenomenal unity covered two distinct phenomenological functions: the act of forming that unity, and the unity itself, so formed. Husserl focused on the latter, assuming the former to be a nonproblematic act performed by the intentional, volitional subject: the subject took a sense that already existed in the "solitary mental life" of the subject and "externalized" it, thereby enabling it to become an object for consideration by other subjects. In this way, expressivity—as the phenomenon of expression—started to bridge the gap between subjective conceptions and objectivity.

But this account was found to be phenomenologically insufficient (most famously by Derrida in *Voice and Phenomenon* but also by Merleau-Ponty, Henry, and others), insofar as it failed to adequately account for the constitution *of* the subject (i.e., of the phenomenal conditions of subjectivity), instead focusing solely on the constitutions performed *by* the subject (i.e., phenomena). Further phenomenological analysis shows us that subjects are able to express only because they are themselves, first and foremost, expressions (of sense, *Stiftungen*, etc.). In making this case, Merleau-Ponty shows us that sense and being are always already intertwined, and therefore the asymmetry that is essential to expressivity (one of the elements is used strictly to draw our attention to the other) can be mutual: we "live through" a *Stiftung* (which is the "mode of being" of sense) so as to engage directly in our being, even as that engagement (in a sort of interrogative mode) causes us to always be reworking and reshaping that *Stiftung*, and hence that sense.

But this more phenomenologically rigorous account of the relation between the subject, sense, and expressivity leads to a new problem: if sense is what is expressed in and through the subject (as expression), then who or what is expressing that sense in and through the subject? Providing some account of the forming of the relationship between expressed and expression is necessary for a genuinely rigorous account of expressivity, though it is not necessary that this relationship be conceived of substantially, that is, as a "who" or "what" that "performs" the expressing. Generativity clarifies how expressing can be understood (in its most basic form) as a kind of self-unfolding process that requires no "who" or "what," and this process of relating (rather than the subject that performs it) is the essential third element of expressivity.

This final point, then, provides a clarification of the last key term of our definition of expression: "phenomenal." For this account of the ongoing, necessary intertwining of sense and being, of expressed and expression, as a self-unfolding process is nothing other than an account of the phenomenalization of phenomenality. By severing this phenomenalization from its need to be performed by a subject outside of itself, expressing helps us see that there is an "immanent causality" or an inherent generativity at work in phenomenality that precedes (and conditions) the "transcendence" of the transcendental subject. This immanent relation, I am arguing, is nothing other than expressivity itself, in its threefold relation of expressing, expressed, and expression. The articulation of the immanent relation between those three elements therefore leads us to the probability (which has not yet been established as a necessity) of a certain type of immanent generativity at work also in phenomenality, since maintaining a notion of a subject that is simply transcendent from sense led to several problems for Husserl, problems that disappear with the innovations of Merleau-Ponty and the "generative" Husserl.[34] This immanent generativity allows us to account for the functioning of phenomenality on its own terms, which are—as this book is attempting to argue—the terms of expressivity. Expressivity offers us an account of the functioning of phenomenality insofar as expressivity explains to us the production of phenomenal unities and therefore the process of phenomenalization.

Expanding on the account of expressivity that has been sketched so far in this chapter will enable us to clarify and solidify this account, while making explicit some of its more significant implications. For the account of expressivity as the "how" of phenomenality outlined in this chapter has huge implications for our understanding of experience—especially regarding its subjective component, how that effects our understanding of knowing and being in the world, and how it transforms our understanding of the political—and for our understanding of phenomenology, especially its methodology and its account of transcendentality. It is these implications, and the details of our account of expressivity that give rise to them, that we must now explicate in the following chapters.

2

Material-Spiritual Flesh
The Subjective Implications of Expressivity

We now turn our attention more explicitly to the claim made in the previous chapter that the account of expressive experience we are developing is committed to the relativization of the subject to sense. This claim seems radical, especially if held against a certain traditional assumption (especially of phenomenology) that is committed rather to the relativization of sense to the subject. To properly understand this relativization, we must examine an expressive account of the subject, of sense, and of their relationship. The subject and sense are intimately interconnected (*Verflechtung*), and the nature of this intertwining is important to clarify. Indeed, the failure to adequately clarify this connection was one of the things that held back Husserl's early account of expression and left him unable to properly appreciate the significance of expressivity for experience. Clarifying this connection requires elaborating an account of the subject as expressive and showing that this account is essential to embodiment, subjective performance, and subjective constitution. This means, at least, that an expressive subject is one that is always both constituted and constituting in a mutually reinforcing way: subjective acts shape the world in which the subject operates, and the subject itself is, in turn, shaped by that world and its ongoing alteration. This, in turn, will lead us to a certain account of sense: one that conditions how subjects are given to us and how the subject is given to itself. As such, it begins to explain an account of experience that lends credence to both the lived nature of the subject's experience (as *Erlebnis*) and the politically constituted nature of that experience by showing that these are not two distinct elements, but that the "dominant discourse" of the politically constitutive community "is in mutual relation with subjective life even as the two are not fully contiguous" (AE, 43).

To articulate this well, the subject-world relationship must be carefully articulated. But such an articulation is problematic, insofar as there does not seem to be one consistent position on this relationship: the subject of §8 of Husserl's first *Logical Investigation* does not seem to have much in common with the subject of Husserl's *Crisis*, much as *Structure and Behavior* seems to offer us a different account from, say, *The Visible and the Invisible*. Here, using the notion of expressivity as our guideline, we will trace the development of a phenomenological articulation of the subject (vis-à-vis the world) from Husserl's articulation of the subject in the first *Logical Investigation* to his later account of the material-spiritual in *Ideas II*, the *Crisis*, and beyond. Then, and again using expressivity as our guide, we will look at how the notion of the material-spiritual moves beyond any notion of simple subject-world correlation toward a more primordial account of phenomenal cogenerativity in which the subject's ability to constitute a world is simply the expression of a deeper constitutive process that first constitutes the subject as an expression. This expressivity, we will see, is necessarily tied to embodiment: our bodies are not simply physical things but material-spiritual expressions of the particular world(s) we occupy. As such, expressivity helps us see that the physical, the meaningful, and the sense-bestowing (*Sinngebung*) are not wholly distinct but are expressively tied together in and as the living body (*Leib*). Therefore, the body is simultaneously politically expressive and living, and subjectivity is necessarily an expressive, living body.

Gestures and Embodied Subjects

We begin this investigation of the expressive understanding of the subject with an issue that bothers many readers and commentators of Husserl's account of expression in *Logical Investigations*: the exclusion of gestures from the realm of expression (LI I, §5). The problem is not simply the claim that gestures are not expressive, properly speaking (though that is problematic and counterintuitive in its own way). Rather, the larger problem is what that exclusion suggests or opens up in Husserl's thought: "Husserl has been accused of privileging volition and intention over reception, presence over absence, speech over writing, and consciousness over corporeality and materiality."[1] This latter is the most important for us in this chapter, and nowhere is that criticism more pointed (or famous) than in *Voice and Phenomenon*, where Derrida moves from Husserl's exclusion of "facial expressions, [and] gestures," to an exclusion of "the whole of the body and the mundane register, in a word, the whole of the visible and spatial as such" (VP, 35).

Derrida attributes this exclusion and devaluing of the body and the physical to Husserl's spiritualism and voluntarism (VP, 35). And, at least in *Logical Investigations*, that accusation seems warranted. In that work, the physical and the meaningful are still considered as two distinct things: "the concrete phenomenon of the sense-informed expression breaks up, on the one hand, into the physical phenomenon, forming the physical side of the expression, and on the other hand, into the acts which give it meaning and possibly also intuitive fullness" (LI I, 191–92). But we can question whether the sharp distinction between, and the privileging of, sense over the physical is, in fact, essential to Husserl's account of expressivity. If we look a little deeper at Husserl's account of gestures and their relationship to expressivity, we see that *Logical Investigations* is not the end of the story for Husserl, as it pertains to gestures, expression, or spiritualism. By *Ideas II*, for example, gestures are considered expressive.[2] How are we to take this obvious departure from the earlier position of the *Logical Investigations* that "facial expressions and the various gestures which involuntarily accompany speech . . . are not expressions in the sense in which a case of speech is an expression" (LI I, 187–88)? Further, given that it is immediately following this latter quote that Husserl equates expression with phenomenal unity, a point that we have made essential to our analysis of expressivity, the question must arise whether a change in Husserl's account of expressivity occurs here and, if so, whether that calls into question our preceding analysis of expressivity.

Sara Heinämaa argues convincingly that it is not Husserl's account of expressivity that changes between *Logical Investigations* and *Ideas II*, but rather his account of embodiment, and more precisely of the way we are to understand the relationship between subject and body. This change enables Husserl to move beyond his early spiritualism to a more "expressive" account of the subject-body relation that will relativize the subject, in a certain way, to sense. Therefore, by appreciating and highlighting the significance of expressivity we can better understand embodiment, subjectivity, and the relations of constitution that hold between the subject, the world, and sense.

Heinämaa argues, "If the body of another person would be given to me, in my concrete factual experience, merely or primarily as an indication of the other, as a mere signal of his existence, then he and his body would be separate, independent in their existence" (EE, 9). Since the *Logical Investigations* clearly claims that there is only an indicative relationship between me and my body (since my bodily gestures must be indications and not expressions), it seems to follow that, in that work at least, the person and the body remain two distinct things, and therefore the charge of spiritualism remains plausible (though not unambiguous, as we will see). But Heinämaa then goes on to cite several examples from *Ideas II* where Husserl clearly "characterize[s] the body as an expressive unity" (EE, 7) with the person:[3]

> This body [*Leibkörper*] . . . is a thing [*Sache*], one that has spiritual meaning, *that serves as expression*, organ etc., for a spiritual being, for a person and his spiritual activity. (Hua 4, 214, translation modified;[4] emphasis added)

> The thoroughly intuitive unity presenting itself when we grasp a person *as such* (e.g. when we, as persons, speak to them as persons, or when we hear them speak, or work together with them, or watch their actions) is the unity of the "*expression*" and the "*expressed*" that belongs to the essence of all comprehensive unities. (Hua 4, 248)

> The human being in the personal world (the world of spirit, we also say, as the domain of the human sciences) is *the unity of the living body as expression* of spirit and of spirit as expressed in the living body, as it is given in the personalistic attitude. (Hua 4, supplement X, 337; emphasis added)

The person-body relationship is here understood in a way analogously similar to how we understand a book: either the book/body is *simply* a material object (black marks on a page; biological and chemical functions) lacking any meaning or "we can see it as an indivisible spiritual-sensuous unity . . . in which all parts are internally tied together and which, due to this articulation, has an orientation and a direction" (EE, 8). If we take the latter option—which the later Husserl clearly opts for—then "the Body is, as Body, filled with the soul through and through. Each movement of the Body is full of soul, the coming and going, the standing and sitting, the walking and dancing, etc." (Hua 4, 252).

This language of a body "full of soul" still has dualist overtones, as if body and soul are two distinct entities in which one (the body) provides the foundation of the other (the soul). At least by the time of the Vienna Lecture, Husserl is adamantly opposed to such a position (see Hua 6, 294–98). But that we ought not think of the body as the foundation for a distinct soul does not mean that we cannot distinguish at all between physical bodies and the notion of a soul (or spirit) that animates or enlivens them. The question is not whether the body-soul distinction makes sense at all, but rather the type of sense that it makes: need we think of one as the foundation of the other, and need we prioritize one over the other, and if so in what way? Such a causal or foundational understanding of the body-soul (or body-person) relationship can only arise, Heinämaa shows, if we first "experience the body as an expressive unit" (EE, 11). Husserl argues "that the *unity of expression* is a *presupposition* for the constitution of the founded reality as one which encloses [two] levels [e.g., body and soul, the physical and the mental], and that it is not already in itself this reality" (Hua 4, 257). In other words, "human beings are given to us in two different ways": "as twofold realities, composed of the reality of the body and the reality of the soul," but also "as expressive units in which no two realities can be distinguished" (EE, 11). This difference in modes of givenness is not simply neutral: "in the order of (genetic) constitution, the expressive body is primary and . . . the mind-body compound with its psycho-physical interaction is secondary and dependent" (EE, 11). It is as an expressive unity that we *primordially* encounter bodies; the dualistic distinctions that "are objects of the sciences of psychology, physiology, and psycho-physiology" (EE, 11) are dependent upon this more primordial, expressive engagement with bodies.

This primacy of our experience of subjects as an expressive unity actually echoes Husserl's claims already in *Logical Investigations* that meaningful communication happens only "if the auditor . . . takes the speaker to be a person, who is not merely producing sounds but *speaking to him*," and that this occurs when "the hearer *intuitively* takes the speaker to be a person who is expressing this or that, or as we certainly can say, *perceives* him as such" (LI I, 189). This claim seems intuitively correct: I cannot intend some sound as meaningful unless I take whatever is producing the sound as the kind of thing capable of understanding and communicating sense. Heinämaa points out, however, that the significance of characterizing this primordial experience as "intuitive" and "perceptual" is lost on Husserl in *Logical Investigations*, and not properly explored until *Ideas II*. For if I perceive the other person as a person, this must mean that I take the person as, in some meaningful sense, one with the body I encounter or perceive. This is not an indicative relationship, requiring a second act of judgment ("if that body makes those sounds, then I guess they must be a person"), but rather an expressive one: I simply take the body as a person—in my lived experience of the person, I "live through" the physical properties of the body so as to "live in" the sense communicated by and with the person— and I do so in my initial intuition, though I can later, through reflection, distinguish, if I want, the physical body I saw from the personal characteristics (e.g., having an "inner mental life") that I took it to express. In this regard, what I encounter when I encounter a person is, phenomenologically speaking, first and foremost "a specific organization or articulation of what is *sensuously* (pre)given" (EE, 12) as a unity. My primordial encounter is not of a merely material body with sense somehow added to it later, nor of an ideality (e.g., a "person") that is somehow encased in a material body, but of a material-spiritual or "sensuous-spiritual" unity (see Hua 4, 250–51; EE, 2).

Our primary encounter with other people, then, is an expressive encounter with a sensuous-spiritual body, and not with a physico-material, or even psycho-physical, world. Husserl's early exclusion of gestures as "merely indicative" does not accord even with his own early intuitions of our engagement with subjects and/as bodies, so it should not surprise us that he later changes his mind about the expressive status of bodily gestures. But the significance of this shift for our understanding of the subject and its relation to others, the self, and the world is *not* a shift in his understanding of expressivity, but precisely the result of Husserl coming to understand more clearly the implications of his account of expressivity and the role it could play in his phenomenological examinations.

The increasing importance of expressivity in Husserl's thought further develops this account of the "sensuous-spiritual" unity. As we move toward Husserl's later works, and especially the concept of spirit that he develops there, we see that the unity is not a collection of distinct, preexisting elements (i.e., the "sensuous" and the "spiritual") but a primary unity out of which the distinct elements emerge. Further, the primacy of this sensuous-spiritual expressive encounter pertains not only to our experience of others, but also, ultimately, to our experience of the world (as *Lebenswelt*) and our experience of ourselves. These latter two points can already be inferred from Heinämaa's argument concerning Husserl's shifting attitudes regarding gestures and embodiment: given that Husserl changes his position on gestures ultimately because he changes his position on embodiment (as Heinämaa argues convincingly), it follows that we can take gestures as expressive only because our bodies *are* us, in some (expressive) way. Clarifying the precise nature of this expressive unity is therefore crucial to properly understanding the subject, embodiment, sense, and the host of issues that come with those problematics. And so it is to this notion of the "sensuous-spiritual"—or its Husserlian variant the "material-spiritual" (Hua 4, 250n1)—that we must now turn.

An Expressive Understanding of Spirituality

We should not, then, take the "sensuous-spiritual" simply as the adding together of two distinct elements, which can bear only an indicative relationship to each other. Rather, the unity between them is an expressive unity that is primordial, before the distinction and division between physical and psychical, between exterior world and interior mental life. It is imperative, therefore, that we come to understand the material and the spiritual on the basis of the earlier expressive unity, rather than attempting to understand the expressive unity as a stitching together of mutually independent parts. To do this, we must understand the relation between them on its own (expressive) terms, rather than define it by the relative position of its constituted relata: we must start by seeking to understand the "relating" that constitutes the nature of both relata. This relating is the expressivity of expressing, in all its generative, co-constitutive force. We can properly understand the "sensuous-spiritual" nature of our experience, then, only by recognizing the uniquely "expressive" nature of that relationship and how it in turn constitutes our understanding of the sensuous and of the spiritual as distinct from and prior to "physical sensation" and "soul."

We can begin to do this by clarifying the concept of spirit (in its late Husserlian sense) as the extension of Husserl's earlier account of expressivity, moving him toward something much closer to the mutually constitutive but still asymmetrical account I attributed primarily to Merleau-Ponty in Chapter 1. Husserl makes at least two claims in the Vienna Lecture that are significant for developing an expressive understanding of spirit: first, that spirit is not merely produced by us but operates in us, constituting us even as it is constituted by us; and second, that spirit is the driving force of our lives, determining both what we care about and what we do. It is, for example, through spirit that "character is given to the persons" (Hua 6, 273). This "character" is not merely a set of personal character traits, moods, or dispositions, but the outgrowth of a spiritual teleology of sense (Hua 6, 273), the acting-out of an inherent entelechy[5] that actively guides development "toward an ideal shape of life" (Hua 6, 275). In this way, it is analogous to an Idea in the Kantian sense,[6] an infinite regulative ideal that "has [not] ever been reached or could be reached," but which rather provides "an infinite idea toward which, in concealment, the whole spiritual becoming aims, so to speak" (Hua 6, 275).

These two seemingly parenthetical insertions in the last quote are essential to an expressive understanding of spirit. First, spirit, while deeply constitutive of persons in their personal and communal life, operates in "concealment,"[7] which is to say, at least in part, that it operates without the persons in whom it is operative being aware that it is operating. Second, describing this spirit as an "idea" toward which something "aims" is not to be taken literally: spirit is not primarily rational, and it is not a utopian ideal or a desired endpoint toward which one strives. It is a dynamic, motivating force, a power that "has its history" (Hua 6, 274) and inhabits that history, or is inhabited by that history, in a way that "bears within itself the future-horizon of infinity" (Hua 6, 277). That is to say, spirit is a historically constituted generative force that shapes the nature of subjects, providing them an impetus or motivation to move forward into the future in particular ways.[8]

This generative force of spirit shapes how subjects bring the world to intuition, and so is essential to the subject's relation to the world and is necessary for any experience whatsoever. We see this through the role that spirit plays in fulfillment. For Husserl, it is the notion of fulfillment that enables us to experience our various perceptions of an object as a single experience of a single object that we can know to be *this* object. This is only possible because of a distinction Husserl makes between "clarifying" and "confirming" modes of intuition. The clarifying mode of intuition seeks to clarify, picture, or prefigure the intended objective sense (Hua 11, 79–80) and so helps narrow the range of possibilities via the horizon of expectations out of which we operate. By filling some of the emptiness of the intended object, the clarifying mode enables the intended object to coincide with a confirming-fulfilling intuition in a synthesis. The confirming mode of intuition, then, is "the specific fulfillment of intuition" that is the "synthesis with an appropriate perception" (Hua 11, 79). Here, "the merely expected object is identified with the actually arriving object, as fulfilling the expectation" (Hua 11, 79). It is in this fulfilled expectation that the object is not only constituted as an object, but is constituted as *this* particular object of *my* experience: it is in fulfillment that I encounter this thing before me as a desk that, like other desks I've previously encountered, I am able to work at, place things upon, and so on.[9] When Husserl describes spirit as operating as a "vital presentiment"[10] (Hua 6, 270), then, he is situating spirit squarely in the clarifying mode of bringing to intuition, a mode that operates preobjectively (*Gegenstandlich*; see Hua 11, §28, and Hua 17, 69) to determine the horizons of expectation that are necessary for the constitution of any experience whatsoever. In the next section of this chapter we will look more closely at how spirit is able to function in this way. For now, our interest is simply in seeing the function that spirit plays in the Husserlian system: the generation of expectations that enable us to "make sense" of our experience according to a pregiven meaningfulness. Because such expectations are "the felt signpost for all discoveries" (Hua 6, 276), spirit, as the force generating such presentiments, is a necessary element of any and all experience.

But what, precisely, is meant by saying that spirit generates presentiments? Husserl is clear that "the attitude [in which spiritual meaning is seen] does not itself constitute the spiritual entity, the material-spiritual is already pre-constituted, pre-thematized, pre-given" (Hua 4, 250n1; see also LE, 127). That is, while spirit is operative in subjective acts of meaning-constitution, that is not the only (or even the primary) way in which it operates. More fundamentally, Husserl speaks of a "spiritual meaning" that is "embodied" in the environment of the lifeworld (Hua 39, 427)[11] in cultural objects such as "houses, bridges, tools, works of art, and so on" (Hua 8, 151) that he sometimes calls "spiritual products" (Hua 6, 270). These objects are not merely "present to us" but "address themselves to us" in the context of our lives, and hence are said to have a "spiritual" meaningfulness (Hua 9, 111, 118, 384, 408; see Hua 4, 236–38) that is "not externally associated, but internally fused within as a meaning belonging to [the cultural object] and as expressed in it" (Hua 9, 112; LE, 125). Indeed, "a reference to subjectivity belongs to that ownmost essential substance" of these cultural objects and therefore "a relatedness to personal community belongs to the very sense of all cultural objects" (Hua 9, 118; see also LE, 124). Cultural objects, then, are not simply physical things that distinct acts of subjective apprehension attach a meaning to but are material-spiritual entities that necessarily carry *within themselves* both an essential meaningfulness and a constitutive relation to subjectivity (as both constituting subjectivity and constituted by it).

Spirit therefore constitutes horizons of expectation, not merely within the mind of individual subjects but in the very fabric of cultural life itself. Both the "meaningfulness" and the objects that carry it are spiritual "products." To speak of the spiritual, therefore, is for Husserl not primarily to speak of one half of a dyad (spiritual vs. material, culture vs. things, meaning vs. matter), but of a necessary relationship (i.e., expressing) that constitutes its relata in a fundamental sense: spirit is why we have bridges and the complex mathematics that enables us to engineer them; spirit is why we have works of art and the creativity that inspires us to create them. Or, to use a more complex example, the current chemical composition of our planet's atmosphere is a spiritual product that carries within itself a particular "meaning," and, as such, it is as spiritual as is the "barbaristic" (Hua 6, 299), anthropocentric cultural milieu that led us to this position.[12]

If we now return to the question of the subject and its embodiment, we can see more clearly why the body is primordially experienced as a "spiritual being which essentially includes the sensuous but which, once again, does not include it as a part" (Hua 4, 251). The material or sensuous is not simply a part of the subject that, when added to the spiritual or soul part, makes up the totality of the subject; rather, the material or sensuous is already a spiritual product, even as spirit itself is a product of the historically material situations in which it is generated. As such, to speak of the "living

body" of the phenomenological subject is not simply to talk about the ani-
mation of neutral material substance by a distinct animating spiritual
principle,[13] but about the submersion of the person within a "suprasubjective" (Hua 6, 270) relating that is constitutive of subjects (shaping
their character, their future goals and endeavors, etc.), even as it is itself
constituted by the activity of subjects. Ultimately, then, it is in the notion
of "spirit"—understood expressively—that Husserl moves fully beyond the
soul-body, person-body type of dualisms, into an (material-spiritual) expressive whole as our primary mode of relating to others (as sensuous-
spiritual bodies), to the world (as *Lebenswelt*), and to ourselves.

Sensing: from Physical to Sensuous

But this is only half of the story. Despite our best efforts to show why this
should not be the case, it remains possible that focusing only on spirit
threatens to be misread as a casting of phenomenology back to some kind
of idealist, perhaps even Hegelian, lens.[14] To avoid this, we must make clear
how spirit is not simply received by people but is constituted in historical,
material conditions that are themselves inherently spiritually constituted,
as we have already shown. To establish that we are not simply founding
the material on the spiritual (which, again, should be clear already from
the expressive account of spirit discussed in the previous section), we must
now also elaborate the account of the "material" or the "sensuous" that is at
work in an essentially expressive understanding of the subject.

Of course, we must make a distinction already here between the strictly
"physical" and the "sensuous." By the former, I mean the world of empirical objects and physical stuff, an empirical world that can be distinguished
from the surrounding world of the subject, but only secondarily and as a
manner of abstraction. The "empirical world" is an abstraction from the
spiritual-material and not vice versa.[15]

In order to develop an expressive understanding of the subject-world
relation, we must explore the "sensuous," that is, the material(-spiritual)
that functions as the primary phenomenological touchpoint of the subject
in the world. As we have already said, the surrounding world is always the
"material-spiritual" or "sensuous-spiritual" world insofar as I intuit or preobjectively encounter things in that surrounding world as always already
connected in particular ways (Hua 6, 276). As such, I "live in" sense, not
by leaving the sensuous or material behind, but precisely by inhabiting it
in a particular way: sense is a way of being in the sensuous, and not simply
a way of thinking about the sensuous. This has important implications for
our understanding of the relationship between ontology and epistemology,

between being and knowing, as we will see in subsequent chapters. For now, our focus is on the implications of this expressive relationship for the subject and its relation to the world. And for that purpose, the material-spiritual ensures that we find the subject always already in contact with the surrounding world.

In *Ideas II*, Husserl coins the term *Empfindnisse* (a portmanteau of *Empfindung*, sensation, and *Erlebnisse*, lived experiences), usually translated as "sensings," to articulate this situation of a subject that is always already in contact with the surrounding world (see Hua 4, §36). *Empfindnisse* constitute, in Alia Al-Saji's words, "a tacit bodily awareness that is lived through without self-ascription or objectification."[16] While this awareness can become objectified or self-aware—"can be made explicit by directing a ray of attention through it" (BaS, 18)—in our primal experience, such "sensings" are not (yet) *my* sensations *of* the world, but rather are the condition of the body as a "sensible and concrete surface in touch with the world" (BaS, 19) that feels that "touch" with the world as "contact, pressure, movement, tension, warmth and cold, pleasure and pain,"[17] and so on. In *Empfindnisse*, we move away from the notion of a person as a separate body that must somehow take in hyletic data from outside itself and then apprehend that data (according to some preestablished categories) so as to constitute a "sensation" of the world. Instead, sensibility is redefined as a primal touching that is always a co-touching:[18] the body does not just touch the world, the body is also touched by the world (Hua 4, 152–53) and is capable of feeling itself as touched. That is, the body does not simply alternate between being a subjective body (actively touching the world) and an objective body (being touched by or in the world), but rather, through the notion of *Empfindnisse*, Husserl is able to articulate that the body senses itself as touched, even as it also senses the world as touched, but in a different way. The body, then, can be understood generally as "a field or spread of sensings" (BaS, 24).

But such a construal of the body does not entirely eliminate my subjectivity or individuality. Indeed, the Husserlian portmanteau *Empfindnisse* includes precisely the *Erlebnis* or "lived" element of experience: sensings are a primordial contact with the world that is already lived or experienced, and hence constitute a kind of phenomenal condition of experiencing (as discussed in Chapter 1) that is simultaneously a contact with the world and a subjective living through of that contact. But this "living through" is not yet individuated; it does not (yet) pertain to this or that particular subject but is the background, field, or (expressive) unity out of which my distinction from the world is constituted. The nature of the difference between the body's sensing itself as touched and its sensing the world as touched constitutes a particular body as "my" body, insofar as it is a kind of nexus of related and localized sensings: this sensing (heat!) motivates a response (move!), which is itself another sensing (the rush of air as my arm moves away) that motivates another response (relief!) that is itself another sensing (relaxation of tensed muscles), and so on. The nexus of these sensings can be localized in one particular body, and that body's "double sensation," its ability to sense itself as touched and as touching, can open up a reflexive space that consciousness is able to use in and as reflection (a point that we will return to in Chapter 5). When this happens, I am able to reflect on this body as "my" body (as opposed to another body in the world), but this reflection is secondary, phenomenologically speaking, to my experiencing and sensing, my touching and being touched by, the world.[19]

This power of being touched by the world is most often called "affectivity" in phenomenology. I am affected by the world in such a way that the world immediately calls me to respond to it in particular ways: I am "pulled" to pay attention to this element of the world rather than another (see Hua 11), or to move in this direction rather than another, or to reach out and caress something rather than pull away in fear. And insofar as it is the complex of related motivations that ties *Empfindnisse* together into and as *my* sensings of *my* body, then the affectivity occasioned by *Empfindnisse* entitles us to conclude that the world itself is part of the "field of sensings" that make up "my" body. In this way, *Empfindnisse*, as sensings, "render indeterminate" the dichotomies of subject-object, and even sensing-sensed (BaS, 23). Prior to the reflection that enables me to distinguish between "my" body and "other" bodies, there is only the field of related motivations and sensings that Michel Henry refers to as the shared "bodily-ownness" (*corps-proprié*) of living beings and the Earth.[20]

We can therefore distinguish between my merely physical or objective body (*Körper*) and my lived body (*Leib*), but we can also distinguish the lived body from my primordial *Empfindnisse* with (and not simply of) the world.[21] This distinction, like the one between *Körper* and *Leib*, is *not* a distinction between different things, but between different attitudes I can take toward the same thing. If I view my lived body as *primarily* mine—already set apart from a world beyond it—I smuggle the subject-object dichotomy of the natural attitude, however surreptitiously, back into my understanding of embodiment.[22] Instead, I must acknowledge that, before it is distinguished from the world as "my" body, that which I call "my" body is first part of the body, the system of related motivations, of the world. This world is not simply the empirical world of physical objects, nor the surrounding world of the subject, but the material-spiritual world of phenomenal expression that Henry calls the Earth.[23]

Calling the Earth a "body" risks a number of misunderstandings. It should be obvious that I do not mean the Earth is an objective body; it may be made of a series of objective bodies, but why should we think that collection of bodies itself constitutes another body? Perhaps, one could argue, it is a body because it is all animated by a single consciousness or spirit.[24] Those who think this, however, would be much more likely to consider the Earth therefore as a *Leib* rather than simply a *Körper*: the point is not that the physical world is a body distinct from its animating impulse, but rather that the Earth is the living body of that impulse, and it is precisely its living status that creates the necessary moral "ought" required to motivate, for example, ecological responsibility.[25]

But it is not as a *Leib* that phenomenology, at this point, considers the Earth a body. Rather, in its expressive primacy, the Earth is, properly speaking, not "a" body but rather is embodiment, incarnation[26] or, perhaps better (since both "embodiment" and "incarnation" still have connotations of some immaterial thing taking up residence within a physical body), flesh. The flesh of the Earth (or the Earth as flesh) is the complex of lived-sensings (*Empfindnisse*) that are capable of the double touching constitutive of the lived body, but prior to the "ray of attention" that alone can begin to distinguish between subject and object, between "my" body and the "flesh" of the "world."[27]

The material-spiritual nature of expressivity, therefore, reveals a phenomenological primacy in which the relation (i.e., expressing) phenomenologically precedes and is constitutive of both its relata. In this regard, trying to describe the elements of this relata as either material or spiritual is prone to misunderstandings: unless we maintain a fierce and rigorous hold on the reduction, we threaten to slide back into the natural attitude[28] (with its subject-object, material-spiritual dichotomies), and therefore misunderstand either term by defining it on its own, apart from the relationship between them. But, as we have seen, we are able to distinguish them only because we first live through the relationship between them: expressing opens the way to define (and redefine) both subject and object, both material and spiritual, in much the same way my friendliness and the acts that show that friendliness are both constantly defined and redefined by the friendship that relates them.

This reversibility (to use Merleau-Pontian language) of material and spiritual can be seen in Levinas's claim that *Ideas II* reveals "a corporeal sphere refractory to the subject/object schema," a corporeal sphere that we can also call "a Spirituality . . . inseparable from localization."[29] The invocation of spirituality as another means of referring to the realm of *Empfindnisse* further entrenches the secondary nature of the spiritual-material, subject-object distinctions vis-à-vis the expressive unity in which we first encounter (proto)subjects (who are, therefore, not yet subjects, if the latter term can only be understood in distinction from objects). It also hearkens back to our description of spirit as an affective force shaping how subjects bring the world to intuition. By suggesting that spirit operates in and as an affectivity,[30] we prefigured the affective nature of *Empfindnisse*. This affectivity is not simply active nor simply passive, but rather situates a place on the border between (or, perhaps, before the distinction between) passive and active. For affectivity includes both the pull exercised by the object on consciousness, but also the "receptivity" of the subject (Hua 4, 347), which must be pregiven for any activity to take place (Hua 11, 84, and BaS, 26), just as spirit was described as "pregiven" in the previous section. This affective receptivity is pregiven as feeling or tendency (Hua 11, 149–50), and is itself constituted within a "temporal, habitual and historical" horizon (BaS, 26),[31] that we might refer to as a "spiritual horizon." In this way, spirit is felt, not as a distinct *sensing* (akin to vision, touch, etc.) or another way of being in contact with the world, but as a necessary, transcendental condition[32] of that contact understood expressively as *Empfindnisse*, given that our tendencies "function to define the relativism of the affective field" (BaS, 27) such that any sensing (such as touch, vision, etc.) already "implies an intricately woven affective and temporal contact within the body and in its relation to the world" (BaS, 27). That is, our sensings already draw on, require, and reveal an inherent contact with the world that is not merely sensation, but is always already shaped by the spiritual horizon of the (proto)subject. Sensings always already employ sense (and not mere sensation), and spirit is therefore a precondition of *Empfindnisse*, even as *Empfindnisse* are a mode of spirit's affectivity.

Again, this is not to found sensings on spirit or vice versa, but to show the necessary and mutual coordination and cogenerativity of the two that emerges when we focus on the expressive unity that precedes the distinctions into subject and object, physical and psychic, and so on. And in this expressive unity, we see that subjective experiencing in the form of *Erlebnis* is always already political insofar as it necessarily draws on a suprasubjective force (spirit) in and for its most basic engagements with "the body," where the latter refers both to the body of the Earth and to its "own" lived body, which can be reflectively distinguished from the body of the Earth. In this way, the subject is always already expressing spirit, even in its own ability to distinguish itself as a (individual) subject. Expressivity is primary, not just in our relation to others (who must be taken as expressive if they are to be taken as genuine Others) and to the world (which must be engaged from horizons that are always already sedimented with spiritual sense), but also in our relation to ourselves.

The Expressive Subject

At this point, it should be clear how the subject is relativized to spirit and so to sense as a phenomenalizing condition. Let us conclude this chapter by reviewing some of the implications this has for an account of the subject and its relation to the world and to sense.

First, and to begin, it is clear that the expressive subject needs to be embodied (in "touch" with the world, sensing, etc.). But it is also clear, once one pays attention to the body as an expressive unity, that the term "embodied" is easily misunderstood as a descriptor of the subject's situation. In common uses of English, the standard meaning of the prefix "em-"[33] is to "put something into" (e.g., entomb). In the context of the subject, this suggests a prior disjunction between subject and body, such that the subject must be "put into" a body. This, as should be clear, cannot be the meaning of a fundamentally expressive account of embodiment. Another meaning of the prefix is "to restrict," normally with the sense of "on all sides" or "completely" (as in encircle, enclose, etc.). But this too carries unhelpful connotations: we do not, I think, want to think of the subject as "restricted" to a body, as if the body is a prison holding or restricting the freedom of our soul (claims that are all too common in Platonic and Cartesian accounts of dualism). Perhaps we could think of the subject as "restricted on all sides" in the sense of a third meaning of the prefix "em-," namely "to cause to be" (e.g., enslave, entangle). This might begin to move us closer to a genuinely expressive account of embodiment, insofar as it suggests that this is not a case of a subject simply being given a body, but rather of the subject *being* a body (as someone who is enslaved *is* a slave). Still, the prefix may give the sense (connotatively at least) that this is something that happens subsequent to an initial state, such that the subject is initially bodiless and then must be caused to be a body as a secondary act. If anything, it is, we have said, quite the opposite: the subject begins as body, and the distinctions between subject and object, between soul and body, between animating and animated are all subsequent to this prior expressive unity. As such, we must be careful that our language does not suggest that the parts begin distinct and must be subsequently brought together, a suggestion that is strongly connoted by the "em-" prefix.

One further grammatical option remains: "em-" can also be used to turn something from a noun or adjective into a verb, and/or to make a verb transitive or give it a transitive marker (e.g., enshield, enliven). Thought this way, we can see the sense in which talk of "embodiment" is phenomenologically fruitful: the "body" does not, at least initially, name a noun, but rather a verb (embodied) that is taken in a necessarily transitive way. While the normal function of transitive verbs is to suggest that the verb requires a direct object, in the expressive state before the subject-object distinction—a state it is difficult to talk about, given the subject-object nature of most English grammar—we can, perhaps, think of this transitivity in a broader way as simply affecting something else. Embodiment is the subject as necessarily affecting the world.

But this latter move works only if we think of embodied in its verb form. In this regard, and technically, it may be better to say that "the subject embodies the world" than to say that "the subject is embodied." Embodiment names, then, not a condition or state of the subject vis-à-vis other possible states or conditions it could occupy (nonembodied, for example), but rather the activity of the subject relating to the world. And this activity is not, primarily, performed by the subject onto or in the world, but rather is the subject's taking up of "the world" in and as the subject itself, before it carries on any other actions: before the subject performs embodied actions in the world, the subject embodies (or simply expresses) the world.[34]

Such a notion of embodiment seems to be captured in the phrase "living body" (*Leib*).[35] The living body "is not a *thing*, it is a situation: it is our grasp upon the world and the outline of our projects," as Simone de Beauvoir states.[36] The living body "means a specific sense of embodiment central in all experiencing of worldly objectivities" (OTU, 6). But this "specific sense of embodiment" can be characterized in different ways. Heinämaa discusses three different fundamental distinctions that orient varying approaches to the living body: the body as viewed from a first-person perspective vs. from the third-person perspective; "being" a body vs. having or possessing a body; and subjective vs. objective bodies (OTU, 6–10.). The account of the living body as an expressive unity helps us see a few things in relation to these varying ways of defining the "living body" and so helps us clarify the "specific sense of embodiment" that is characteristic of the living body.

Insofar as spirit is necessary for the expressive unity of any given body (including my own body), and insofar as spirit is necessarily suprasubjective, then the distinctions between subject-bodies and object-bodies and between first- and third-person perspectives begin to be weakened. For if my experience of my own body, not as "scientific thing" but even already as my way of moving or being in the world,[37] is one that necessarily expresses a spirit that is suprasubjective—a necessary implication if our living body is premised on a field or connection of *Empfindnisse* and if spirit is a transcendental condition of *Empfindnisse*—then my own first-person perspective already opens on to another perspective that, while perhaps not the full-blown third-person perspective of objectivity, is nonetheless a certain kind of third-person perspective: my experience of myself always already involves the input of others (though not yet other "subjects").[38] Indeed, *Empfindnisse* precede the distinction between first- and third-person perspectives, so trying to understand the subject's primordial mode of embodiment by applying the first-person rather than the third-person perspective risks missing something essential to the subject as an expressive unity:[39] namely, that the subject is always already the expression or embodiment of a suprasubjective force that, as my later analyses will show, is both constitutive of subjectivity (and objectivity) and is itself partially constituted by the actions of subjects. Our spiritual situation, therefore, has political consequences already in the constitution of subjectivity itself.

Our expressive account of the subject therefore has something to contribute to the question of whether the living body is egoic or nonegoic.[40] We have already distinguished between the body as an inherently spiritually expressive unity (perhaps the "tactile body" or, to prefigure our later analyses, the body as "tactility") and the postreflexive body that is able to conceive of itself as "my" body. In this regard, we agree wholeheartedly with Heinämaa's claim that the "mineness of the living body would thus be a secondary formation, resulting from a subsequent objectification and thematization that works on the primary system of non-egoic sensings" (OTU, 10). The body as expressive unity precedes the distinctions between subject and object, self and other. The expressive body, then, is certainly nonegoic, as Alia Al-Saji claims. But is the *living* body also nonegoic? To answer this question, we must determine whether the living body is always already *my* living body. If we can distinguish between the living body and *my* living body, then it is possible to equate the living body with the body as expressive unity. If, however, part of what makes the body "living" is its conscious, postreflective nature—if life is always *my* life or *your* life, if *Erlebnis* must be the *Erlebnis* of *this* or *that* subject—then the living body must necessarily be egoic, and therefore distinct from the primal, expressive, "tactile body." Al-Saji does not seem to rigorously distinguish the tactile body from the living body. If the two are conflated, then it is clearly the case that the living body is nonegoic. If they are not conflated, one would need to come up with a plausible argument for distinguishing them.[41]

Such an argument is required because the notion of the body as expressive unity also calls into question the simple distinction between the constituted body and the constituting body.[42] If our primary experience of bodies is as a sensuous-spiritual expressive unity, then our very constituting abilities are themselves premised upon our being-constituted within certain spiritual conditions, conditions that are themselves both constitutive of subjects and world and constituted within the world by the acts of subjects. Hence, the "ambiguity" of Husserl's use of *Leib* criticized by Crowell may prove to be not ambiguous, but primordial.[43] *Before* the distinction between "the body with constitutive functions" and the body "as part of the pre-given world,"[44] Husserl locates the *Leib*, the living body "constituted as a dynamic intertwinement of sensings and sensed qualities, internality and externality, subjectivity and objectivity" (OTU, 21)—and, we might add, of sensuous and spiritual.

In this way, thinking the living body as an expressive unity complicates the first-person perspective that is taken to be a hallmark of phenomenological investigations in many nonphilosophical disciplines. It introduces social and political concerns into the subject's experience even of its own body: it is not simply *other* bodies that I encounter primordially as a spiritual-sensuous unity, but also *my own* body. That is to say, the subject's experience of its own body is not universal, but already politically constituted and hence politically situated. George Yancy, for example, discusses the experience of Black bodies as "confiscated/taken," where "the black body is taken, torn away, and then thrown back, *spread out* before [the black person] as the 'Nigger' that the white gaze objectifies [them] to be." This leads, Yancy argues, to "a form of embodiment . . . where one feels alienated from that sense of being one's own body."[45] One can find similar analyses in the work of Frantz Fanon, Cornel West, W. E. B. Du Bois, Sarah Ahmed, Gayle Salomon, and Judith Butler.[46] Judith Butler goes so far as to say that my body, with "its invariably public dimension . . . is and is not mine."[47]

Our embodiment, therefore, should not be simply contrasted with "normative cultural practices and structures of meaning" (FE, 14), but is itself the first expression of such cultural practices and structures of meaning. The distinction between sex and gender or between skin color and race is a methodological distinction that is secondary to their expressive unity in the lived reality of our embodiment.[48] Sex is already a normative cultural practice (as the practice of "assigning sex" at birth makes clear), and gender, as a set of normative cultural practices, is a particular way (or ways) of embodying the world. This is not to do away entirely with the distinction, nor to reduce the duality simply to one of its relata; rather, we can agree that studying gender or race philosophically cannot "be settled just by studying bodies" but "must also encompass a study of the culturally specific ontological schemas in which those bodies and experiences gain value and meaning" (FE, 100–101), precisely because bodies are never "just bodies" but are living bodies that, *qua* expressive, already are embodiments of the material-spiritual, not simply as ontological schemas but as phenomenal conditions of experiencing as such.

But how can we speak still of "experiencing as such," given the political nature of subjectivity? For if *all* subjects' relation to themselves is necessarily politically constituted (as this chapter has been arguing) and this political constitution alters even one's sense of the "mineness" of one's own body (as Yancy, Fanon, West, Du Bois, Ahmed, Heinämaa, de Beauvoir, Salomon, and Butler argue), then it seems that all subjects' first-person perspective—the entirety of every subject's *Erlebnis*—is affected by its political constitution. And it is not simply that individual subjects are shaped in some particular details by the historical and empirical circumstances in which they find themselves, but the entirety of subjective experiencing itself is constituted, to its core, within particular political contexts. All of my experience, as a subject, is politically constituted. And if this is true, then the very promise and project of phenomenology seems called into question. If the distinction between how I appear to myself and how other things appear to me is shown to be a secondary distinction, founded on a more phenomenologically primordial encounter with myself as an expressive unity, then the methodological use of the "first-person perspective" in all the fields in which phenomenology is used in "fruitful ways" (including "the neurosciences, psychopathology, social psychology, qualitative sociology, political science and critical anthropology . . . gender studies, race studies, disability studies and nursing studies"; OTU, 1) requires further methodological grounding if it is to be viable. Put simply: unless a better justification of the first-person methodology can be found, phenomenology threatens to lose its helpfulness in a variety of fields. For insofar as the subject is always already communal and social before it is individualized, there is and can be no "phenomenological monad," except as a methodological device, just as there can be no rigid sex/gender or biology/culture distinction.

But therein also lies the hope. For that these distinctions are not primary does not mean they have no methodological value. We can still concede that it may be helpful, at times, to treat the subject *as if* it were a monad, or sex and gender *as if* they were distinct phenomena, so as to allow us to focus on other parts of our analysis.[49] Such uses are not ruled out of bounds by the current analysis of the expressive nature of subjectivity; they simply require further methodological justification. Treating the subject *as if* it were a monad, for example, would require a bracketing of the communal nature of the subject that is phenomenologically prior to any attempt to single it out. In this way, taking the subject as monadic would require a more complex methodology, and perhaps even an additional reduction.[50] This is not, then, to say that we can never speak phenomenologically of the subject or the Ego; but we must remember that "the living subject is the subject of his surrounding world, including . . . his personal and social surrounding world" such that "this subject is a person among persons, a citizen of a state, a legal subject, a member of a union, an officer, etc." (Hua 4, Supplement XIII, 382). For Husserl, the phenomenological subject is always already intersubjective, and can be defined as "an intersubjectivity *for itself*" (Hua 4, 315). This implies that the subject clearly has its own "for-itself" character, and that this character arises out of its intersubjective (or sociopolitical) context. To properly understand even the egoism of the subject, then, we must understand it in relation to the (political or communal) sense or spirit at work in its every intuitive encounter with a body— its own, those of others, and of objective bodies in the world.

Expression, therefore, helps us make sense of how subjective life and "dominant discourses" or social constitution are in mutual relation without being reduced one to the other (see AE, 43).[51] For the subject—whether conceived as a living body or methodologically as an isolated monad—is always already relative to the expressive sensuous-spiritual unity that phenomenologically precedes and constitutes it. This relativity means that the expressive subject is always conditional, indexed even in its self-understanding to a spiritual sensing that is constitutive of it, even as it is not wholly contained or exhausted by that constitution. But this constitutive indexing is not merely epistemological: the subject does not just require recourse to spirit in order to *understand* itself reflectively, or to articulate itself theoretically. As we have seen—and as we must still examine more closely— the generative force of spirit is not simply epistemological, but also ontological and practical. The subject is indexed to spirit in such a way that even its very being is constituted in and by this indexicality, for the "sense" of spirit is a phenomenal sensing and not merely an epistemological sense. As such, the expressive subject is not simply in-bodied, but the embodiment of the spiritual-material world it incarnates, an embodiment that can be understood both spiritually/mentally and materially/physically only because it is first a material-spiritual expressive unity. And since expressivity names also the power of relating epistemology and ontology, sense and being, the expressive functioning of spirit within phenomenality entails a not simply epistemological understanding of sense that our analysis of expressivity can help us clarify further. It is to this question that we must now turn.

3

From Sense to Sensings
The Epistemological Implications of Expressivity

In the previous chapter, we suggested that "spirit," as it operates in this expressive unity, is always already related to sense such that one can almost use the terms interchangeably. This near-interchangeability suggests a certain understanding of sense that is important to bring explicitly to light for reasons both phenomenological (i.e., pertaining to the constitution of experience) and epistemological. Phenomenologically, it suggests that sense is not primarily a thing distinct from subjects that they can draw upon in performing certain actions (e.g., meaning-conferring acts of expression, in Husserl's *Logical Investigations*) but rather is something constitutive of subjects that is, therefore, neither merely intrasubjective nor extrasubjective, but "supra-subjective" (Hua 6, 270): we are constituted within a sense that is simultaneously within us and exceeds us. Epistemologically, it suggests that *episteme* is not the most basic form of knowledge (or of engaging with the world "knowingly"), and hence that epistemology is neither first philosophy nor, perhaps, even first in the philosophical study of knowledge. Indeed, as we will see, the distinction between epistemology and ontology begins to break down as we recognize the expressive relation with the world that is both ontologically and epistemologically primary.

To make sense of this, we must trace the ontology-epistemology relation back to its expressive core. We saw a glimpse of this already in previous chapters when we began to move away from the language of "sense" toward language of "sensings" (*Empfindnisse*). But to fully appreciate this transition, we must begin from the expressive sensuous-spiritual unity of "flesh" and trace the outline of the ontological nature of sense while highlighting how even such an ontological sense continues to operate epistemologically. Ultimately, we will see that sense is generated within being itself and functions as an orientation or direction of being such that the sense-being relationship is not a simple founded-founding relation, but a more complex, reversible relation that is nothing other than the relation of expressing. As such, it is a kind of generative process or unfolding that is operative in phenomenality as a kind of *poiesis*. Hence, in the move toward something like "ontoepistemology,"[1] we will be able to see the tying together of being, knowing, and doing in the phenomenological knot that constitutes the core of human experiencing.

Sense and Sensings

We begin, then, with the sensuous-spiritual expressive unity that we called "flesh." Phenomenologically prior to the distinction between subject and world, flesh is characterized, in part, by sensings (*Empfindnisse*), which function as the motivational connections of affectivity that are the contact generating "subject" and "world." But the affectivity at work in such sensings, as I have said, is not simply a passive reception (such as the taking in of hyletic data) but is always already a "feeling" or "tendency" (Hua 11, 149–50) that draws on social horizons and spirit for its operation. Such spirit, we will also recall, functions preobjectively, helping shape the horizons of expectations that we necessarily draw on in our intuition of the world, in part by shaping our "presentiments" or "clarifying intuitions," and so, in terms of its impact on questions of intuition and fulfillment, we can see an epistemological significance to spirit—it clearly shapes how we come to "know" the world. But does this epistemological significance extend even to spirit's function in sensings, such that sensings are themselves already epistemological, a matter of "sense"?

Before we too hastily answer in the affirmative, we must consider more carefully what we are asking. If we return to Frege's notion of sense, whose elaboration is the purpose for Husserl's deployment and development of expression,[2] we begin to see the strangeness of the question. Sense, for Frege, is a mode of presenting referents to and for individual acts of knowing (SR, 210). Sense, therefore, has to be distinguished both from the subjective conceptions of each person's individual mental acts and from the "objective" referents that alone attribute truth value to sense-filled propositions and claims (SR 216). Hence, we can infer two things about "sense" as Frege understands it: on the one hand, sense is distinct from conceptions insofar as sense can "be the common property of many [people] and therefore [is] not a part or a mode of the individual mind" (SR, 212), while conceptions are, by definition, individual and subjective. On the other hand, sense is not a "common property" in the same way that referents are, insofar as sense is "one-sided and dependent upon the standpoint of observation," though, despite this "one-sidedness," sense remains nevertheless "still objective, inasmuch as it can be used by several observers" or, at least, "it could be arranged for several to use it simultaneously" (SR, 213). This bigger-than-subjective-but-not-quite-fully-objective nature of sense is not elaborated on by Frege,[3] but simply illustrated through this example: imagine someone is looking at the Moon through a telescope: the Moon is clearly the referent; the "real image projected by the object glass in the interior of the telescope" is sense; and the "retinal image" of any observer is the conception (SR 213). Sense, we can infer, has an objectivity to it, insofar as— like the image in the telescope—it could be used or seen by multiple people, which would result in each of those people's having their own conception of what was seen. Yet it still remains conditioned and localized by its particular mode of presentation (in this case, by the operation of the telescope), though this conditionality and localization are not individual, but are in principle available to multiple individuals.

Sensings may therefore seem to have little to do with sense, insofar as sensings seem purely subjective and therefore not objective or available to multiple people. But this initial supposition, while plausible from the perspective of a subject (my sensations are certainly mine, and not available to other people in the way they are available to me), is not quite accurate regarding the *Empfindnisse* of the sensuous-spiritual unity. Sensings are never simply "one-way streets." The mutual asymmetry of expressivity is seen already here, in the "reversibility" that Husserl says characterizes sensings: the body does not just touch the world; the body is also touched by the world (Hua 4, 152–53).[4] In this regard, sensings are not simply *my* sensations of X, but rather the condition of sensibility itself; not simply my touching of the world, for example, but rather Touch itself. Now, these conditions of sensibility are not simply physical conditions nor the activity of consciousness, but are rather the phenomenal unity that can be expressed in either direction: I can "live through" my touching of the world so as to "live in" my being touched by the world, or vice versa. And while I—as a fully formed subject—cannot do both simultaneously, this is only because of the nature of expressivity and the phenomenal unity it engenders. It is, you will recall, reflection that enables me to distinguish between the distinct elements of the phenomenal unity—in my initial experience, they are taken precisely as a unity. But such reflection is limited by my own attention and the intentional "rays" of my consciousness: I can only focus on one or the other element at a time, in my reflections on the phenomenal situation, and hence I can reflect on myself only as touching or as touched.[5] But this does not mean (contra the Merleau-Ponty of *The Phenomenology of Perception*) that the "reversibility" or "double touching" itself cannot be simultaneous: as we discussed in the previous chapter, in the phenomenality of the expressive unity there is touching and being touched at the same time.

Sensings, therefore, are characterized by this reversibility, and as such are phenomenologically prior to the unique conceptions (i.e., sensations) I later come to form on the basis of those sensings. And because of that reversibility—or, rather, because of the shared body of Earth as a "field of sensings" that is part and parcel of that reversibility—sensings have a certain objectivity to them. They are in principle shareable by other people, and they can even be used by other knowers simultaneously: the touch that is expressed in my touching of the world is also available for you to use in your touching of the world or in your touching of me. But this objectivity (which is clearly not the full objectivity of referents or individual things in the world) is not without its own one-sidedness. While Frege characterized this one-sidedness as a "dependence on the standpoint of the observer," this one-sidedness appears in the sensuous-spiritual unity of flesh as the localization of a particular connection of motivations: while we may share "visibility," it is still the case that that visibility is conditioned by our particular worldly locations—this is visible here, from this angle, in this lighting, in this social context, with these cultural presuppositions, and so forth.

In this way, sensings—touch, vision, taste, and so on—make possible the presentation of (or, at this point, perhaps it is better to say: the contact between) the world and subjects, and therefore functions (at least structurally) akin to sense in Frege. As such, sensings can be considered epistemological elements that help us "know" the world. But "know" must be used cautiously, in quotation marks, for it is also the case that sensings make possible the presentation of subjects to the world, and hence they also make it possible for the world to "know" subjects. Sensings, then, are epistemological elements that call into question the priority of the subject in and for knowing. Knowing ceases to be relative to the subject and becomes instead a process, a mode of engagement, in which subjects participate both as knowers and as known.

To the extent that sensings are a mode of engagement in which subjects can function both as knowers and as known, they remain pertinent to epistemology. But as a process or mode of engagement that is not conditioned or controlled by the subject, but rather confirms that the subject is always already taken up in a larger context that is not merely epistemological, but political, supra-subjective, historical, and so forth, sensings seem to take us beyond epistemology. In this way, we might begin to wonder whether sensings are best described as epistemological at all; rather, they seem to describe the (meta-epistemological? phenomenal? ontological?) conditions out of which knowledge can arise. We could say that sensings are perhaps the process by which sense is generated, or (like expressing vis-à-vis the expressed and expression) the relation that constitutes both sense and sensible.[6] In such a scenario, sensings would seem to be "supra-epistemological," that is, at once deeply constitutive of epistemology and also beyond or exceeding the "merely epistemological."

The nature of this "beyond" begins to emerge when we recognize the significance of the plurality of sensings. There are multiple sensings, yielding therefore multiple senses and multiple sensibles. We have talked of the sense of touch and its corresponding tactility; we could speak also of the sense of sight and visibility, the sense of hearing and audibility, and so on. But we need not restrict the types of sensings merely to the physical senses: Merleau-Ponty, for example, discusses at length language as a type of sensing, akin to visibility or touch, enabling us to talk also of the "sense of language" (or linguistic sense) and linguisticality (the proper object of the study of linguistics, perhaps). Sense, while retaining its epistemological character, therefore moves beyond mere epistemology into questions of language (and therefore sociality) and ontology.

But this full scope of sense was only revealed when attention was paid to the expressive unity that makes sense possible. For Frege, sense is merely a matter of language and linguisticality (or perhaps of symbolism or syntax, insofar as he would speak also of mathematical expressions), and therefore the only interesting question for expression is how that sense is able to express referents and their truth conditions. This linguistic account of sense is taken up by Husserl, whose phenomenological bent pushes him to consider—as his primary expressive concern in *Logical Investigation*—the question of how sense (with its objective but still one-sided and conditional nature) can make the mental acts of one person available for the objective scrutiny of others. Expressivity was phenomenologically interesting initially only insofar as it was the means by which subjective acts of sense-making were pushed out (ex-pressed) into the objective world. However, studying sense and expression phenomenologically opened Husserl's eyes to the phenomenological structure of expressivity, a structure that further analysis enabled him to see was constitutive even of language (and other such sensings) itself. As such, the need arose to shift the focus from the function of expression within logic or within a "logically complete language" such as Frege's *Begriffsschrift* (see SR, 222) to a broader horizon in which sense and its expression are operative.

Ultimately, I am trying to show that the broadest (or most phenomenologically basic) horizon in which sense and its expression functions is in the horizon of phenomenality itself. For each of these sensings—necessarily rooted in the structure of expressivity—provides a unique mode of engaging phenomena, but each requires the conditions of phenomenality in order to operate. That is, sensings make sense within the conditions of the sensuous-spiritual unity we have characterized as "flesh." And in seeking to elaborate the "ontology of flesh," Merleau-Ponty therefore neither abandons phenomenology and its pursuit of sense nor reduces that pursuit merely to ontology (as Heidegger perhaps did), but rather comes to see—perhaps for the first time in phenomenology—that sense cannot be separated from ontology,[7] even as it cannot be wholly conflated with it either. Rather, what needs to be explored is precisely the unique relation between sense and being—a relation that we would call expressive.

Flesh and the Ontology of Sense

To further explore and justify this claim of the expressive relationship between epistemology and ontology at work in the notion of sensings—and, if that notion is accurate, at work also in the core of human experiencing—we must first look at the peculiar ontological nature of "flesh." Once that has become clear, we will turn, in the next section, to how sense is generated within that ontology. The nature of this generation, as we will see, is such that we cannot say that sense is founded on ontology, nor ontology on sense, but rather both are intertwined (or, following the language of Chapter 1, we might also say "cogenerated," "co-constituted," or "co-delimited") in a peculiar way in "flesh." That way, we will argue, is expressivity.

We turn our immediate attention, then, to the ontology of flesh, which is elaborated in Merleau-Ponty's later works *The Visible and the Invisible*, "Eye and Mind," and "The Philosopher and His Shadow," and explained in Barbaras's *The Being of the Phenomenon*.[8] This ontology is best summarized by the phrase "the world is made of the same stuff as the body."[9] But we must be careful to recognize that this "stuff" is not merely physical stuff, nor is it stuff in a substantialist sense (i.e., that which remains itself, beneath or despite its changing appearances, properties, etc.). Flesh is not "a multiplicity of individuals synchronically and diachronically distributed" who are simply made of the same atomic elements; rather, flesh is "a spatial and temporal pulp where the individuals are formed by differentiation" (VI, 114). Flesh, then, is a kind of matrix of differentiating processes, and so is the ontology it presupposes. This makes sense only through a fundamental reorientation of the account of being, one that is consistent with the broader phenomenological reorientation of being (explicated most notably by Heidegger): being is not a collection of individuals arrayed before me like a photograph (or a movie playing on a screen, if you want to simply add in the temporal element to this substantialist picture), but a process, an unfolding, "a certain manner of being, in the active sense, a certain *Wesen*, in the sense that, says Heidegger, this word has when it is used as a verb" (VI, 115).[10]

To speak of the ontological nature of flesh, then, is to speak not of "what is," in the sense of a collection of objects, but to speak of the processes of differentiation out of which things are generated. This is a generative ontology that would prefer to speak of the (modes of) be-ing that characterizes human experience rather than of "the human being."[11] Take, for example, our earlier discussion of sensings, and how they open a reflexive space that enables "my body" to distinguish itself from the body of the world. Here, my body emerges as a thing, a being, but it precisely *emerges* as such out of a background that is somehow primed to enable such an emergence. This background is not merely a "background state," but is the sum total of conditions necessary for the emergence of things. These conditions include processes, activities, and the like that are not merely carried out within being (as the "stage" containing the collection of objects) but are themselves modes or ways of being: it is the body (of the Earth) as a "field of sensings," as we discussed in Chapter 2.

Knowledge, in the broad sense of "making sense of the world," is one of these activities. That is, knowledge is not merely the reproduction or representation of "being" within the realm of a consciousness that would be distinct from being,[12] but a project taken up within being and as part of being (as we will see in Chapter 5). But to speak of knowing as a process of being is not to equate being with knowing, nor knowing with the making of "a system of everything that is possible before the eyes of a pure spectator" (VI, 108). That is, the type of knowing at work in flesh—the primordial type of knowing that is intertwined with a particular kind of being—is not the kind of objectivity sought or accomplished in science, in *episteme*, any more than the being of flesh is a stable state or collection of what just "is." Flesh, then, is not the conflation of ontology and epistemology but rather the prior condition(s) that make possible the emergence of ontology and epistemology as distinct practices, and that is constitutive of those practices. We ought not understand being on the basis of (objectivist) epistemology, nor epistemology on the basis of (objectivist) being, nor flesh on the basis of either (or both). Rather, flesh constitutes the prior matrix that must condition our understanding of being and epistemology, insofar as they emerge out of flesh.

This emergence is a generation within being, since ontology and episte-mology remain activities of being. The knowing subject does not stand "in front of" or "behind" being but is surrounded by it and traversed by it, such that "my vision of Being [is] not forming itself from elsewhere, but from the midst of Being" (VI, 114). Ideas are "already encrusted in [my body's] joints" (VI, 114), because my body itself is "made of the same stuff as the world." This does not make ideas merely empirical artifacts any more than it makes of my body "merely" a "thing in the world," because my body is a "very remarkable variant" of being (VI, 136) insofar as it is, as we have already discussed, doubled or reversible: it is the "sensible sentient" (ibid.), the touching that can be touched, the see-r that can be seen.

But this variant is *not* remarkable because it is doubled: being itself is doubled, is full of folds that create gaps (*écarts*) and dehiscences (VI, 153), differences, and differends.[13] The particular doubling of my living body is "remarkable," rather, because it generates *a certain kind* of difference (sen-tience vis-à-vis sensibility), a certain gap (between consciousness and world), a certain dehiscence (between subject and objects). The emergence of con-sciousness is no more or less remarkable, in and for being, than the emer-gence of different kinds of sloths or the gap between living and nonliving beings, though it seems more remarkable (and is certainly more remarked on, in Western philosophy) to us as conscious subjects so generated. We find it remarkable because we experience and live the gap, and therefore we seek to explain it, to "make sense" of it, to wrestle and understand this dimension of being that we experience directly, alongside other dimensions of being we experience (and, perhaps, in addition to further dimensions that we do not experience).

If this desire to explain, to "make sense," is unique to humans (and Merleau-Ponty's work on nature and animal behaviors should cause us to wonder whether it is, in fact, unique to humans), it is unique only in the types of questions it asks, and the type of (epistemic) answers that it tries to give, and not in asking questions of itself or of being. For (theoretical) think-ing is and always remains a mode of being that is produced within being—within flesh—and therefore sense, too, is part of being, produced within being. For, as discussed already in Chapter 1, "the existing world exists in the interrogative mode" (VI, 103), and so questioning the world around us is the most natural thing in the world, for all beings. Looking for food is a type of questioning of the world (which we could reframe, in a lin-guistic sense, as "What will keep me alive and healthy?"). Searching for a mate is a questioning of the world ("How will I reproduce?"). Seeking com-panionship in groups, marking one's territory, even just taking up space are all concrete modes of questioning the world. They are distinct modes from the (epistemological) mode of sense, but they are modes of questioning nonetheless.

Epistemological sense, then, is one mode of questioning the world, and is therefore one mode of being for humans, though obviously not the only one. Indeed, as discussed earlier, sense is already multiple modes of questioning the world, multiple ways of being: visible, tactile, linguistic, and so forth. And each of these sensings, in turn, find their existence, their mode of being, in the world in some *Stiftung*[14] or other. This is not to say that sensings are *Stiftungen*, but simply that they *exist* or take on concrete modes of being only within various *Stiftungen*.[15] Visibility, for example, exists only in and through various visual *Stiftungen* (as Merleau-Ponty makes clear in "Eye and Mind").[16] Each sensing, therefore, comes to us via traditions or institutions that precede us, shape our engagements with the world, and thereby affect how we interrogate the world. As such, each sensing itself can be given in multiple ways: the painter does not see the world the same way the engineer does, and the musician does not hear the world the same way an ornithologist does.

What is significant for us here is that this multiplicity of sensings and their various senses precede and condition individual subjects. For while they all emerge within flesh and are distinguishable only as various folds or doublings of flesh—various ways that flesh has unfolded (physically, temporally, culturally, etc.)—sensings remain "natural": part of a nature that is understood, not simply as the constituted opposing correlate of culture, but as "the primordial—that is, the nonconstructed, the noninstituted. . . . Nature is . . . our soil [*sol*]—not what is in front of us, facing us, but rather, that which carries us" (N, 4).[17] Nature is noninstituted (i.e., is not itself a *Stiftung* but is the condition of all *Stiftungen*) precisely because it has no founder, no inaugurator to give it a purpose.[18] Nature is "what has meaning, without this meaning being posited by thought: it is the autoproduction of meaning" (N, 3). *Qua* nature, sensings are the conditions that necessarily, and on their own, give rise to various inaugurated *Stiftungen*. Within these *Stiftungen* sense develops not by the intervention of people or culture into a distinct, "natural" setting, but within and out of the unfolding of nature itself. In other words, sense and meaning are not created by a thinker in a concrete act of thought; rather, thinking articulates, in a "new" linguistic way, a sense that exists latently in nature, and in articulating it in a new way, it alters it from within. That is to say, thinking expresses sensing. Sense and sensings are not *created* by humans or by subjects but are always already circulating in being, a being that is already under way before any individual self emerges.[19] Sense, therefore, is a necessary element in being, even as being is a necessary element in sense. The distinction between sense and being, like that between epistemology and ontology, is a product of the processes and unfolding of the expressive unity of flesh, and so neither term can be properly understood without accounting for their generation out of flesh.

Genesis and the Sense of Ontology

The process of generating sense within being is, therefore, a self-differentiation within being itself (N, 176). It is not a process that must be carried out by an agent or by a doer that is distinct from being, but rather is the result of being's own unfolding as temporalizing and spatializing. Martina Ferrari refers to these as "processes of self-differentiation whereby being phenomenalizes itself as beings," a process she equates with flesh.[20] Not only does this repeat and confirm our earlier analysis of flesh as the expressive and ultratranscendental[21] unity out of which subject and world, subject and object, and so on are differentiated and constituted, but it also clearly associates these processes of differentiation with phenomenalization itself as an act that is not controlled by the subject but an act that subjects undergo within, and as constituted by, the being of flesh.

In speaking of the processes of differentiation (including spatializing and temporalizing) as "phenomenalization," we mean to say that they are the way in which nature or "the Earth," that is, that which in flesh precedes the distinction between subject and world, and so that which can be considered the shared "bodily ownness" of "subject" and "world" (see BR, 45) "makes sense" of things.[22] But this "making sense" is not, then, the (cultural) imposition of meaning on a neutral and inherently meaningless substrate (nature),[23] but rather the constitution or generation of things within being as the beings that they themselves are. That is, and as we saw with the way that spirit constitutes horizons both within the subject and in the generation of cultural objects ("houses, bridges, tools, works of art and so on"; Hua 8, 151), the process (phenomenalization) that makes sense cannot be distinguished from the process of "materialization" whereby individual beings are constituted as individual beings.

Phenomenality, therefore, is always already the intertwining of being and meaning, not as the same thing nor as wholly different things but as the (phenomenal) unity of being and meaning—that is, the unity of being and meaning in and as phenomenality, a unity that is not a simple identity insofar as later reflection is able to distinguish them but is not simply difference because I experience it as a unity and not as a difference. It is, quite simply, phenomenalization as expressivity.

We can note, then, two significant aspects of this account of phenomenalization (as the self-differentiation of being into beings) that we have been discussing in this chapter: first, making sense is not, primarily, something performed by subjects but is a "natural" process that precedes and conditions subjects—we are "made of sense" at least as much as we "make sense"; and second, phenomenalization occurs always already as "institution," and so materialization—the generation of individual beings—is already part of a *Stiftung* laden with sense.[24] These aspects have significant implications for our understanding of the phenomenological core of human experience and of the phenomenology by which we try to understand it. The first makes clear that sense is a "natural" product and begins to suggest, since such phenomenalization is a self-differentiation of being, that being (as flesh) can be understood as the autoproduction of meaning (N, 3), that being simply is the process of producing sense. The second makes clear that, because phenomenalization is a process of flesh's autoproduction of meaning, meaning and materialization are always already laden with tradition or with purpose, that is, are always already both situated somewhere concrete (both socially and materially, though we can see now how that very distinction breaks down in the expressive unity of flesh) and going somewhere and/or doing something. Indeed, sense—in its mode of being as *Stiftung*, but also in its doubling of, its reversibility with, materialization—is perhaps nothing more than this directedness within being itself.[25] Sense as doubled sensibility—sensings—is the way in which being unfolds itself, not according to a predetermined and externally given *telos*[26] but according to the internal, generative force of spirit discussed in the previous chapter. The generation of sense, then, is not some distinct process within being, but is simply the unfolding of being itself in and through processes of (self-)differentiation. As such, "the generation of sense is not exclusive to human life but, rather, is an irreducible element of nature's dynamics" (PT, 391). This, in turn, "means that I am not the wholly active constituter of sense, for the institution of sense requires an activity that surpasses me."[27] That is all to say: *I* do not generate sense, nature (i.e., being-as-flesh) does. And, in generating sense (first and foremost through the processes of sensings), nature also generates subjects, which must be understood relative to the sensing(s) that generate them.

Because of this autogeneration, "we must admit in the very fabric of physical elements a transtemporal and transspatial element" (N, 176). That is, not only is physicality (the "just physical" world of the natural sciences) an expression of a deeper materiality, as we discussed in Chapter 2, but that materiality is also an expression of a deeper relating that is not simply temporal and/or spatial, but temporal*izing*, spatial*izing*. Flesh is the transcendental process(es) by which the very fabric of physical elements is generated, processes that are known as "phenomenalization."[28] Phenomenalization, therefore, is simultaneously an epistemological process (insofar as it generates sense) and an ontological process (insofar as it generates sensibility and sensible "things"), and sensings are the "latent sense" guiding nature's unfolding, including our articulation of that sense linguistically, visually (in perception and in art), tactilely, audibly (the "music of the world"), and so on. And because this latent sense is a "living plan" (N, 176) or an "incarnate principle" (VI, 139) that shapes or guides the unfolding of being from within, "nature is *poiesis*,[29] an incarnate process of *self-differentiation* traceable in and through the visible . . . whereby its phenomenalizing entails the continual renewal of being and the sense of the sensible" (PT, 393).

As poietic, this sense is not primarily propositional or theoretical, but a creative process, a "silent persuasion" (VI, 214) that emerges through its showing, through its doing, by being "lived in" like the difference between right and left (VI 216–17):[30] the sense of right and left cannot be articulated in strictly theoretical terms,[31] and it cannot be articulated using only one of the relata. Rather, it is a sense that emerges in and as a way of relating (to the world and to each other) that must be *experienced* to be sensible. That is, sense "is not an object appearing to and graspable by a subject" (PT, 395) but primarily a way of engaging or "living in" the world (sensing) that is a necessary condition for our experience, but a "necessary condition" not in the sense of a logical necessity but as a kind of "call to follow" (IP, 77) that affects us as we live in the world, pulling us in this direction or that direction, asking us to take up this question or that question, helping us to see this problem but not that one.

Such a sense/sensing, therefore, is both meaning and orientation—a point captured in the French sense of *sens*. And this dual connotation implies an intertwining, not just of meaning and being but of meaning, being, and doing: if nature is the autopoiesis of sense in and as beings, then we can see in the expressive unity of flesh a unity of sense, being, and a process (or "doing"), a unity that is a phenomenal unity insofar as it is the unity of phenomenalization itself. That is, phenomenality—the nature of experience *qua* experiencing—is a particular way of relating knowing, being, and doing. Epistemology is always already caught up in both ontology and doing/poiesis,[32] where the latter is an ongoing unfolding that differentiates (and relates) beings as beings, sensings as sense and sensible— and all as *Stiftung*, which are sense's mode of being and being's mode of sensing.

The Epistemological Implications of Expression

In seeing sense as both a meaning and an orientation, we seem to have come a long way from Frege's notion of "sense." But this does not, I think, entail that we have simply left that notion behind and so made any talk of "sense," meaning, or epistemology simply ambiguous or equivocal. Rather, Frege's notion of sense—that which is able to present (objective) referents in, to and for the personal conceptions of individual subjects—is now expanded and contextualized. While Frege seems to assume that such sense is univocally epistemological, our analysis of sense in terms of expressivity has shown us that the epistemic is only *one* way of presenting referents in, to, and for subjects, and therefore *one* way of knowing. We usually call this way of knowing "objective" knowing. It certainly presents us a certain picture of objectivity: disinterested, dispassionate, disaggregated knowing at a distance—the object as (epistemologically) standing against [*gegen-stand*] or before the subject.[33] If we are willing to concede that this is what we mean by objectivity, then it must be clear that objectivity is not our primary way of knowing or engaging the world; things in our world are *not* primarily objects but something else. In both Henry and Heidegger, we encounter things first as tools, that is, useful elements of our practical engagements with the world (see BR, 45; BT, 68–69). Our way of "knowing" them, then, is first of all practical, not epistemic. With Husserl, we saw in the last chapter that we encounter things as "spiritual products" (Hua 6, 270): as things carrying a "spiritual meaning" as an inherent part of their own being (Hua 9, 112). Their meaningfulness is not primarily a matter of theoretical or objective knowledge—disinterested and at a distance—but of preobjective (*Gegenstandlich*) spiritual connection: we "feel" or are affected by things before we objectify them. In Merleau-Ponty, we share a sensibility with things before we formulate sense *about* things. All these offer primary ways in which things present themselves in, to and for subjects that precede or condition any kind of objective presentation.

This does not, however, entail that objective knowing—*episteme*—is somehow illegitimate. We may, for various reasons, choose to focus on our engagement with things in their form as constituted objects. Just like the methodological choice discussed at the end of the last chapter to view the subject sometimes as a monad, this is a permissible, and perhaps at times even necessary, methodological decision. But it is precisely a methodological decision, one that carries with it certain presuppositions (e.g., that things are "objects," that there is a qualitative difference between things and the knower of those things, etc.) that will affect our analysis of the situation. As such, it is a methodological decision that should be entered into consciously and purposefully, and ideally with an awareness of how that decision may affect the results of our investigation.

Such a methodological decision seems to lie in the domain of theoretical thought. This is to say, it is the product and domain of a particular *Stiftung*, instituted to engage the world in a particular way for particular purposes. As *Stiftung*, theoretical thought is animated by a certain "sense" of the world that orients "knowers" in the world in a particular way that alters, not just how they understand the world, but how they engage it: we treat, for example, bodies differently when we think of them primarily as objects than we do when we think of them as subjective or living bodies. Both sexual objectification and environmental indifference illustrate this point. If a body is primarily an object before my gaze, I am free to "intend" it however I see fit: as coworker, as potential sexual partner, as aesthetic object, as (human or natural) resource, as tool, as fuel, as economic possibility, and so forth. If I encounter a body, however, as an expressive unity with a person and therefore as a subject in and of itself, I must take account of its intentions in how I intend it: I am no longer free to engage with it however I see fit, but am compelled (or, at least, called or solicited) to engage with it in the mode it chooses to give itself to me, insofar as I now understand it as an agent capable of choice in its mode of givenness and seeking mutuality in our relationship. And this will not only affect how I see or "intend" the body encountered, but also how I act toward it (Do I ask it for advice or for a phone number? Do I ask it questions, or give it commands? Do I seek consent or engage solely on my own terms?), the role I assign it in my practical engagement with the world (partner, foe, tool, etc.), the things I find it capable of doing (objects don't have subjectivity, so even if one of them is making noise I must assume such noise isn't inherently meaningful but is governed solely by how *I*, as the subject, interpret the situation: "Don't get all bent out of shape! That's not what I meant"), and even the shape or form future such bodies can or will take (if feminine bodies exist for the male gaze, then their actual physical characteristics will be altered to remain more appealing to that gaze, as in some forms of cosmetic surgery.[34] In another register, if animal bodies are mere economic products of the agricultural-industrial complex, then breeding and genetic manipulation to increase economically desirable traits and minimize economically undesirable ones are both sensible and materially determinative: what pigs or chickens "are" will be altered by the sense with which we approach our engagement with them). Taking a particular stance on knowledge (e.g., an epistemological stance that privileges *episteme*), therefore, is not *simply* an epistemological choice with epistemological consequences, but a social, ethical, and perhaps even ontological choice with social, ethical, and ontological consequences.

For phenomenology, it is a basic tenet that before things are encountered as objects or even as tools, they must be encountered as phenomena. After our discourse on expression, perhaps we are able to appreciate this basic tenet more fully. A "phenomenon" is not an "appearing" of the thing as opposed to its actual (objective) "being" (BT, 25–28): it is not to be understood in juxtaposition to a presumed noumenal realm that, by relation, renders the phenomenal simply "the best we can do." Phenomena are not concessions to human finitude judged against the normative standard of a presumed infinitude (of God or the God's-eye view) or a direct, unmediated access (as some may presume happens, e.g., in mathematics). Phenomena, rather, are "the basic units of existence."[35]

In this regard, Karen Barad is articulating a very phenomenological point in her "ontoepistemology." Her claim is that phenomena (and phenomenality) are not primarily epistemological entities, "mark[ing] the epistemological inseparability of 'observer' and 'observed,'" but rather "*phenomena are ontological entanglement.*"[36] From our analysis so far, we can see that at least materiality, *Stiftung*, spirit, and individuality are all entangled in and as a phenomenon. In the concrete case of a pregnant woman getting an ultrasound, for example, this means that "the medical professionals who acquire, operate, and maintain the apparatus and analyze the images it produces belong to the same phenomenon as the machine itself, the pregnant woman and her fetus, and the social, economic, geographic and political conditions under which the examination is performed."[37] Or, to return to Frege's example, the telescope, its constituent parts, and the people using it remain part of the phenomenon of viewing the Moon. The phenomenon, therefore, is not simply the thing (*das Ding*), but the whole complex of material, spiritual, sensing, political, and related forces that have enabled nature to unfold itself in this particular way at this particular time.

This is the significance of phenomenology's mantra—"To the things themselves!"—being a pursuit of the *Sachen selbst* and not the *Ding-an-Sich*. For phenomenology, a phenomenon is always a *Sache* and never merely a *Ding*, not because phenomenology has abandoned objectivity in favor of relativism but because the only way to be "objective," to understand the object on its own terms, is to understand the *Stiftungen* out of which it arose and which provide it its sense, that is, both its meaning and its orientation within being or existence. If we want to understand the "things" of the world, we have to recognize that things are not primarily objects—disconnected, disinterested, distinct—but always already things-in-relation, or, perhaps better: always already the relating-of-things.

Barad confirms this point with her claim, "Phenomena are ontologically primitive relations—relations without pre-existing relata."[38] The last part of that phrase is especially telling in the context of our analysis of expressivity here, for she highlights that—as we discovered in expressivity—the relata do not constitute their own relation but rather are constituted by the prior relating, the relation*ship*, that gives the relata both their meaning and their being. Such an epistemology (which is also, we have seen, an ontology, and therefore perhaps should just be called: a philosophy) of phenomena denies a "correspondence relation" between sense and things in favor of what Barad calls "a causal explanation of how discursive practices are related to material phenomena."[39] Given our analyses in this work, we might choose to expand phenomenology's claim to offer a causal explanation of how *expressive* practices (and not merely discursive ones) are related to material phenomena. This is not merely a semantic difference, but one that gets at the heart of why phenomenology can be called an "ontoepistemology" but not, perhaps, an "agential realism" (both terms are fundamental to Barad's project): the latter suggests the necessity of "agents," which, while necessary to discursive practices, are not yet operative in expression in its most fundamental sense.[40] That is, while phenomenology certainly does not want to get rid of talk of "agents" or even presubjective "agencies," such individual agencies are not the primordial cause of action. Phenomenologically speaking, we can discern a prior unity (Earth, nature, flesh, etc.) out of which agencies are differentiated, not by a primordial agent but by an autopoietic unfolding that is not substantial (i.e., there is no substance standing behind or beneath its processes of unfolding): there is no "Nature naturing" and "Nature natured," to use Spinoza's distinction; there is only the sense of nature always interrogating itself, in its very being, as and through beings. And because of that (phenomenological) priority, agents and agencies must be understood relative to that primordial sense (spirit, *Stiftung*, etc.): phenomenalization happens before agencies, and the latter are the result of the former. That is, before agents can produce phenomena, phenomenalization must produce agents/agencies.

Two significant implications arise from this, one epistemological and one methodological. Epistemologically, we must acknowledge that *episteme* are relative to other, more primordial means of engaging/knowing/sensing the world. These other modes are not subject-generated but are processes that are both subject- and object-constitutive. Hence, if epistemology means the "study of how we know the world," we must recognize that the primary object of epistemology is not reflective or theoretical thought, and not, perhaps, even techne or praxis, but poiesis. That is, we must recognize that epistemology is necessarily entwined with our primordial engagements with the world: it is a matter, not just of "knowing" (in the traditional, cognitive sense) but of a "making" or "creating"—a generating of phenomena—that always includes elements of being and doing. Epistemology must always be onto-epistemology.

And this is true, even if "epistemology" is taken, not as the study of how we know the world, but simply as the study of *episteme* (of theoretical knowledge). Even such an understanding of epistemology (which then loses, I think, any claim to being "first philosophy") must still be understood as a type of cultural production, insofar as theoretical knowledge is taken as either a phenomenon in itself or as a type of *Stiftung* productive of various phenomena. In either case, as should be clear from our analyses in this chapter, *episteme* are expressions of some deeper (material, spiritual, and natural) forces, and epistemology therefore remains onto-epistemology.

This leads us to the methodological implications raised by this chapter. In offering "a causal explanation of how discursive practices are related to material phenomena,"[41] Barad's work begins to provide a response to the methodological questions raised by Oksala and Heyes in the Introduction. Our expressive analyses extend that response further: by preserving the agency of subjects but suggesting that subjects/agents also arise out of the processes of phenomenalization, I have suggested that subjects can be considered a type of material phenomena which can then, following Barad, be causally connected to discursive practices.[42] In doing so, we can begin to clarify the method whereby we can trace how subjects (and even perhaps subjectivity itself) are formed in particular political contexts without eliminating the power and force of the "lived" quality of individual experience that accrues to them *qua* subjects (and not merely *qua* phenomena). But if this explanation is merely empirical, we will simply have reduced subjectivity to a product of discourse (as the Introduction suggested some poststructuralist discourses do), and hence will have lost the power and force of *Erlebnis*. To preserve this power, we must maintain a dimension to and for subjective experience that is not simply empirical: we must find a way to consider the social, economic, geographic, and political conditions under which a phenomenon occurs as nonempirical elements of the phenomenon of sense and sense-constitution.

Such a nonempirical significance for these elements emerges only when we begin to ask not just what we see but *how* we are able to see it phenomenologically: when we begin to investigate phenomenality as the conditions of experiencing. Such investigation brings two things to the table methodologically, two tasks that must be explored further if we are to properly understand both the political generation of subjectivity and the method whereby we can come to understand and articulate it. First, to truly understand individual phenomena in the world, it is not sufficient to ask, "What are they?" (the question of essence). Rather, we must ask, "How did they come to be here? Why did the phenomenon take this form at this time? When and where did certain events transpire to cause this transformation rather than another?" This shift—from questions of "What" to questions of "How much? Who? How? Where and when?"[43]—mirrors the phenomenological shift from "static" or "eidetic" phenomenology to "genetic" phenomenology.[44] It is a shift away from a concern with possibility (essences as the realm of what is possible to know) toward a concern with the actual, which includes not just individual phenomena but also their emergence within what Gina Zavota calls "the social, economic, geographic and political conditions" that are "entangled" with them *qua* phenomena. To explain this more fully, we must still account for the actual generation of subjectivity within the expressive unity of flesh (Chapter 5) and the generation of subjects within particular political communities and contexts (Chapter 6).

Second, this concern with the actual must have "a transcendental scope, beyond empirical examples" that can be accounted for philosophically.[45] This transcendental scope of actuality is accounted for in the move from genetic to generative phenomenology, which alone enables us to make sense of the "social world as *transcendental* historicity, materiality, and sociality" (HB, 15; emphasis added). This "transcendental" move is simply an inquiry into "the constitution of sense" (HB, 12), a constitution that generativity reveals to occur always within particular historical, social, and political contexts. Hence, accounting for the role of these contexts as nonempirical elements of the phenomenon of sense and sense-constitution requires us to pay attention in a particular way (which we can call generative and transcendental) to how experience has actually unfolded: "the task of a generative phenomenology is precisely to inquire after how historical and intersubjective structures themselves become meaningful at all, how these structures are and can be generated" (HB, 260) in a way that is more concrete than simple static or genetic analyses alone.[46]

We have seen this generative, transcendental move already in how we have paid attention to the generation of subjects (Chapter 2) and of sense (Chapter 3) within the prior expressive unity of phenomenalization. From those analyses, we have learned that thinking expressively requires us to think of the actual primarily as a process (actualization) rather than as the set of "what is." Actualization is thereby understood as the process by which things emerge or are generated out of a differentiated and self-unfolding field (e.g., nature, flesh, etc.) rather than being realized out of a set of possibilities. Possibilities are traditionally understood as preexisting the real such that "the whole of existence is here related to a pre-formed element, from which everything is supposed to emerge by a simple 'realization.'"[47] Conversely, actualization is the self-unfolding inherent to a differential relationship in which relata are determined by their relationship, and so no "thing" within the relationship can be predetermined in advance: the field can be defined or explained only by the actual processes that give rise to the differentiated relata and their relationship ("How did they come to be here? Why did the phenomenon take this form at this time?," etc.), even as the unfolding of that relationship also guides or generates those processes. The expressive co-constitution and cogeneration of sense and being in phenomenalization entails that actualization is the very force of differentiation itself.[48] Actualization is one facet of the expressive force of phenomenalization, and the poietic generation of phenomenalization is therefore autopoietic.

Let us use the *langue-parole* distinction from Saussurean linguistics as an example of how this works. Sausseure is infamous for describing *langue* as the differentiated structure of language (the possible semantic and syntactic combinations, the rules of grammar, existing sets of connotations and denotations, etc.) that provide the "rules" by which everyday uses of language (*parole*) function. This differentiated structure operates in the background of *parole*, not as a set of discrete things (e.g., rules, letters, words, etc.) that subjects can choose to draw upon if they wish to exercise some latent "linguistic possibility" that resides within them, but as a field that necessarily actualizes itself in and through people's use of language (*parole*), that is, through people's writing, speaking, and so on. Its structure, as a series of differential relations that are reciprocally determinative ("B" is what it is in relation to "A," "C," etc.; "cat" means what it does in relation to "rat," "car," "cut," but also "feline," "mammal," "amusing internet videos," etc.), is actualized in its use, even as that use shapes and alters that structure: the "rules" of language change according to how language is used, even as an utterance must function according to those "rules" in order to be a use of language. This is an account of Saussurean linguistic structures inherently animated by their own expressive force: it is not that people simply choose to take up these structures as a means of articulating some independently formed sense, but that these structures shape the sense that can be formed within them, even as that sense is partially constitutive of the people who think it.

Epistemologically, this example helps us see that sense always operates within structures or rules that shape the sense we make of empirical conditions even as those structures are cogenerated with the sense they make of those conditions. That is, the unfolding of sense is simultaneously generative of empirical conditions and the "rules" of sense that condition our understanding of those conditions, and so the relation between structuring conditions (e.g., *langue*) and what they condition (i.e., empirical conditions like *parole*) can be properly explained only by contextualizing them within the expressive relation, the phenomenal unity that precedes and generates them via processes of actualization.

It is only by understanding the actual processes that give rise to actual conditions, then, that we can properly clarify the relationship between subjects, subjective processes, and particular political contexts. We have said that such an understanding must be generative and transcendental. But to see how and why these processes of actualization must be transcendentally operative—to clarify how this is not merely empirical production but transcendental generation—the next step of our clarification of expressivity and its implications must be a clarification of the notion of the "transcendental" in its relation to the "empirical." It is to this that we must now turn in the next chapter.

4

Making Sense of Experience
The Transcendental Implications of Expressivity

There are two important issues to consider as we seek to clarify the relation between conditions and what they condition. The first is whether concrete "empirical" phenomena can alter the transcendental condition(s) of their own appearing. Insofar as we said that phenomena (defined as the "basic units of existence" that occur as "ontological entanglements"[1] of, at least, materiality, *Stiftung*, spirit and individuality) are able to alter both phenomenality and phenomenalization, it seems that they can. But then to what extent are those conditions transcendental and not simply empirical? This question is crucial to a proper understanding of critical phenomenology, and of the role that factors such as race, gender, sexuality, and the like play in the constitution of experience or of subjectivity itself, and not simply of particular experiences of particular individuals. Are racism, sexism, heteronormativity, and so forth matters of transcendental significance, or are they simply "empirical" concerns?

Of course, much trades on the definition and understanding of "transcendental." Our previous discussions have suggested that the transcendental should be conceived primarily as a field and not a (transcendental) subject. This brings us to the second important issue opened up by the relation between conditions and what they condition. For if the conditions are not themselves subjective but are suprasubjective (i.e., somehow constitutive of subjectivity without themselves being strictly confined within subjectivity), we must ask about the type of *experience* (if any) we can have of the transcendental,[2] or whether the transcendental is only (and necessarily) a deduction to the necessary conditions for our current experience. This is a question concerning the nature of the transcendental as it functions in our inquiry into expression, but also a methodological question concerning the validity of talking phenomenologically about phenomenality and phenomenalization and, more broadly, about the first-personal nature of phenomenology's mode of inquiry. After all, if the transcendental is not primarily subjective but a field, then why should self-reflection on our own subjective experience be a legitimate method for analyzing or accessing the transcendental? Why should phenomenology have something meaningful to say, not simply about individual *experiences* of racism, sexism, and so on, but about structural or institutional racism or sexism?

At issue, then, is whether we can ever speak phenomenologically about anything other than the particular conditions of a particular empirical instance: can we speak coherently about "experience" itself, or only of my particular experience of this particular phenomenon? Can *Erlebnis* ever meaningfully get us to some kind of connected and publicly shared experience? These questions, of course, have been with us since our discussion of Johanna Oksala and Cressida Heyes in the Introduction. Clarifying the precise nature of the transcendental will help us see that phenomenological transcendentality is fundamentally consistent with a "transcendental empiricism": being altered by empirical phenomena is, in fact, a transcendental and constitutive necessity of transcendentality in the phenomenological sense. In other words, the transcendental is not just a "condition of possibility" for experience but is itself an element of actual experience. It is therefore experienceable, though not as a phenomenon; rather, it is the experiencing of our experience, something we can only recognize or experience directly through the phenomenological reduction. Therefore, the transcendental will be confirmed as something we can talk meaningfully about in relation to expressive experience, but only insofar as we acknowledge the way that our particular experiences shape our understanding of the transcendental.

But the transcendental also shapes our particular engagements with the world, acting like the "rules" of experiencing within particular contexts. Therefore, understanding any given experience requires also understanding the transcendental conditions that (partially) give it sense. But understanding transcendental conditions is not simple, insofar as they are operative as conditions of experience and not as distinct phenomena. Articulating an understanding of them is therefore to generate a phenomenon, a concept or idea about transcendental conditions, that never simply describes the transcendental "as it is," but always, *qua* generative expression, alters both the transcendental and empirical conditions it is purporting to describe. Transcendental phenomenology is therefore revealed to be a necessarily political and critical endeavor—articulating the rules by which we make sense of our experience in a way that contributes to the alteration and transformation of social structures and the experience of subjects within those structures—not least because the transcendental is itself both politically constituted and politically constitutive. And critical phenomenology is also revealed to be necessarily transcendental: concepts like gender and race do not name merely empirical phenomena, but transcendental processes (racialization, genderization) that make sense of experience itself.

The Empirical and the Transcendental

We turn first to the status of transcendentality and its relation to factual existence and "empirical" happenings. The significance of language of the transcendental has been a consistent and major theme of (meta)phenomenological reflection at least since Husserl's "Origin of Geometry" (if not earlier) and Heidegger's *Being and Time*. Like its Kantian predecessor, the transcendental refers to "an investigation into the senses operative in our experiences" (MHC, 2).[3] However, whereas Kant considers transcendental only those logical necessities which make possible our cognition *a priori*, that is, apart from experience,[4] phenomenology is interested in the conditions *of* experience, and not those devoid of experience.[5] Husserl, in one notable example of this, marks the distinction between himself and Kant by the account each gives of the givenness of subjectivity itself: while Kant assumes subjectivity is simply given, a priori, Husserl is interested in how subjectivity itself is constituted (see Hua 11, 126).

If the conditions of subjective constitution are therefore important transcendental elements for phenomenology, the fact that they are "only conceivable in genesis" (Hua 11, 125), that is, within the unfolding of phenomenality (as we discussed in Chapter 4) means that they cannot be, strictly speaking, conditions of *possibility*. Given the significance of expressivity for this unfolding, the constitution of subjectivity cannot be understood along the lines of "conditions of possibility" because such conditions (if A exists, B must exist or must have existed) apply to indicative relations, and not expressive ones.[6] The (transcendental) conditions of subjectivity, then, cannot simply be (logical, ontological, or even phenomenological) possibilities that happen to be realized in some particular instance. Rather, they are the (virtual) structures that are actualized in and through our experience.[7] This is to say that (empirical) experience does not simply *require* its transcendental conditions; it *expresses* them.

This difference is not simply semantic. Insofar as experience expresses its transcendental conditions, the transcendental and the empirical are established in a particular type of relation. The transcendental conditions function as the background field that gives rise, via its own self-differentiating movement, to the individual phenomena of our experience. That is to say, the transcendental and the empirical elements of our experience are not distinct from each other as discrete phenomena (i.e., with their own content or their own "location," e.g., ideal vs. real, or transcendent, beyond experience, vs. immanent, experienced), but as modes or axes of a phenomenon.[8] The transcendental does not simply name the "conditions of possibility" in a logical or ontological sense, but the generative conditions that give rise to actual experience. And within these generative conditions, we can distinguish the transcendental axis/mode/dimension from the empirical or historical axis/mode/dimension, just as we can distinguish, as discussed briefly in the last chapter, between *langue* and *parole*.

The importance of maintaining this distinction and its unique character as axis and not as discrete phenomena is essential to understanding both the relationship between the transcendental and the empirical and the transcendental itself (which is determined by its relationship with the empirical).[9] The transcendental is an axis *of* experience, not something distinct from experience (e.g., as a logical *a priori* structure, as in Kant) having some different "content" than our experience. These two axes, rather, run parallel to each other (Hua 1, §14), a distinction that makes no difference (of content) but is only a difference of relation, a difference that nevertheless necessarily changes everything.[10]

This distinction in axis is part of the expressive nature of experience as such, in which that distinction is simultaneously distinguished but experienced as a unity. And the co-delimited and cogenerative nature of expressivity ensures that changes in one level necessarily also alter the other level, since there is no difference (of content) between them: in being expressed, an expression does not simply manifest the expressed, but also necessarily alters (if only infinitesimally) the relation to the expressed, and therefore the context or conditions of expression, as discussed in Chapter 1.

While the significance of that alteration may seem insignificant in some cases, in "The Origin of Geometry as Historical-Intentional Problem," the significance of this alteration for our understanding of the transcendental emerges relatively clearly. There, Husserl makes plain that geometry (which is here standing in for ideal knowledge, including all scientific or objective knowledge, if not even for all *Stiftungen*) "must have arisen out of a *first* acquisition, out of first creative activities" (Hua 6, 355). It moves forward not simply as a process from "one set of acquisitions to another" but as a "continuous synthesis in which all acquisitions maintain their validity, all make up a totality such that, at every present stage, the total acquisition is, so to speak, the total premise for the acquisition of the new level" (Hua 6, 355). As such, geometry (and science more broadly) necessarily relies on actual geometers/scientists "who are the accomplishing subjectivity of the whole living science" (Hua 6, 356).

This enables Husserl to distinguish between the "sensible utterances that have spatiotemporal individuation in the world like all corporeal occurrences" and "the spiritual form itself, which is called an ideal object" (Hua 6, 357). Both of these have a kind of repeatability or iterability that is necessary to them, but in different ways: actual utterances are necessarily individual but theoretically or ideally repeatable (while said in one particular language by one person in one time and place, the same sentence can, in theory, be repeated in different places and different times), while the "spiritual form" of the ideal or transcendental domain is necessarily repeatable but theoretically or ideally individual (that is, it is the same thought that is thought in every individual conscious act of thinking, e.g., that the sum of the angles of a triangle must equal 180 degrees). Through these complimentary notions of repetition, Husserl is able to claim that ideal objects "do exist objectively in the world," but "only in virtue of these two-leveled repetitions and ultimately in virtue of sensibly embodying repetitions" (Hua 6, 357). Hence, geometry is able to "proceed from its primary intrapersonal origin, where it is a structure within the conscious space of the first inventor's soul, to its ideal objectivity" through language (Hua 6, 357–58), which is itself "inseparably intertwined" (*Verflechtung*) with the world (Hua 6, 359): original acts of intuitive self-evidence are virtualized so that they can be both "sedimented" (become part of the "total premise" of what is already known) and "reactivated" (Hua 6, 362). Language, therefore, is essential to the unfolding of geometry (and all scientific and objective knowledge), both accidentally and necessarily: it is, perhaps, an accident that the first inventor had the original insight, but it is necessary that that insight, once achieved, can be virtualized and so part of the "field" for further knowledge acquisition and development.

What we see here, in this account of the development of ideal knowledge, is both the affirmation of the process of generative actualization discussed in the last chapter and its necessary connection to the transcendental, understood as an axis, dimension, or "level" of the phenomenon distinct from (but necessarily related to) its expression in individual, empirical circumstances. The insight of the "proto-geometer" cannot be divorced from language and its virtualization; both are necessary conditions of objectivity and ideality, within which can, therefore, be distinguished, as different dimensions, the empirical axis (e.g., it was Euclid who made the discovery, in Greece, in the Greek language, etc.) and the transcendental axis (e.g., that that discovery inaugurated the "tradition" or *Stiftung* of "geometry"). These different dimensions or levels are present not simply in the original insight or its "transmission" in language but at every step in the journey: in the original insight we can distinguish between the intrasubjective mental act by which the insight "came to mind" and the transcendental necessity of any insight, in general, necessarily "coming to mind"; in the coding of that insight in language (which itself occurs doubly, in the original thinking of the insight within the structures of knowledge available to the proto-geometer and in the "transmission" of that insight to others) we can distinguish between the actual coding of that insight into the actual Greek language of that day and age and the transcendental necessity of the coding of any such insight; in the writing down of that insight, we can distinguish between its actual inscription by this or that stylus on this or that parchment and the transcendental necessity of making the language, in principle, available to any possible thinker, whether present or not; in the sedimentation of that written insight into the body of knowledge of "geometry," we can distinguish between empirical cases of actual individual people learning geometry and the transcendental necessity of a "total premise" for the acquisition of new insights; and so on.[11]

Like the relation between *langue* and *parole* in Saussurean linguistics, then, the relation between transcendental and empirical is one of a productive, mutually coordinated tension: what happens in one necessarily affects the other without the two being wholly conflated. Instead, the two are presented, in our experience, as a phenomenal unity in which we "live through" the transcendental conditions so as to "live in" our empirical lives, even as we "live through" the factuality of the empirical examples so as to "live in" in the (transcendental) sense embodied therein.[12] That is to say, the relation between transcendental and empirical is an expressive one.

Making Sense of the Transcendental (as) Field

The expressive nature of the transcendental/empirical relation helps us account for the differential nature of sense. The differential, you will recall, entails that things mean what they mean, not simply on their own, but always in relation to other things: something's positive definition is found only in its relation to (and implicitly its differences from) other things. Internet memes might prove to be a helpful example to illustrate this point. Richard Dawkins coined the term "meme" to refer to "a unit of cultural transmission,"[13] and Internet "memes" take up this meaning. But each of these "units," each particular meme, is not simply a self-contained "unit," a self-identical "point" on a line of possible or actual uses of a linguistic structure, but rather the necessary relation of three distinct semantic structures "folded into" the meme itself: first, a linguistic structure (e.g., the "folding" of previous connotations or uses of the word into this particular use of the word, giving "layers of meaning" to its current use); second, a visual structure (i.e., the use of the particular image, which itself is "folded" over with the connotations of its previous uses, other images to which it alludes, etc.); and third, an intersection of linguistic structures and visual structures in the virtual structure "Internet meme" (i.e., each meme is also "folded over" with the connotations of other memes, whose use, *qua* meme, therefore impacts the reception of the current meme). A meme, then, can never be understood on its own terms but is always composed of its (implicit or explicit) relations to other memes (the image; the words used; their mutual connection under the concept "meme"), and each meme, as a "unit," stands alone only in a particular, interconnected and enfolded way: while we can distinguish this meme from that meme (they are differentiated as distinct phenomena), we can only make sense of each meme by seeing it as an internal differentiation of various multiplicities of language, image, and so on, whose multiplicity of connotations, uses, and the like must all be "folded into" the meaning of the current meme. Each meme is individual, but no meme stands alone.

This differential account complicates our earlier account of expression in terms of Y being expressed in context X as expression Z. Earlier, we acknowledged that the expression of Z alters X (into X+Z), thereby calling for a new expression of Y. But we can now see that X itself is not simply a stable collection of individual meanings, but an interconnection or web of various differential relations. Hence, Y's expression as Z is not merely an addition (as if X were simply a set that now has one additional member), but rather requires a repositioning of everything in the differential web of relations: once another anchor point is made in the web, all the previous nodes can connect with this new node, but also many of the previous connections between existing nodes would also be altered, as "space" must be made for this new node; new nodes would be further created as new intersections occur between lines connecting previous nodes and lines connecting to this new node; and so forth. As such, the unfolding of X+Z requires not just a new expression of Y, but also of all the other nodes that initially made up X: a new expression of A, of B, of C, and so on. X+Z is not simply an expansion of X, but a fundamental alteration of it.

Compare this now to a nondifferential conception of sense, in which each distinct idea is conceived of as a distinct statement of an individual sense (idea A, B, C, etc.). In such a case, we can understand some new idea (I) as being realized out of the old possibilities (P), in such a way that I is now added to P, either replacing an earlier idea (E) or simply being added to it. P is now either (P + I) or (P − E + I)—but nothing else in P is altered by the emergence of I: P is simply a collection of ideas that now includes one new such statement, I. As such, I remains fixed in its meaning, and changes to other elements of P (A, B, C) do not necessarily affect I or vice versa: I can be critiqued, or defended, or defeated, and doing so alters nothing essentially about A, B, or C, and alters P only insofar as I is, perhaps, removed from P (if I is "defeated" as an unfeasible idea). In such a conception—which, it seems to me, is broadly consistent with the traditional logic of predication, based as it is on distinct individuals—one needs to engage with I only if one wants to understand I; no engagement with P or any of its constitutive elements is necessary (though one *can* talk about A, B, or C, for example if you think the addition of I to P can give us a new way of thinking about A or B or C). As such, "new" concepts can emerge and be added to P simply be engaging those new concepts: I do not need to engage with all of P, I can simply articulate and discuss I on its own, and understanding I need not alter or affect the rest of P.

As should by now be clear, on the type of autopoietic sense that is constitutive of our expressive account of phenomenality, one does not understand the expressed (Y) simply by understanding Y on its own. Rather, one understands Y by tracing out all the alterations made in X by Y's expression as Z. Seeing these alterations helps us better understand the differential relationship between Y and X, and therefore helps us better understand Y, not on its own, but precisely in its entanglement or mutual intertwining with all the elements of X. Or, to return to the terms of the previous paragraph, we would say that P is a web of connections (between A, B, C, etc.), such that the introduction of I would necessarily alter the whole of P (shifting A to Ai, B to Bi, C to Ci, etc.). Of course, I could not just be "introduced" from without, either, but would have been generated from the relations within P (AB, AC, BC, etc.), and their ongoing attempts to articulate themselves anew within the shifting context of P (which would always be P+n, where n designates the latest expression [Z] of a concept [Y]).[14]

We can, then, understand new ideas or concepts in two distinct ways: what it "means" (its definition, or essence—what it is), but also the work it does to transform what everything else means. The former is the broadly empirical or mundane sense of sense and it provides a "technical" understanding of a concept or idea. The second, insofar as it provides an "inquiry into the constitution of sense" (HB, 12), is the transcendental account of sense, and accounting for it requires us to "reactivate" the way that the concept transforms our entire intuitive take on the world. Both ways of understanding concepts are legitimate, and so something is lost if I pay attention to only of them: the full sense of some concept or idea is not found simply in its (denotative) meaning (i.e., the position it occupies in the semantic system of its *Stiftung*) but also in its capacity to connect or engage us with the world in a particular (preobjective) way. When we lose the expressive nature of phenomenality—which, we can now see, is always multiple, expressions piled upon expressions in a series of folds and levels—we lose the true, interconnected (or intertwined [*Verflechtung*]) nature of the phenomena themselves, which are never only "in themselves," but always relating to, and thereby altering, other phenomena and the conditions of their generation.

Hence, acknowledging this expressive nature reveals the "pure relation with an object [or phenomenon]—a relation in which the subject and object are reciprocally engendered and governed" (IOG, 142). This "pure" "objective" relation is the "pure possibility of a genetic relation" that marks "the subject's, *as well as* the object's, genealogically secondary and dependent status," and, through that, "their primordial interdependence" (IOG, 143). Hence, the duality of modes of understanding is not simply about (cognitive) understanding, but is about phenomenal experiencing as such, which always maintains this "psycho-phenomenological parallelism" (there is my [psychological] experience of something, and there is the way that experience [phenomenologically] alters how I "make sense" of all my other experiences), and which leads "in truth to the idea of *reciprocal envelopment*" (PS, 102) that we have already encountered in the notion of flesh as a predifferentiated field of sensings.

In marking, then, the inherent connection between expressivity and the transcendental-empirical dyad, we clarify the phenomenological way of understanding the transcendental: not as the (logical) conditions of possibility of empirical experience, but as the parallel (sense-bestowing, "sensing," etc.) axis, dimension, or level expressed in and through that empirical experience. The empirical is not the accidental realization of the possibilities inherent in the transcendental structures that exist outside experience, but the actuality generated by the transcendental at work in expressive phenomenality. This does not reduce the "transcendental" simply to being a product of empirical history because a transcendental structure is not simply a phenomenon to be understood "in-itself" but rather marks the generative relation necessarily at work in phenomena operating transcendentally. A historicist understanding of the transcendental fails to adequately mark the different axes or dimensions at work in the transcendental and the empirical. While such a historicist understanding is not inherently wrong (there is, in fact, a constitutive relation also between empirical, historical actions and the transcendental), but rather misguided: to critique the late Husserl's work as historicist is to fail to adequately perform or maintain the reduction, and hence to fail to intend that work in a sufficiently phenomenological fashion, insofar as it ignores the (essential) phenomenological insight that history is transcendentally (and not simply empirically) significant.[15]

Experiencing the Transcendental

Once the transcendental is understood in phenomenology as a difference of axis rather than of content, then we can see that we do in fact "experience" the transcendental, though not as a particular phenomenon or object of our experience. Rather, the transcendental is experienced precisely as the experienc*ing* of our experience. As such, it is present in our experiences, even if it is not, itself, the direct object of a singular experience.[16]

The transcendental, we said, is a field of differentiated relationships that generates discrete individuals: there are transcendental structures that produce distinct experiences of distinct phenomena. But the field itself is never one of the discrete individuals (in physics, the field/wave is never a discrete particle).[17] As such, we do not directly experience the transcendental (e.g., we do not experience flesh or linguisticality), but only the discrete individuals (e.g., we experience distinct subjects and objects; we experience English or French).

But how, then, do we experience the relationship between our own subjectivity and its transcendental conditions, if we can only experience the subjectivity and not the conditions? The answer, to be precise, is that we experience the *relationship* between them. This relationship, we have said, is a differential relation in which the relationship itself constitutes the relata. Further, we have said that this relationship is characterized or marked by expressivity. To experience the relationship is, then, to experience a differential expression. This might seem like a strange thing to experience, but it seems quite obvious that we use language in differentially expressive ways: words change meaning over time; we use metaphors to relate elements of our linguistic structure that we wouldn't normally relate to each other, yet somehow makes sense to relate; we use memes to relate words, images, and other memes together in a current phenomenon that is what it is precisely in relation to the previous uses of those words and images in other memes. All of these in some way bring to the fore the differential aspect of our language use.

Of course, in our everyday lives we do not focus on that differential aspect; we focus mainly on the meaning of the words used. If we are made to think historically, we can concede that words certainly change meaning over time (remembering what words used to mean or the force they used to have in an earlier time and comparing that to our current experience of those words), and can then perhaps infer that words have an ability to change their meaning over time, and can postulate that, perhaps, it happens bit by bit rather than all at once. In this way, we could base an understanding of the differential aspect of language on our experience, but this is quite different from experiencing it.

Our experience of the differential aspect of language, it seems to me, comes not in the meaning of words and their change over time, but rather in the freedom we feel when using language: the power or ability to make new words or give new meaning to words, to refold language in creative ways, or to redeploy words or images in new ways or in new contexts. We speak ironically or sarcastically, and suddenly a word takes on a whole new meaning. We speak to our parents, our children, or our friends from work, and in each case we easily (and probably without thinking) speak slightly differently, using different language, different slang, and different tones of voice to communicate the same (or similar) ideas. We use swear words to express our joy when we are with friends in a way we may not do to express joy at work or with our kids. In all these ways, we *experience* the differential expressive nature of language without thematizing it as such or having a direct experience *of* it: we would not say (normally) that we have an experience *of* the freedom of language, so much as we assume that freedom in our other linguistic experiences. But nonetheless, that freedom is there, as part of the experience. And we can draw attention to it in various ways: we read a poem or hear a song that uses words in a different way; a child asks us, "How come we can't say that word when Nana is around?"; a miscommunication happens with a coworker, and we are left trying to figure out where things went wrong; a phenomenologist asks us to think differently. In all these cases (and more) we are prompted to look differently at our linguistic experience, and in doing so we can come to realize something that had always been there, but of which we were not consciously aware, even as it structured the entirety of our experience and our use of language. So, too, would be the case for all the transcendental conditions of experience vis-à-vis our empirical experiences pertaining to them.

But this is not simply the case of drawing our attention to that which is already part of our perceptual field, but which we simply aren't paying attention to (like when someone mentions the buzzing of the lights, and then we suddenly recognize we have been hearing them the whole time, though consciously we have filtered it out). That is, the shift does not simply concern *where* we direct the ray of our conscious attention. Rather, the difference between our experience of particular words and our experience of the freedom of using language is a difference also of *how* these things give themselves to us in our intuition. It is not simply a matter of *what* we pay attention to, but of *how* we pay attention to it: our normal experience of particular words is given to us as a present experience (of a phenomenon) that can be re-presented; our experience of the freedom of language, on the other hand, is given to us as a condition of another present experience, rather than as a present experience itself. It is there, in the experience, but not as a distinct phenomenon of its own. Rather, it is "in" the experience as a dimension of our experiencing of that experience (we experience our talking as a way of actualizing our ideas). To notice it, we must shift not only the direction of our conscious regard, but also the level of experience at which we are looking: no longer simply at concrete experiences, but at how we experience those experiences.

So, while we experience the transcendental, we do not say we have an experience *of* the transcendental. Rather, we experience the transcendental as conditioning our other experiences. We do legitimately experience it; we don't simply deduce or infer it. But we cannot simply single out our experience of it and separate it from our experiences of other things. We become aware of it only obliquely, on the periphery of our experience.[18]

Expression and Transcendental Phenomenology

But in becoming aware of the transcendental, we experience or express it differently, and thereby alter both the transcendental and the role it plays in constituting our empirical experiences. For if the transcendental functions as a condition of our experiencing, trying to express it (linguistically or experientially) as a distinct experience would lose the true sense of the "matter" under consideration,[19] precisely because the "matter" of the transcendental is a field of processes (e.g., differentiation, actualization, generation) and not of subjects or "things (-in-) themselves." This means that, given the differential nature of expressivity—how each expression necessarily alters the conditions of expressing, and thereby alters (however infinitesimally) the expressed and the expressions themselves, requiring an autoproduction or a necessary auto-unfolding of expression—transcendental phenomenology should not expect to express a transcendental condition via one single term or proposition with a fixed denotative reference, and assign that term to represent that condition forever. Doing so would be internally incoherent and would cause us to miss precisely the matter under consideration.

Rather, acknowledging the transcendental (field) as an ongoing process that generates individuation through autopoietic expression (and therefore makes a logic of predication viable), provides us a new way to talk about the transcendental. To "make sense" of the transcendental is not simply to refine my propositions about it so as to get the sense of my words to resemble most closely the state of my experience but is rather to produce the concepts and ideas—to produce the sense—that will enable us to see *and experience* the transcendental anew.[20] Articulating the transcendental, then, is not simply a descriptive enterprise, but always already a generative one.

This generativity necessarily has two aspects that are crucial to our understanding of transcendental conditions and the way they condition (and are conditioned by) the empirical. First, we make sense of the transcendental by tracing the effects it has on our experiencing of the empirical. We cannot divorce the transcendental from its empirical effects. Second, in making sense of or articulating the transcendental, we necessarily express the transcendental within particular conditions, and thereby alter both the expressed (the transcendental), the conditions (the empirical), and the relation between them. As such, paying attention to the transcendental never merely defines or describes either the transcendental or the empirical, but necessarily generatively alters both.

Because the transcendental names processes by which experiencing is transformed, to articulate it directly as a distinct "thing" is to lose sight of its transcendental (and processual) character: it is, for example, to conflate one mode by which something was actualized with actualization itself. Therefore, we can best talk about the transcendental indirectly, via the way it has been actualized in empirical phenomena. Transcendental phenomenology must distinguish, then, between three different levels of analysis: the empirical phenomena themselves (such as a particular concept, idea, or use of language—an instance of *parole*); the (quasi-) transcendental functions these empirical phenomena perform within the particular regimes of sense (i.e., the *Stiftungen*) in which they find themselves (such as *langue*, which is already deployed within a particular understanding of language, and finds content only as determinate semantic, syntactic, etc. rules governing particular, determinate languages); and the transcendental processes themselves (such as linguisticality, which is the sensing that enables language to transform our experiencing of the world). A fourth possible level emerges if one distinguishes between the transcendental process (such as linguisticality) and the "ultratranscendental" processes that enable the transcendental processes to work transcendentally (such as "transcendental subjectivity," "Being," "flesh," or "differance").

We can call these the empirical, the transcendental empirical, the transcendental, and the ultratranscendental levels of analysis.[21] They distinguish phenomena, the processes that produce *these* phenomena, the processes that produce *any* phenomena (of this type), and the processes that produce the processes that produce phenomena. While there may seem to be a problem of infinite regress here (are there processes that produce the processes that produce the processes that produce phenomena, etc.),[22] that problem is mollified by the fact that the difference between these levels is a matter of paying attention not to distinct phenomena but to phenomenality; it is a phenomenological (rather than an ontological or logical) difference that cannot be infinite because of our finite capacity for reflection. These levels, then, are distinguishable as phenomenological functions, not as distinct phenomena: the transcendental empiricals are quasi-transcendental, insofar as they perform a transcendental function (i.e., they help explain the constitution of sense) only within a particular *Stiftung*. This is phenomenologically distinguishable from the transcendental function itself, even if the two functions are "performed" by the "same" phenomena: linguisticality, within the *Stiftung* of, say, academic English, is nothing other than the rules of semantics and syntax (the *langue*) pertaining to academic English. But they can be distinguished insofar as one is interested in understanding how meaning can be made in this particular *Stiftung* (the domain of linguistics, perhaps) vis-à-vis understanding how meaning can be made *in general*, beginning from subject matter located within this particular *Stiftung* (the domain of a phenomenology of language). The ultratranscendentals, then, operate via a similar distinction, but now exclusively on the level of the transcendental: how meaning can be made *in general* (linguisticality) can be reflectively distinguished from how the function of meaning-making itself is possible (via the will of the transcendental subject, say, or via the functioning of expressivity). Ultratranscendentals arise, then, when the expression of transcendental processes (e.g., in an articulation or explanation) themselves must be explained.

The task of transcendental phenomenology is to generate the concepts (transcendental or ultratranscendental) that help us make sense of the transcendental functioning of the transcendental (empirical) and how it constitutes phenomena in our experience. Transcendental phenomenology achieves this task, not simply by describing my experience of particular phenomena, but by describing how my experiencing, when understood this way rather than that way (according to *this* structure rather than *that* structure), alters my experiences by altering the transcendental empirical processes that transform my experiencing of phenomena as such. Terms like "transcendental subjectivity" or "Being" do not simply name phenomena ("things themselves") or even transcendental processes, but processes that constitute or enable the transcendental functioning of any "thing itself" whatsoever. And they are understood, as we discussed earlier, not simply "on their own terms" (what Husserl means by "transcendental subjectivity") but by looking at how their articulation alters the whole of our phenomenal experience (how does "transcendental subjectivity" function to "make sense" of any experience whatsoever?).

To understand them, we must, as rigorously and painstakingly as possible, trace the constant, infinitesimal alterations made to the entire system of experiencing through each attempt to articulate the transcendental. At times, this will lead to singular transformations, as we discover the need—given the alterations made in the rest of the structure—to find a different way of articulating the transcendental, a way that better produces the sense that will enable us to see and understand our own experiencing of the transcendental. In the history of phenomenology, one can map these singular transformations by name: transcendental subjectivity in Husserl; the Being of beings in Heidegger; flesh in Merleau-Ponty; givenness in Marion; differance in Derrida; and so on. Expressivity as the trifold relation of expressing an expressed via an expression is my attempt here to map this transformation anew. That is, with expressivity I am attempting to name the differential relating (and not merely the relationship) that is characteristic of the transcendental function in phenomenology itself. This is distinctly *not* to equate the transcendental with an individual relata in the relationship (as, one could argue, transcendental subjectivity did in the early work of Husserl), but rather an attempt to name the relating that constitutes those relata. It is therefore an attempt to articulate a process, a happening, an unfolding, and to give it sense, not as a fixed meaning, but as a sensing, that is, a mode of engaging the world.

Let us return to our earlier algebraic language in the hopes that this will clarify things further. Earlier, we said that Y (our friendliness) is expressed as Z (a smile) in X conditions (my friendship with a coworker), and that once Y is expressed as Z, it introduces Z also into X. Because X is constituted as differentiated relata, adding Z fundamentally alters all the other nodes that initially made up X (A, B, C, etc.). As such, X is altered, not simply into X+Z, but into a series of alterations that transforms X and all its constitutive parts and relations (A given Z, B given Z, but also AB given Z, BC given Z, A given the alteration to BC caused by Z, etc.). The transcendental, therefore, is not simply a new term or integer, but a rate of change that is altering both Y and X.

This rate of change is the transcendental functioning that transcendental phenomenology seeks to account for, and it cannot simply be denoted by a single term (even if, given our current linguistic constraints, that might be the only way we have of "naming" it), since "the transcendental" is both the expressed (Y) and the rate of change that enables expressing to express. Hopefully, this algebraic formulation clarifies why the articulation especially of the transcendentals and the "pure" transcendentals—which we are constantly experiencing but of which we have no direct experience—often happens through a "reading" of the philosophical tradition in which (and out of which) one is working. For if the transcendental is a rate of change that cannot show up "as itself," then the only way for us to talk about it is through the alterations its expression makes in X. And the way to do that is by first noting the role that Y's early expression (as Z) played in X, and then noticing how a later expression (a change in meaning or a shift in emphasis; Z1), in its turn, alters X (and all its constitutive elements) in a slightly different way. Noting these shifts helps us not only better understand the transcendental as rate of change, but also better express it: at some point, we might recognize that the role that Z and its descendants (Z1, Z2, etc.) play in X has become an insufficient expression of the transcendental and a singular change must be made in its expression, if we are to continue to express it, rather than something else.

This is because, as soon as we try to talk about this rate of change, we turn it into an expressed (Y) needing expression (as Z) in a particular context (X). To truly articulate the transcendental (e.g., as transcendental subjectivity, the Being of beings, givenness, flesh, differance, etc.), therefore, requires not just a "definition" of these terms as terms, but an articulation of their generation: they cannot be spoken of simply by answering the question "What is it?" but only by answering the questions of how it got here, when and where it is articulated and by whom, how many and which alterations have been made to the concept and how that has altered the value it holds in its relationship with the empirical, and so forth. And one method of doing this—perhaps the *only* method of doing this—is by offering a "reading" of earlier work concerning the "pure" transcendentals. This is done to show how the current attempted articulation of the transcendental as rate of change is generated within the actual unfolding of the tradition. The various alterations its expressions of the transcendental have made in the linguistic and conceptual structures of that tradition, is, perhaps, what the term really "means," and its proper expression requires the hearer/reader not simply to understand the transcendental as expressed in Z, but to enact the rate of change that the transcendental truly is within the mental configuration of the hearer/reader. That is, to truly appreciate the transcendental functioning of transcendentals, one must reactivate the sensing unique to the transcendental, and not simply understand the sense of some particular expression of the transcendental.

To "read" phenomenology well, one must, as Fink says, always "perform . . . the investigations themselves."[23] "Reading the Tradition" of transcendental phenomenology is not simply a matter of "carrying on a legacy" or "being faithful" to the work of a predecessor; it is a matter of articulating the transcendental by showing how that articulation is "inscribed" in the "edifice" of a particular tradition,[24] and how changing the articulation of one term or one claim causes shifts and alterations throughout the whole edifice. Differance, for example, did not just happen to be mentioned for the first time in a discussion of Husserl's theory of expression; it was generated from Derrida's engagement with that theory, in ways that alter not just Derrida's understanding of Husserlian expression, but of the entirety of Husserlian phenomenology (as a work like *Voice and Phenomenon* makes plain): Husserl's articulation of the transcendental as "transcendental subjectivity," as an initial attempt to articulate a "pure" transcendental, is revealed in its guise as a "transcendental empirical," insofar as Derrida shows it to require an account of subjectivity that was necessarily empirical, operating only within a particular *Stiftung* (of a "metaphysics of presence," of "phal-logo-centrism," etc.). Its "transcendental" capabilities were possible, Derrida maintains, only because of "ultratranscendental" processes he calls differance (VP, 15).

This "new" account or name of an ultratranscendental was not a more faithful representation of what the "pure" transcendental "just is," any more than were the other such names that came before it (transcendental subjectivity, Being, flesh, etc.). Rather, they are all attempts to express that ultratranscendental (as a rate of change) as best as possible in the current context(s) of phenomenology, to re-awaken the sensing of the transcendental within the *Stiftung* of phenomenology. As such, these names or concepts are not simply discovered; they are produced or generated within and out of the ongoing unfolding of phenomenology, which can be understood, like all philosophical traditions, as the necessary production of concepts.[25]

We see, then, that the transcendental can best be articulated (as a kind of sensing) by tracing the impacts its various expressions have within empirical phenomena like particular concepts, texts, or ideas. *Qua* rate of change, the transcendental can never be articulated "as it is"; one can only trace the generation of concepts it produces as it works itself out in transcendental phenomenology.

Transcendental (as) Critique

As a rate of change, the transcendental is always altering itself, the empirical conditions in which it is expressed, and the relationship between them. Paying attention to the transcendental as phenomenal condition therefore never merely defines or describes either the transcendental or the empirical but necessarily generatively alters both. Articulations of the transcendental, then, are never merely descriptive (of what happens), though they retain a certain descriptive element.[26] They also, *qua* expressive, introduce alteration into our articulation of the relationship between transcendental and empirical and, therefore, into our understanding of both the transcendental and the empirical itself. That is, articulating the transcendental alters our experience (however infinitesimally), insofar as it alters our experiencing in general.

This claim might seem grandiose, but it is actually both small and observably true. Small, in the sense that, as with all differential relationships, most of the alterations are so infinitesimally small as to be virtually unnoticeable, except by the most precise (and abstract) of calculations or speculations. We do not feel or notice the alterations to our experiencing at work in these "micropractices"[27] any more than we feel or notice the alteration to our language with every use of a word. Yet, the alteration is, in another sense, observable: most students of phenomenology, for example, admit that, once they "get it," they experience the world differently. As Husserl said, the task of phenomenology is "having to look upon the obvious as questionable" (Hua 6, 180). While this is done within the reduction, its effects can remain, even when we go back to our everyday life, as Hanne Jacobs notes.[28] If earlier we discussed how the transcendental is generated within the empirical, we see here that articulating or paying attention to the transcendental alters or generates new empirical conditions as well. There is an asymmetry (this alters that; A effaces itself so that we pay attention to B), but the asymmetry moves in both directions.

This reasserts that even "pure" transcendentals are generated in the autopoiesis of expressive sense: the purity of the "pure" transcendentals is not that they are purified, in principle, of any relation to the empirical, but again that they are the expressive correlate of the empirical, necessarily coordinated with it by the differential relation that connects them. This coordination is, we have said, one of mutual delimitation: the transcendental is delimited in its delimitation of the empirical, and vice versa; phenomenality establishes itself in establishing phenomena, and phenomena are established only in and through the establishing of phenomenality.

Let us extend this analysis further. In Husserl's example of the origin of geometry, we have seen that we must take up (and potentially reactivate) the linguistically sedimented insights of previous generations if we are to work within a *Stiftung*. And since we necessarily engage all phenomena out of some *Stiftung* or other—because phenomena are nothing other than the "ontological entanglement" of, at least, materiality, *Stiftung*, spirit, and individuality, as we discussed in the last chapter—we can conclude that all of our engagements with phenomena therefore necessarily involve drawing on various transcendental structures, including linguistic and/or conceptual ones, and so engaging with the linguistic and/or ideal structures that are (partially) constitutive of our engagements with phenomena is part of all of our engagements with phenomena. Therefore, any attempt to get to "the things themselves" will require an additional attempt to understand properly the role that linguistic, ideal, and other transcendental structures play in the phenomena.

For such transcendental structures constitute the intelligibility of all our social practices, the "rules" of their game.[29] And since phenomenalization itself is a social practice (constituted within political contexts of suprasubjective spirit, etc. as we saw in the last chapter), this implies that our transcendental structures are the "rules" of phenomenalization itself. And because those structures are generated out of empirical conditions (as with *langue* and *parole*), we can say both that transcendental structures operate as "the glasses through which reality shows itself to us" (FE, 27), and that they are also part of the "matter" out of which "reality" is generated and actualized. Hence, an appreciation of the expressive nature of the transcendental helps us see that "reality cannot be understood independent of the historical and cultural community of experiencing subjects" (FE, 5).[30] This is true, not simply on the level of distinct empirical subjects, but also on the transcendental (and transcendental empirical) levels of the functioning of particular *Stiftung*, of concepts/ideas within that *Stiftung*, and of spirit as well, which is necessarily both politically constituted (i.e., constituted within particular sense-giving configurations of society) and politically constitutive (i.e., constitutive of both subjects and phenomena). That is, we cannot understand reality without accounting for the transcendental role played by (at least) *Stiftung* and spirit, and we cannot understand them without accounting for how they have arisen out of particular empirical conditions that they nevertheless transcendentally condition.

This should perhaps not surprise us, insofar as we have already said that the line between transcendental and empirical is not a line marking two distinct contents, but rather a line marking two distinct functions, two distinct axes of experience, performed by the same content. Insofar as altering our approach (either transcendentally or empirically) will also alter the content (given the expressive relationship at play), this entails that transcendental expressions (including linguistic articulations) have empirical consequences, and empirical expressions (including conceptual articulations) have transcendental consequences. The former implies that transcendental phenomenology is never merely descriptive but is always altering that which it seeks to describe. As such, transcendental phenomenology "becomes a normative project of contributing to the way in which the a priori structures of society develop historically as they are being described," insofar as its analyses take part "in the ethical becoming of social structures or essences that the phenomenologist describes" (HB, 15). The latter implies that factors that are known to affect our empirical conditions—such as gender, race, sexual orientation, class, and ability—likely also have transcendental affect: "experience itself . . . is constituted by practices of knowledge and power . . . but it also importantly contains a self-reflexive and *meaning-constitutive* dimension" (FE, 57; emphasis added). That this meaning-constitutive dimension is transcendentally operative means that "such socially variable experiences as racial fear or feminine bodily comportment" are not simply "immanent conditions" as opposed to "transcendental" ones, but are empirical conditions that have transcendental significance.[31]

This opens new ways of understanding the claims of critical phenomenology. Heinämaa's phenomenological reading of de Beauvoir, for example, opens up new ways of understanding the force that gender plays in experience. While even nonphenomenological understandings of gender would suggest that gender has empirical impact (i.e., particular subjects do particular things differently because of the influence of gender), the phenomenological reading implies that gender also operates as a transcendental empirical (i.e., sense or experience is constituted differently within the particular *Stiftung* of, say, French society in the twentieth century). It may even suggest that gender also functions "purely" transcendentally (i.e., "gender" names a fundamental mode of sensing the world that is operative in all experiencing, such that "phenomenologically [speaking] sexual difference should be understood as a difference between two embodied styles of being"; FE, 100).

We can see the importance of the transcendental function of empirical conditions also in Yancy's description of the "elevator effect,"[32] by which white people, upon encountering a Black person in an elevator, react in ways that show their inherent fear, suspicion, or mistrust of Black bodies (e.g., clutching their purse close to their bodies; huddling in the far corner of the elevator; physically turning their body away). It is clear from such examples that white people's perception of Black bodies is significantly shaped by the (perceived) race of the person involved. If a "Black man" is encountered as dangerous and untrustworthy in our immediate intuition of the situation (such that we unconsciously cover our purse or visibly turn our bodies away), then part of what is at stake in such an experience is the "concept" of Blackness as an operative (and not simply theoretical) concept.[33] If we understand Yancy to be making an *empirical* claim ("all white people react this way to all Black bodies"), the claim is easily falsifiable, and hence can be called out as "Bullshit."[34] But it should be clear that Yancy is not making simply an empirical claim (and certainly not *that* empirical claim). At the least, Yancy is making a transcendental empirical claim about how the sense of Blackness is both constituted and at work as a transcendental empirical operative concept within a particular *Stiftung* (say, American whiteness); at most, he may be making a larger claim about how race might function in the constitution of any experience whatsoever.

Yet these transcendental claims in no way diminish the empirical location of the "sense" of Blackness at stake in Yancy's example. That sense of Blackness is an ongoing, generatively constituted notion that has developed and continues to develop over time, in and through its varied expressions, in particular *Stiftungen*. As such, explaining how it functions transcendentally to "make sense" of that particular situation requires us also to understand how it developed, what caused it to have the meaning it currently has as opposed to meanings it may have had in previous generations, who employs that meaning in what contexts, and so on. That is, the concept of "Blackness" needs to be genealogically reconstructed, painstakingly looked at in all its constitutive parts to see how those parts were put together so as to generate the current notion of Blackness, so that we can understand how that notion of Blackness is playing a role in our current experience of the situation.

The concept of Blackness, then, plays a transcendental (empirical) role in terms of our experience of the person in the elevator. It occupies a particular place in the phenomenal structures of the *Stiftungen* we are drawing on in our intuition of the empirical situation, and as such, it conditions that experience. But the concept of Blackness also, undoubtedly, has an empirical quality to it: it has a particular genesis in a particular situation (is Blackness constituted differently in, say, the United States than it is in Vienna or Johannesburg or Kampala?); it has an actual, empirical history that can be researched through historical archives; it takes a place in an actual, empirical language that can be studied through empirical linguistics; and so on. It functions transcendentally, but it remains also empirical: it is a "transcendental empirical" notion.

The call for a "transcendental empiricism,"[35] therefore, is a call to examine the actual generation of those things which occupy a transcendental position in conditioning our experiences. This does not obviate the need for "pure" transcendental investigation of the transcendental component of that which functions transcendentally (virtual structures, linguisticality, transcendental writing, etc.), but rather reminds us that the transcendental is, in actuality, always located empirically. Given the expressive relationship between transcendental and empirical conditions, this means that any transcendental analysis must necessarily account for the political context of the empirical conditions in which the transcendental is operative, even as the transcendental will necessarily function, in its transcendental functioning, to constitute or shape subjects and phenomena in ways that are reflective of the political context that is expressed in those transcendental conditions. In this regard, the transcendental is necessarily political in both senses: it is politically constituted (it has a particular internal makeup) and politically constitutive (it is a force that constitutes its relata according to that makeup). And insofar as articulating the transcendental necessarily alters the transcendental and the conditions in which it is operative, speaking of the transcendental both describes a political reality and alters that political reality in particular ways or for particular purposes.

This is just to say that transcendental phenomenology is always, necessarily, critical phenomenology, and that critique is a fundamental aspect of transcendental phenomenology. This claim may seem surprising, insofar as we think of phenomenology as the description of our first-person accounts of our experience of phenomena, and critique seems to take us away from our experience, into a world of social and political engagements. But given what we just said about the role transcendental structures play in our experience of phenomena, it seems like robust descriptions of that experience (especially, but perhaps not exclusively, of the transcendental element of our experiencing) require us also to pay attention to how that experience is filtered through the particular *Stiftungen* we inhabit or employ in that experience. And to pay attention to that filtering requires us to recognize how our experience is shaped by particular ideal structures that condition our experience. Given the generative nature of our experience, articulating that role requires giving a certain account of the generation of those structures, of our experience, and of the relation between them. Such a generative account will, by necessity, need to trace some historical development of the structures in order to account for their current generative role in our present experience, but it will also alter those structures, precisely in expressing them (linguistically). This is all to say that we can better describe the various facets of our present experience if we can articulate how it developed, where and when transformations took place that are singularly important for our present experience—that is, if we ask the kinds of genetic questions that Deleuze claims have "a transcendental scope" (MD, 95).

In that regard, critique remains a question of the transcendental dimension of phenomenological method. What I am trying to argue here, though, is that this has implications even for those inquiries where the transcendental is not the object of the inquiry: illuminating at least some of the transcendental elements (e.g., the virtual structure) will shine light on the empirical object of phenomenological inquiry, even if we don't try to articulate the transcendental itself (i.e., even if we are content to describe only the "empirical" side of the transcendental element).

The Transcendental Implications of Expression

Phenomenology remains, then, a rigorous description of our experience—but one that recognizes that such a description requires the articulation of the transcendental conditions of our experiencing, conditions that never appear as phenomena but only via the expression of their differential relations in and through our experiences. Recovering the inherently expressive nature of phenomenality therefore helps us recover (or rearticulate) the necessarily transcendental and critical character of phenomenological inquiry. While some of that inquiry may have the *appearance* of being based on something other than experience, in *actuality* it is precisely an articulation of the conditions of our experiencing via reflections on (the consequences of) reflections on that experience. Such "meta-phenomenology"[36] remains an important element of phenomenology, insofar as it is nothing other than the attempt to rigorously describe an (transcendental) element of our experiences—perhaps, as Merleau-Ponty claims, via a kind of "hyper-reflection" (VI, 38) that would enable phenomenology to become genetic phenomenology (PhP, 126).[37]

But our analysis of expressivity has shown us that phenomenology is not merely genetic, it is also generative. *Qua* generative, it must account for how even the transcendental is necessarily rooted in empirical conditions that are thoroughly political (constituted by *Stiftungen* as modes of spiritual materiality), and which necessarily alter the transcendental, even as they themselves are altered by it. Hence, while "the task of a generative phenomenology is precisely to inquire after how historical and intersubjective structures themselves become meaningful at all, how these structures are and can be generated,"[38] our analysis of expressivity reveals this task to be an inherently critical task in which the "descriptive and transformative dimensions of this practice reciprocally invoke one another; there is no meaningful change without an interrogation of meaning, and yet the process of scrutinizing and naming one's experience already begins to change its meaning."[39] Phenomenology never merely describes; it also always alters.

The reciprocal relationship between these descriptive and transformative elements suggests that the task of transcendental phenomenology—"reflecting on the quasi-transcendental social structures that make our experience of the world possible and meaningful"—is necessarily expressed in critical fashion, by "engaging in a material practice of 'restructuring the world' in order to generate new and liberatory possibilities for meaningful experience and existence."[40] This restructuring is necessary, even if it isn't always purposeful. It is necessary because issues such as gender and race are not simply elements within our empirical conditions or transcendental empirical concepts within our transcendental structure; they also operate as transcendental processes (gendering, racializing) that therefore shape all of our experiencing, including our experiences of reflecting on our transcendental structures. This is to say, race and gender are transcendental conditions of transcendental phenomenologizing, and not simply elements of some phenomenologies. As long as race and gender are transcendentally operative, they are expressed in all our expressions, including the linguistic and conceptual articulation of those transcendental processes, and we must therefore acknowledge that Husserl, Heidegger, and Merleau-Ponty, too, offer racialized and gendered phenomenologies, even if none of them offers an explicit phenomenology "of race" or "of gender." It is not simply "Blackness" that colors our experience of the world, but also "whiteness"; not simply "femininity" but also "masculinity" that shapes our experiences, our experiencing, and our articulation of both via phenomenology.

This, in turn, suggests that *who* is doing the transcendental phenomenology might end up having a large impact on the transcendental phenomenology that is produced, insofar as both the transcendental empiricals and the "pure" transcendentals might be revealed differently to those with different experiences. We can return to our language of "home" to see again why this is the case.

You will recall that earlier we used "home" to describe a generative power that transcends and precedes the constitutive power of the subject: home is the force that enables me to *experience* the world in a characteristic and normative way insofar as the conditions of my home(world) enable me to experience the alien(world). But this experience is mutually co-delimiting: home is constituted in its relationship with the alien, and vice versa. If I always experience "there" from "here," my "here" is not fixed, but always in transformation by my experiences with "there." "Home" therefore "names a belonging that is tenuous, complex, and *forged* by our practices rather than simply given."[41] Hence, Mariana Ortega speaks of "hometactics" as "micropractices of lived experience" by which "multiplicitous selves engage (or are already engaging) in practices that yield a sense of much needed familiarity and ease."[42] But it is primarily the experience of those who feel uncomfortable and ill at ease in their environments, those who feel the need to "make" a "home" because they don't already feel "at home," that brings these hometactics to our attention: though they perform them all the time, these practices are not noticed as such by those with "dominant identities," for whom the homemaking purpose of hometactics is hidden, precisely because they feel "familiarity and ease" already in their own environments. While our practices necessarily restructure the world, then, it is possible that they do not always do so purposefully: we are replicating and altering our "home" contexts, even (and perhaps especially) when we do not realize we are doing so.

If it is precisely because our transcendental structures are so normative and familiar that we may express them without realizing it, then it may be the case that we can uncover them only through encounters with "alien" or different structures. The phenomenological reduction is one way of encountering the world as "alien." But the relation between transcendental and empirical conditions and the familiarity we have with our own transcendental conditions imply that the phenomenological reflections of people with substantively different experiences (people from different racial, gendered, sexual, class, ability, geographic, temporal, etc. contexts) may be essential to uncovering certain transcendental phenomenological structures that may otherwise remain hidden. And those transcendental structures that have already been articulated by the "masters" of the tradition may, in fact, be only transcendental empiricals that need to be better situated in their particular *Stiftungen* in order for their truly transcendental nature (as rate of change) to be truly appreciated.[43] For the concepts that are produced as articulations of the transcendental are produced out of a particular kind of attention paid to our experience itself, a kind of attention that is made possible only through the transcendental and phenomenological reductions. But the compelling force of those articulations is reliant on the resonance they generate with our experiencing of experience: the evidence for them remains bound to our experience, even if our articulation of them comes from paying attention to texts or concepts, as well as to our experiences.

We cannot therefore fully separate any of these questions from issues of phenomenological method. Our transcendental structures are expressively related with empirical conditions, and as such they are "irrevocably tied up with our methods of reflection" (FE, 71). Therefore, if those structures are always changing and thereby altering our world and our experience of it, we must have a method that is able to account for all that alteration if we are to properly make sense of our world and our experiences of it. We have sketched one potential mode of that method in this chapter ("reading" the tradition), but it does not seem to accord well with what is traditionally taken to be the phenomenological method. This methodological gap seems to grow wider in light of the political nature of the transcendental that has emerged in this chapter, and the relativization of the subject to sense that emerged previously. Can the first-person reflective method that characterizes phenomenology still be an effective way of coming to know the world, if we also want to acknowledge the generative development of the transcendental structures that shape (as we are claiming here) both the content and the functioning of phenomenological reflection? If "transcendental phenomenology is a phenomenology of transcendence, and not necessarily of subjectivity," as Steinbock claims (HB, 14), then is the phenomenological method still the most appropriate way of coming to understand phenomena and the phenomenal conditions by which we experience them, or does its seeming emphasis on subjective reflection rule it out as a viable method for understanding a force that we have seen exceeds and constitutes subjects and subjectivity? These questions are about the relation between the transcendental and the empirical, but also about the relation between sensings, sense, and *Stiftung*. Both of these relations are opened up, we have said, by the reduction, normally taken to be a cornerstone of the phenomenological method. So let us now turn to these broader methodological questions, to see how our analysis of expression in phenomenology can help us further clarify both phenomenology and phenomenality.

5

The Subject, Reduction, and Uses of Phenomenology
The Methodological Implications of Expressivity

In clarifying the transcendental element of experience in the previous chapter, we saw that accounting for empirical experience is necessary to properly understand the transcendental. Our analyses there also suggested that the reverse should be true: to properly understand empirical experiences, we must account for the transcendental. But how far can we take this latter claim? Is an exploration of the transcendental element necessary for any phenomenological elaboration of (an) experience?[1]

This question has two parts to it. First, must the transcendental be accounted for in *any* elaboration of experience? And second, is phenomenology the best way to account for that elaboration? This twofold question grows necessarily out of the expressive account of phenomenality we have been outlining in this work: insofar as empirical conditions are expressions of the transcendental conditions that condition them, it seems that both the empirical and the transcendental can properly be understood only in relation to each other and to the (expressive) relation that constitutes them. Conditions of phenomenality, then, cannot be understood apart from the phenomenal conditions in which they arise, and phenomena cannot be understood apart from the conditions of phenomenality that give rise to them. In the language used and justified in the last chapter, we could say instead that experiencing cannot be understood apart from experience and experience(s) cannot be understood apart from experiencing.

Clarifying the nature of experiencing therefore seems essential to any rigorous attempt to understand experience. This is crucial for justifying phenomenology as a methodological choice, insofar as phenomenology is interested in clarifying the nature of experiencing itself. But this raises serious questions for phenomenological methodology and our understanding of it: insofar as phenomenology's method is traditionally understood to be premised on the validity and legitimating authority of first-person experience, how can it simultaneously be called on to explain or clarify experiencing and the political conditions that impact it?

This problem is exacerbated by the processual and expressive nature of phenomenalization we have been articulating here: If phenomenalization is explicitly and necessarily *not* ultimately founded in a subject because the subject is itself phenomenalized, how can reflection on subjective experience provide us legitimate access to that phenomenalization? We may wonder, following Oksala: "does the phenomenological method need to be modified for it to be able [to] study . . . the constitutive importance of culture, language, and historicity" (FE, 105)? These methodological questions, then, aren't just about applying the "right" method; they are also about accounting for the "constitutive importance of culture, language, and historicity"—that is, the political—in our experiencing of any phenomena whatsoever. At stake is whether it is necessary to account for these transcendental, political features in making sense of any empirical phenomena and how one best accounts for them.

My claim, following on the expressive account of phenomenalization I am laying out here, is that phenomenology provides us a unique method to account for these transcendental structures, and accounting for them is valuable in our understanding of any phenomenon whatsoever. Phenomenology's methodological focus on subjective experience is crucial precisely *because* subjectivity is itself phenomenalized and therefore can provide access to phenomenalization. That is, because subjective experience arises within phenomenality, it can shed light on that phenomenality itself in a way that is important to our understanding of any phenomenon whatsoever.

To understand why this is the case, we must first clarify something that has been mentioned at several points in our analysis so far but never yet fully explained: how the subject is generated out of the autopoiesis of expressive flesh. For in articulating the type of expressive doubling that is at work in the generation of subjects, we are open to see the relation between the subject and the transcendental and understand the transcendental as a field that is expressed (in one of its expressions) in the mode of subjectivity. Everything about the phenomenological method relies on this relation, and it is only via this method that phenomenology, in its philosophical provenance, is able to achieve its purpose: the clarification of sense/sensing as the relation between subjective and objective. Once the genesis of subjectivity has been clarified, we will then be able to see how the reduction (and only the reduction) is able to lay bare this relation of (transcendental) subjectivity, after (and, in our current social and spiritual situation at least, *only* after) the "natural attitude" has been bracketed. This, in turn, will enable us to understand anew the "principle of principles," and how it justifies the turn to first-person reflection as a legitimate source of cognition.

The phenomenological method, then, is rooted firmly in the expressive nature of subjectivity as a mode of phenomenalization revealed by the reduction, and it is (at least in our current social and spiritual situation) only through phenomenology that we can adequately account for this subjectivity and therefore the experiencing that is essential to all of our experience(s). This is to say that the phenomenological method reveals something essential about our understanding of experience such that we cannot fully clarify any phenomenon we encounter without recourse to phenomenology. Clarifying how and why this is the case will put us in position, finally, to speak to the question, first raised in the preceding chapter, of whether the phenomenological method can be employed merely "technically" and without a reactivation of the sense of its original insights. We can reframe this question as one about method: Does one have to understand the phenomenological method and its justification in order to use that method? But we can also reframe it in terms of outcomes: Is something important lost if we approach phenomenology with such merely technical uses? The answer to the first question partially depends, as we will see, on various ways that phenomenology is used: as a collection of insights or ideas, an ongoing and unfolding *Stiftung*, or a particular way of sensing the world. Insofar as phenomenology is, in principle as well as in fact, all three of these, the first question can have no one simple answer. As for the second question, something important *is* lost if the entire phenomenological way of sensing is absent from an account of a particular phenomenon: the implicit force that any phenomenon has to alter us transcendentally loses some of its politically transformative power if we fail to account critically for the role that transcendental structures play in empirical phenomena.

The Subject as a Self-Actualization of Flesh

We begin, then, with an account of how the subject is phenomenalized such that it is capable of phenomenalizing. In Chapter 1, I said that this move—to conceive of the subject no longer as the primary or foundational source of phenomenalizing and of expression—occurs in Merleau-Ponty's later work. We will now turn to that work to explore his analysis of this move.[2]

This will enable us to expand on what was said in Chapters 2 (concerning the body as a locus of sensings that, because of its "double sensation," is able to sense itself as touched and as touching) and 3 (concerning knowledge as a mode of being that arises within, and as a result of, processes of being, thereby fundamentally intertwining knowing, being, and doing). For it is precisely the doubling of flesh that enables consciousness, and the subject, to emerge within flesh as a distinct mode of fleshly sensing.

This emergence of the subject must be understood in light of the expressive body articulated in Chapter 2. That is, the subject that emerges—in consciousness, in "interiority," and so forth—is necessarily an embodiment of the world (to use the language we argued for in that chapter), and has its consciousness, its "subjectivity," spread out over its whole body. It is not simply mental awareness that is subjective, but visibility, tangibility, linguisticality, and so on, are all part of the "consciousness" that constitutes subjectivity. Merleau-Ponty considers these to be "little subjectivities" (VI, 141) that are spread throughout the whole of flesh. In other words, consciousness is not something defined in opposition to materiality but must be understood as "the other side" of the body: just as the transcendental is "the other side" of the empirical, so, too, is interiority "the other side" of exteriority, subjectivity "the other side" of objectivity.[3]

To understand this better, we can return to the example of tactility as a mode of sensing. In touching the world, I necessarily open onto a tactile world that necessarily includes both touching and touched.[4] Indeed, it is only because the touching is also touched that touching provides us a genuine sensing (tactility) of the world. This "crisscrossing . . . of the touching and the tangible" (VI, 133) provides three distinct but overlapping experiences: "a touching of the sleek and the rough, a touching of the things—a passive sentiment of the body and of its space—and finally a veritable touching of the touch" (VI, 133). From these overlapping (we might say parallel) experiences, we can distinguish two distinct "doublings" or "folds" (VI, 146): tangibility is folded into distinct touchable things, and some of those things are themselves folded into an "interior" aspect—that which touches—and an "exterior" aspect—that which is touched. This is to say, for Merleau-Ponty, that through "ontogenesis" (VI, 136) flesh is differentiated into distinct things, and some of those things develop depth, subjective capacities that are not an exiting of flesh, but a doubling or folding of it: "it is as flesh offered to flesh that the [tangible][5] has its aseity, and that it is mine" (VI, 131n1).

Subjectivity, therefore, is a folding within flesh, necessarily coordinated with objectivity as "the other side" of itself. Hence, the activities of subjectivity—the "little subjectivities" or sensings that enable us to engage the world—are inherently coordinated with the very things they engage: "the look . . . envelops, palpates, espouses the visible things," not in a manner of controlling or manipulating them, but "as though it were in a relationship of pre-established harmony with them . . . so that finally one cannot say if it is the look or if it is the things that command" (VI, 133). The invocation of "pre-established harmony" is not accidental here: it is an obvious appeal to Leibniz, whose account of that harmony is not separable from the expressive nature of the differential calculus, as Deleuze makes clear.[6] Merleau-Ponty's invocation of the "pre-established harmony" or coordination between subjectivity and objectivity therefore functions to show coordination to be the result of the expressive and differential relation that constitutes them.

From this, we can learn that subjectivity and objectivity are necessarily coordinated, not by the correlating power of the subject (e.g., "I make objects"), nor by mere logical coordination as "conditions of possibility" (e.g., "if I can see something, there must be something there to be seen") but by the expressive force of (expressive) flesh. Subjects are an expression of flesh, a nexus of localized processes (the visible, the tactile, etc.).[7] Subjectivity is not simply the realization of certain latent possibilities inherent in flesh; rather, subjectivity is an actualization of the flesh in its very coordination with the objectivity it touches and thinks about. Subjectivity is nothing else than one of the coordinated poles of sensings (visibility, tactility, etc.), which themselves are nothing else than the self-actualization of flesh: "There is a question of subjectivity only by virtue of the fact that the world's visibility is realized in me. . . . It is for this reason that Merleau-Ponty uses such expressions as Being sees in me, touches in me; because these things happen, there arises something like an 'I,' a subject" (PE, 41).

A subject, then, is a localization of a series of these "little subjectivities," as we discussed in Chapter 2 regarding the living or expressive body. For consciousness is a (lived, expressive) body:[8] "it assembles into a cluster the 'consciousnesses' adherent to its hands, to its eyes by an operation that is in relation to them lateral, transversal" (VI, 141). Calling this relation "lateral" is significant here: consciousness does not pull these sensings together from some place outside or above these sensings (as, for example, in Kant's unity of apperception). Rather, its assemblage is on the same "plane" (to use Deleuze's terminology, which is also Merleau-Ponty's)[9] as the sensings: it is not a transcendent organization of them, according to a plan that is external to the world of sensings, but an assemblage of them according to a "living plan" (PT, 393) that is part of that world itself. Each of the sensings, therefore, is not "a private little world . . . juxtaposed to the world of all the others" but is "surrounded by" the shared world of all sensings, "sustained, subtended, by the prereflective and preobjective unity of my body" (VI, 141–42) in which "all together are a Sentient in general before a Sensible in general" (VI, 142).

This sentience, in turn, opens the space for a kind of "reflexivity" as a certain kind of fold within flesh—precisely the fold that produces, for instance, the touching and the touched from out of the tactile world, or the seer and the seen from out of the visible world. This reflexivity is the difference between the experienced (the touched, the seen) and the experiencing of it (the touching, the seeing). And just as "there is a reflexivity of the touch, of sight, and of the touch-vision system, there is a reflexivity of the movement of phonation and of hearing" that "have their sonorous inscription" and their "motor echo" in me (VI, 144). This "new reflexivity" provides for the emergence of linguistic expression, expressed by a subject: "the insertion of speaking and thinking in the world of silence" (VI, 145). Linguisticality, therefore, as with ideality more broadly, is a sensing of the world, akin to other sensings.

At this point, Merleau-Ponty has inserted into his own text a parenthetical addition that is crucial to understanding the relation between ideal thinking (including language) and the sensings we have been discussing.[10] In that addition he asserts that "from the moment we said *seeing, visible,* and described the dehiscence [i.e., the doubling or reversal] of the sensible, we were, if one likes, in the order of thought" (VI, 145). Thinking, *qua* subjective activity, is part of every sensing: the "seeing" of the seen is already a type of thinking. Granted, this is not yet full representational thought ("it appears to me that . . ."), but simply a "there is,"[11] a prepersonal subjectivity that is a folding of flesh itself. Merleau-Ponty is arguing precisely that representational thought "is comprehensible only as the accomplishment by other means of the will of the *there is*" (VI, 145),[12] which is to say that representational thought is an accomplishment of subjectivity, and not merely of individual subjects: representational thought is a continuation of the thinking found in seeing, touching, and so on. Rather than offer a radical break from the world, ideal thought (as a kind of "second or figurative meaning of vision"; VI, 145) is therefore in a relation of reversibility with concrete acts of thinking: "Thus between sound and meaning, speech and what it means to say, there is still the relation of reversibility, and no question of priority, since the exchange of words is exactly the differentiation of which the thought is the integral" (VI, 145). Thought, too, like other sensings, is an expressive and differential relating.

Thought is therefore defined as "a relationship with oneself and with the world" (VI, 145),[13] such that ideas "owe their authority, their fascinating indestructible power," to "the fact" that they lie in the "heart" of the sensible (VI, 150). Defining thought in terms of this kind of relationship to the world is just to say, in the language of the present work, that thought (including ideality, linguisticality, etc.) is a sensing, with all the meaning we gave to that word in Chapters 2 and 3. Sentience and the sensible (which is here both "physical" and "sense-able") are therefore intertwined in the world in and by a relationship we have been calling "expressive." This expressivity is, as we saw in Chapter 2, inscribed directly into the subject-as-body, which is at once both objective (i.e., a thing in the world) and phenomenal (VI, 136), both "sensible" and "sentient" (VI, 136). In trying to understand the "abyss" that separates these "two 'sides' of our body" (VI, 136), then, Merleau-Ponty does not want us to think in terms of space (with its discrete individuals) but of motion, of sensings themselves (visibility, tactility, linguisticality, etc.) "sometimes wandering and sometimes reassembled" (VI, 138), the (expressive) body being "one sole movement in its two phases" (VI, 138). This understanding of the expressive body applies equally to the subject-as-body (that is, to the subject as living, expressive body) and to "the whole of the sensible of which it is a part, and to the world" (VI, 138). Subjectivity, then, is unique, not ontologically or substantively, but simply expressively: it is not a distinct "thing" from the world, or a different kind of "thing" than objectivity, but a new function performed within the unity of flesh, "a certain visible turn[ed] back upon the whole of the visible" (VI, 139), that is to say, a folding of sensings, and ultimately of flesh, back onto itself. Nonetheless, there remains a certain *kind* of difference between subjectivity and objectivity, between seer and seen, a difference that necessarily coordinates them with each other like a series of images reflected between two mirrors facing each other, "which belong really to neither of the two surfaces . . . and which therefore form a couple, a couple more real than either of them" alone (VI, 139).

We can recognize this coordinated difference as the differential relation of expressivity, and like all expressions, it is expressed only within a context that both constitutes it and which it, in turn, constitutes. Just as my words express meaning within a linguistic context (twenty-first-century Canadian English) that they also (infinitesimally) alter by their very expression within it, so, too, do both subjectivity and objectivity (for it is more precise, at this point, to talk of subjectivity and objectivity as processes or collections of processes than of subjects and objects as distinct things or subjects) express themselves within a context (sensings, the sensible/sentient world) that they also alter by their very expression within it.

This immersion of subjectivity in its context(s) yields two methodological implications: first, that immersion grants subjectivity access to that context, and the ability to express that context in a unique way, such that there is something to learn about the context from subjectivity; second, that immersion entails that subjective activity necessarily alters that context, such that any attempt to access or understand that context "in itself" will necessarily have to account for those alterations by understanding and clarifying also subjective activity and the alterations it makes to the context. Both of these implications are essential to the phenomenological method: the first justifies first-person reflection as a legitimate mode of understanding something beyond "just" the subject, while the second requires the explication of subjective activity in order to provide a robust account of "the things themselves." That is, the first gives us the essential "how" of the phenomenological method, while the second gives us the "why" that justifies the need for the phenomenological method.

The Phenomenological "How": Reduction and the First-Person Perspective

Subjectivity's genesis within flesh, therefore, provides its mode of access to flesh and to all the differences actualized by flesh in its differentiations. Our sensings are able to give us access to the world because both "sides" of the sensings are part of one and the same world: I can trust what I see, because my seeing and what is seen are part of visibility, of the visible (world), and are expressions of it (PE, 44). Since subjectivity is a unique kind of expression, one that privileges the sentience side of the movement between sentience and the sensible, subjectivity therefore gives us a unique way of knowing what is expressed: thinking is not simply visibility, tactility, and so forth, though it is rooted in them and connected to them inherently. Hence, we can know flesh, and know the world, by better understanding subjectivity, and we can better understand sentience by understanding it as a mode of engaging the world (i.e., as intentionality). These are fundamental tenets of the phenomenological method.

Of course, it is not unproblematic to speak of "the" phenomenological method. There remains a great deal of debate both about the extent to which the method is essential to phenomenology and about the content or practice of the method itself.[14] However, we will see that at least the *epoché* and the reduction are necessary for phenomenology to yield a particular account of intentionality that works in service of the "principle of principles" to justify phenomenological inquiry, broadly construed.

Let us begin, then, with that so-called principle of principles. This is the claim, stated most explicitly in *Ideas I*, that: *"every originary presentive intuition is a legitimizing source of cognition,* that *everything originarily* (so to speak, in its 'personal' authority) *offered* to us in 'intuition' is to be *accepted simply as what it is presented as being,* but also *only within the limits in which it is presented there*" (Hua 3, 43–44; emphasis original). This principle is controversial, but it is equally (or perhaps even more so) necessary: the "first-person perspective" that is crucial to phenomenology in all its guises requires something like this principle if it is to be at all meaningful.[15] For the principle of principles teaches us two things: (1) that the appearing of things to me is a "legitimizing source of cognition" but (2) only insofar as we take them (only) as presented, having wholly bracketed the question of a Kantian "thing in itself" (*Ding an sich*) and considering only the matters (of consciousness, of givenness, etc.) themselves (*der Sachen selbst*). Without a principle like this, it is not at all clear how or why our first-person reflections should in any way count as legitimate sources of evidence.

To see why this is the case, we must understand the relationship between self and world that underlies and justifies the principle of principles. In phenomenological methodology, this relationship is discussed under the label "intentionality," which is construed most simply in the formula that "consciousness is always consciousness of . . ." But if we begin, as many of us in the West do,[16] with the subject/object split (which we will take up later), we are driven, almost by necessity, to posit this connection in terms of an individual being (subject) that has some X as the direct object of its consciousness. Intentionality then becomes consciousness of X, in one of two different ways, both of which phenomenology inherently critiques.

The first possibility is that any individual experience of X is construed as, at best, a way of (subjectively) glimpsing certain elements of what is, in reality, "just there" on its own, that is, objectively and, at worst, a deception, "mere appearance," a veil hiding the thing-in-itself.[17] To truly understand X "in itself," we would then have to subjugate or subordinate our personal experiences and find a more "objective" way to gather information about X as it "really is." On such an account, still relatively dominant in the natural sciences,[18] there is no room for first-person description in legitimate scientific inquiry about the world:[19] we seek objective truths, not subjective ones. This would be to give in to the empiricist view on the self-world relationship: the world is simply there objectively, and the self is simply a moment within that world.

The second possibility, historically, is to take X as knowable to us only on the basis of my unique (and wholly distinct) subjective experience. In this regard, the world is simply a product or creation of myself as subject. There is no possibility of common ground between different subjects here, since there is nothing more foundational than individual subjective experiences, and so scientific inquiry becomes merely a means by which one person or group can exercise the dominion of its world over all other possible (and actual) worlds. Such a view—popular in some humanistic and social scientific critiques of objectivity—is the idealist view of the self/world relationship, and it undercuts the possibility of "legitimizing sources of cognition" outside the will of the subject, and so it, too, undercuts the legitimacy of first-person description as a *scientific* methodology.

Phenomenology, by contrast, does not posit an X as the correlated object of consciousness:[20] consciousness is consciousness of . . . but *not* consciousness of X. Consciousness is an openness or mode of engagement not with some particular object X but with flesh, that is, with a particular (differential) relation that generates self and world as expressions. It is this expressive, generative relation, we saw above, that legitimates first-person reflection as a legitimate mode of access to the world: it is because I am part of the visible that I can see, part of the tangible that I can touch, part of the sensible that I can be sentient. And because I am part of the world, the access I provide is necessarily access to that world of which I (and what I see, what I touch, etc.) am a part. Subject and object are not distinguished as radically different things, but as differentiated and differentiating expressive functions (subjectivity, objectivity) of the differential relation of flesh. As such, consciousness is a functional connection, a particular mode of the self-expression of flesh that opens a unique engagement with the world. Since this unique mode of engagement is expressed via subjectivity (one of whose functions is consciousness), and because subjectivity is constitutive of individual subjective experiences, reflecting (in a particular way) on those experiences enables us to make sense of subjectivity and, through it, of the world in a particular way. Without such a justification for the validity of the first-person perspective, the principle of principles[21] threatens to devolve phenomenology into either a question concerning merely how things appear to us (as opposed to how things actually are) or a discipline based on the (as yet undemonstrated) naïve assumption that things as they give themselves to me are, in fact, things as they are in themselves. In either case, phenomenology would be methodologically insufficient, requiring further justification to establish the relationship (epistemological or otherwise) between its findings and the states of affairs in the world.

Thankfully, expressivity has enabled us to clarify this apparent ambiguity in the principle of principles. For not only have we clarified the nature of expressivity itself (in Chapter 1), but we have also come across a series of expressive relationships, each of them in some way essential to our understanding of subjectivity: there is the expressive relation between the subject and the body from Chapter 2; the expressive relationship between being and sense in Chapter 3; the expressive relationship between the transcendental and the empirical within subjectivity in Chapter 4; and the expressive relation between subjectivity, objectivity and the flesh discussed in the first part of this chapter. One of the key elements of our account of expression is that it is a type of relation that holds two things together in a kind of coordinated tension. Such a tension is subjectively experienced as a phenomenal unity, but not a unity of substance, ontology, or logical identity. As such later reflection is always able to distinguish between the two elements of an expression, even if, in the moment, I do not experience two distinct elements. In phenomenology, the name given to the type of (methodological) reflection that takes what seems like a simple, unified experience and distinguishes within that experience differing (and differentially related) elements is "the reduction." And what the reduction reveals is precisely that every act of consciousness always already contains at least two distinct elements in such a way that the distinction between them is crucially important but wholly unthematized. This distinction is not simply between a (subjective) thought and its (objective) correlate, as a simple representational model of consciousness would have us think. Rather, the distinction is one of differential expression between the (transcendental) conditions and what they condition (empirical experience), between the (empirical) phenomena and the (transcendental) way they affect the conditions of phenomenality. This distinction is, as we have seen, mutually asymmetrical: *qua* sensing, sentience enables us to encounter and "live in" the world in a particular way, but it is already itself also a matter of the "world" (the visible, the tactile, the sensible, etc.). Therefore, the world is immanent to thought in at least a twofold sense: first, (ultra)transcendentally speaking, thought is a process or folding of flesh, and, as such, the flesh that constitutes the "world" is already present "within" thought-as-flesh (i.e., within thinking/sentience as a mode of sensing the world), which is simply another expression or unfolding of the expressive world or Earth; and second, any particular thought is always already shaped in both its "content," so to speak, and its functioning/thinking by transcendental (empirical) elements (e.g., spirit, sedimented horizons of expectation, etc.) drawn from the "empirical" world.

Now, as discussed in Chapter 4, the "immeasurably profound" difference between these two facets of thought's "inherent worldliness" is not a difference in content, but of the nature of the relationship to the world at stake in them (Hua 1, §14). As such, when we see the expressive relationship inherent to subjectivity we can see also that the two realms of evidence, the two types of exploration, differ, not in terms of content but in how that content is approached or evaluated.[22] Hence, as I said, the transcendental axis always runs parallel with the axis of naïve or everyday ("empirical") experience, distinguished not by radically different content but by the approach one takes to that content. But this raises the question—a question that Derrida points out is endemic to the (philosophical) phenomenological project itself—of the nature of the relationship between these two parallel realms: Do they "sustain simply an *indicative* or metaphorical relation between themselves" (VP, 10; emphasis added) or, instead, do they constitute "a difference which, without altering anything, changes all the signs" (VP, 11)? If we remember the "essential distinction" at the beginning of the *Logical Investigations*, we will see that the alternative to this "simply indicative" relation must be, precisely, an "expressive" relation. Expression, then, creates a situation in which the content of the differing elements does not differ, but yet the two elements are marked as wholly different.

We can see, then, why Husserl would claim that phenomenological research, properly speaking, is "inseparable from undeviating observation" of the reduction (CM, §14), insofar as "the reduction" names the type of methodological reflection that reveals the proper understanding of the relationship between these parallel realms that are presented, in our everyday experience, as a phenomenal unity. This parallel understanding must be revealed precisely because it is *not* what is presumed in our current spiritual situation. For the most part, our shared horizon of expectations, in the West, is one that presumes a sharp distinction between subjective and objective taken in a substantial sense: the "world" is made up of a series of distinct and discrete individual things, called "objects," each of which has its own identity in itself; the subject, insofar as it is not simply an object, is characterized by the things it does to try to access or understand these objects from its own, separate and distinct, vantage point. By definition, these "subjective" processes are not themselves "objects," and as such they are not part of the "objective" world or its fundamental truths (which are best accessed by "objective" means that minimize "subjective" interpretations as much as possible: mathematics, quantitative logic, or other universalizable, purely formal methods are the most "objective" means we currently have at our disposal). Indeed, subject and object name an opposition, perhaps an antithesis or even an antinomy: they are necessarily irreconcilable, insofar as what is true of one is, by necessity, not true of the other, like Descartes's understanding of *res cogitans* and *res extensa*.

Beginning with this subject-object split, our "commonsense" intuitions about the world then suggest that the world is what it is, apart from subjects and subjective activity. Whether or not this is how we answer the philosophical questions about ontology and epistemology in academic philosophical circles, this tends to be how we intuit the world, such that even the notion of intuition is commonly understood to be a subjective feeling about things that is not a legitimate source for objective knowledge about the actual world itself. We are, intuitively, by and large, a culture of substance dualists[23] who are steeped in that kind of mutually exclusive distinction: subjective freedom vs. objective determinism; mind/spiritual vs. matter/material; humanities and art vs. "hard" science; interpretation vs. "true" knowledge; and so forth. These distinctions function not philosophically but prethematically, preobjectively: they are how we engage the world when we are not thinking (philosophically) about how we engage the world. They constitute a kind of natural or normal attitude we take in our "naïve" everyday life.

It is this "natural attitude," "an attitude where our ontological preunderstanding of the world is not visible to us at all" (FE, 108), that must be bracketed in the *epoché* if we are going to be able to perform the reduction at all. For we will never look to understand the nature of the relationship between the subjective and the objective if we simply assume it to be one of substantially distinct subjects and objects. The bracketing, therefore, is not a denial of the existence of an external world (as if we were all subjective idealists), but rather a suspension of any and all naïve pre-understandings of the self-world relationship (which can be rooted in empiricism or idealism), so as to be free to better understand the relationship on its own terms. And the reduction, then, helps us see a necessary coordination of subject and world that does not begin with the distinction between them, but which produces that difference out of the differential nature of the relationship itself.

Therefore, we might say that if you begin with subjectivity and objectivity as radically and definitionally distinct, you will never find a way to truly get them connected. The *epoché*, therefore, is not the positing of a particular relationship between them (e.g., "there is no world, there is only the subject"), but merely the suspension of our natural (that is, spiritually conditioned) inclination to presuppose one possible understanding of that relationship so that we can see if another understanding might be plausible. It does not say "the external world does not exist," so much as it opens space for us to ask, "Is an *external* world of objects the primary mode of subject-world relations, or is subjectivity (and not just 'subjects' construed as 'things in the world') fundamentally *in* the world?"

While the *epoché* does not answer that final question, it opens space for the reduction to reveal to us the internal distinction(s) within our seemingly "simple" experience of the world. And when the reduction reveals the expressive relationships inherent to subjectivity, Husserl is able to posit a fundamental connection or engagement between subject and world. This is what Husserl means by his concept of intentionality. To say that consciousness is always intentional, that it is always consciousness *of* . . . is *not* to say that consciousness always (successfully) points to or indicates a world that exists outside itself: consciousness of . . . is *not* the same as consciousness of X. Rather, it is to describe the "universal fundamental property of consciousness," namely, that "a cogito, [bears] within itself its *cogitatum*" and not merely its *cogitationes* (Hua 1, §14): the world is within my thinking, not just as a represented object, but within the very process of thinking itself. This is just to say that the *cogitationes* are not mere indications (e.g., of the world) but are to be understood fundamentally as expressions:[24] *thinking* itself, and not simply the content of particular thoughts, is an expression of the world, of the sensings, spirit, *Stiftungen*—and, ultimately, of the flesh[25]—that are the necessary conditions of the generation of both "the world" and "consciousness."

The Phenomenological "Why": Understanding Subjectivity to Understand the World

The expressive nature of subjectivity, then, can only be revealed by bracketing our "natural attitude" so as to permit us to use the reduction to reflect on the coordinated distinction(s) of our subjective experience (like the transcendental-empirical distinction highlighted in Chapter 4). Such thinking definitely helps us understand subjectivity better, but it is perhaps not yet clear why understanding subjectivity better is necessary for understanding whatever "things themselves" may be under consideration in any given phenomenological inquiry. After all, if I'm not doing a phenomenology of the subject, then it is not obvious why I must understand subjectivity (and its various operative expressive relations). Understanding subjectivity—and therefore employing the *epoché* and the reduction that are jointly necessary to understand that subjectivity—would seem to be necessary only for those phenomenologies that are seeking to explicate or explore philosophical questions related to the subject and its various relations to the world (knowing, being, doing, etc.). In nonphilosophical uses of phenomenology,[26] where we might have a different object of inquiry, it may not be necessary to understand subjectivity in order to understand the actual object of our inquiry.

However, given what we have learned in our analysis of expression so far, it should be clear that, no matter the object, a phenomenological investigation into "the matters themselves" will necessarily have to account for subjectivity. This is because the "matters" in question are phenomena, and not objects. As such, they are always entangled with spirit, *Stiftungen*, materiality, and so on—and two of those three seem to have a necessarily subjective (which is not to say individual) component that is essential to understanding the matter at hand. Insofar as we understand phenomena as entangled—a point that also follows from our analyses of the interrelation of visibility, tactility, linguisticality, ideality, and so forth as various sensings—we must understand their entanglements in order to properly understand the phenomena. And insofar as some of those entanglements are necessarily subjective—that is, insofar as they result from that unique type of folding or doubling of flesh that generates "little subjectivities"—we must understand subjectivity to understand those entanglements, and therefore to properly understand the phenomena. Indeed, this is precisely the justification for the first-person mode of phenomenological inquiry: reflecting (in a particular way) on one subject's experience can help us understand subjectivity; understanding subjectivity helps us understand some of the phenomenon's entanglements and therefore understand the phenomenon; therefore, reflecting on one subject's experience can help us better understand the phenomenon in question.

The question, then, is how we must reflect on a subject's experience, in order for such a reflection to help us understand subjectivity. Transcendental phenomenology has a straightforward (if sometimes difficult) answer: the "subject" is a name we give to a certain nexus of located subjective functions; such subjective functions, *qua* subjectivity, are an expression of flesh, so understanding subjectivity helps us understand flesh. Phenomena are also expressions of flesh; therefore, understanding flesh will help us understand something of phenomena.

But certainly it is not necessary to go all the way back to "flesh" to understand every phenomenon: is it not enough, for example, to understand the relevant "empirical transcendentals" in order to understand a particular phenomenon? Perhaps. But in order to understand even how empirical transcendentals shape a phenomenon, we have to understand the nature of expressivity. And once we do that, we realize that every expression (infinitesimally) alters the context in which it is expressed, thereby altering both the expressed and its ongoing expression. Without accounting for those ongoing and infinitesimal alterations (without identifying the "differential equation" that explains the rate of change), we can never fully understand the entanglements of any given phenomenon. And if we limit ourselves only to one such entanglement (to one "empirical transcendental," for example), we may learn interesting things about the phenomenon, but we will not learn as much as we can about the phenomenon as a whole (which is characterized by the convergences and divergences, the foldings, of various empirical transcendentals), nor even about the one empirical transcendental (which itself is also characterized by its being-situated in a broader context that is itself always being infinitesimally altered). To get the most rigorous and robust understanding of a phenomenon, then, we must trace it back as much as possible to flesh itself (or whatever other name we give to the ultratranscendental processes that condition the transcendentals).

Put simply, phenomena are entangled with subjectivity, so understanding subjectivity and its processes helps us understand the phenomena that are entangled with it—and we will never properly understand phenomena if we don't understand their entanglement with subjectivity. This is the justification of the first-person reflective methodology that characterizes so many (perhaps all) interdisciplinary uses of phenomenology. But it also suggests that phenomena, therefore, can most rigorously be understood if they are traced back to their transcendental conditions.

Disambiguating Phenomenology

But that conclusion, in turn, presumes that we are searching for a rigorous explanation of phenomena. Is this, in fact, the case: must every account necessarily provide the most rigorous explanation possible of the phenomenon in question? This is not simply a question of distinguishing good or bad accounts of a phenomenon, but rather a question about the nature of giving an account itself: What, precisely, are we trying to do when we give an account (a *logos*, perhaps?) of a phenomenon?

Note that such a potential description of phenomenology—giving a *logos* of a phenomenon—differs from the description provided in the introduction of this book, namely offering a logic of phenomenality (a phenomenologic). We can, hopefully, see the connection between these two accounts: providing a rigorous account of a phenomenon requires us, as we have now seen, to also give an explanation of the logic of the phenomenality that conditions the phenomenon. To describe the phenomenon as best we can, we must account also for the power it has to transform our understanding of other phenomena we experience and the power which transforms the phenomenon vis-à-vis other phenomena and our phenomenalizing of it. This is to say, in the language of the last chapter, that the better our descriptions of phenomena are, the more they must also account for the fact that our descriptions never merely describe, but always transform.

Our analyses of expressivity have therefore awakened us to new distinctions that might help us disambiguate what happens under the name "phenomenology." So far, we have distinguished between at least three different levels of phenomenological analysis: the empirical (e.g., what someone actually says), the transcendental (e.g., linguisticality), and the transcendental empiricals (e.g., English as a linguistic structure). We could apply these levels to phenomenology, in light of some of our earlier analyses, by construing phenomenology variously as a collection of insights: a method for reflectively accessing phenomena in their autopoietic self-unfolding (i.e., a sensing), or as a *Stiftung*, respectively.

Such disambiguation helps us better think through the potential necessity of accounting for the transcendental conditions of phenomenality (i.e., outlining a phenomeno-logic) within any account of a phenomenon. At the beginning of this chapter, we discussed this problem in terms of whether a simply "technical" understanding of phenomenology was sufficient for giving an account of some phenomenon. Now we can see how ambiguity about the nature of phenomenology plays an important role in how one answers this question. If we begin by considering phenomenology as a collection of insights, for example, then it seems apparent that these insights could be used without any appreciation for the transformative power of transcendental processes. So, for example, notions such as lifeworld, prereflective (or pretheoretical) experience, intentionality, empathy (which we will discuss in the next chapter) and the lived body could prove very helpful in a wide variety of disciplines, either to critique some assumptions operative within those disciplines (e.g., using the notion of living body to counter the primacy of the "objective" body in certain biological and health sciences) or to bolster assumptions within those disciplines (e.g., using the notion of lifeworld to ground the notion of "systemic" influences on personal action in sociology or anthropology), or for any of a number of other purposes. Since we would consider these terms to be used "well" when they effectively accomplish the task assigned to them in whichever discipline they are being used, there seems no reason to restrict their understanding to specifically philosophical understandings, let alone to restrict their use to those researchers who "first master the theoretical intricacies of the epoché and the reduction."[27] That is to say, it seems entirely plausible to think those notions could be effective, even if they are used differently in the various disciplines, with only the thinnest of connections to their original development in the work of some famous phenomenologist. And given that, there seems no reason whatsoever to think the notions could only be used helpfully if someone has a deep appreciation of the role of transcendental processes in the self-transformation of our experiencing of experience. There seems to be no necessity for the reduction, then, when we are speaking simply about using phenomenology as a collection of insights or ideas: performing the reduction might help us come up with new insights, or might help us understand those insights differently, but it would be perfectly possible to use phenomenological insights without any kind of transcendental concern, and hence without any need for the reduction.

But we have also said that phenomenology can function as a *Stiftung*, in addition to being a collection of insights. Are transcendental aims and goals necessary for the *Stiftung* of phenomenology, such that the *epoché* and the reduction, as the means for achieving those goals, also become necessary? Certainly for the strand of phenomenology known as "transcendental phenomenology," the *epoché* and the reduction are necessary. They may even be necessary for *philosophical* uses of phenomenology more broadly, insofar as philosophy uses phenomenology to answer questions regarding the status of the subject, the relation between the subject and the world, the possibility of knowing truths about the world, and so on. The phenomenological answer to these questions seems to rely on some notion of the transcendental (e.g., the inherent connection between subject and world) in order to be persuasive and legitimate, and therefore would require the *epoché* and the reduction.

But phenomenology can also be used to address a variety of issues or problems in health sciences, sport science, psychology, anthropology, nursing studies, and more. In such cases, they would deal with problems inherent to those disciplines, and not (explicitly) with philosophical concerns. Do such uses of phenomenology maintain a continuity with the *Stiftung* of phenomenology, and so also require some account of transcendental processes? On the one hand, we could simply consider each of these to be its own *Stiftung*: there is a tradition or institution of phenomenological psychology or phenomenological nursing and such. In that case, there is no *prima facie* reason to suggest that each of these *Stiftungen* must be interested in the issues of phenomenological philosophy, and therefore no reason to think that they must all require some recourse to the transcendental. Perhaps, if I am working in phenomenological theories of education, it is enough to appeal to Max van Manen,[28] without having to appeal to Husserl or Merleau-Ponty.

On the other hand, if these traditions are not to be entirely equivocal with their use of the term "phenomenology," then it seems they must, at some point, have recourse to a broader tradition of phenomenology, of which each of them is their own offshoot. If this were to be true, I think the majority of researchers would be justified in merely referring to those within their own (sub-)*Stiftung*, without having to appeal to the broader one. It would then be the case that at least *some* people in each offshoot should be able to articulate the ways in which that particular sub-*Stiftung* branches off from the main *Stiftung*, and so give a theoretical (and methodological) justification for the continuity of that sub-*Stiftung* with the broader *Stiftung*. These people would then be the "method" people within the "applied phenomenology" and would seem to function structurally analogous to the "transcendental empiricals" in the analysis of Chapter 4: they are not engaged in transcendental phenomenology, per se, nor in simply "applied" or "empirical" uses of phenomenology, but rather study the way that transcendental concerns impinge upon the use of phenomenology in that particular sub-*Stiftung*.[29] Assuming they do their job well,[30] those working in the relevant applied fields would be methodologically justified in referring to their work, without having to go beyond them back to the broader *Stiftung* themselves.

Such a move—considering each sub-*Stiftung* as a *Stiftung* in its own right, with its own methodological justification—would allow "qualitative researchers [to] engage with the phenomena themselves" without leading "them astray by making them choke on methodological metareflections" they may not be equipped to deal with, while still dealing with the concerns of Giorgi and Morley that phenomenology offers a unique approach that is radically different from, say, naturalistic approaches to "empirical" or applied fields.[31] While Zahavi might be correct that "most qualitative researchers" would not agree that their work must "constantly [be] supported by a transcendental–philosophical framework,"[32] this does not mean, methodologically, that those researchers are correct in their assumption. In other words, one thing we can learn from philosophical phenomenology is that our approach to the world (including our theoretical approach when we are doing scientific study, broadly construed) is based on certain (philosophical) accounts of transcendental processes (e.g., of subjectivity, of intentionality, etc.) that influence our theorizing and the results of our theorizing, whether we are aware of them or not. Indeed, a major theme of the *Crisis* is Husserl's contention that contemporary science was driven by a spirit that it was almost entirely unaware of, and which was contributing directly to the dehumanization of the sciences, and of the broader lifeworld.

To say, therefore, that no one needs to be concerned with the methodological presumptions of scientific inquiries (in their various disciplinary forms) would fail to acknowledge either the tradition or the insights of phenomenology. But, to say that *every* individual researcher must be able to ground their methodological reflections all the way to the transcendental levels analyzed by Husserl, Merleau-Ponty, and others would fail to acknowledge the limits of finite human researchers: we simply cannot expect one researcher to be an expert in transcendental phenomenology *and* in the objects, aims, and means of the particular applied discipline(s) in question. Hence, asking a few researchers to play the mediating role of translating transcendental phenomenology into the language of applied phenomenologies seems a kind of solid middle ground.[33]

This is not a question of trying to establish who can legitimately use the name "phenomenology" in their research, and even less about trying to police the boundaries of the phenomenological *Stiftung*. Rather, there is a real concern, simultaneously methodological and political, at stake in this discussion: do we need to understand things as "entangled phenomena," necessarily caught up in a web of related processes, spirits, and idealities (including processes such as genderization, racialization, etc., discussed in Chapter 4), or can we understand them only as isolated objects? Philosophical phenomenology makes a (I think compelling) case for the former, but our "natural attitude" still seems to lean toward the latter (though perhaps less so than in Husserl's time). Indeed, as discussed above, without the *epoché* and the reduction being used, implicitly or explicitly, we (at least in our current spiritual situation) are likely to construe our theoretical investigations in either empiricist or idealist terms,[34] and, as such, *not* in phenomenological terms—at least when phenomenology refers to a unique mode of engaging the world (i.e., as a world of phenomena, not of objects).

By claiming that the *epoché* and the reduction can be used implicitly or explicitly, I am granting that not every researcher needs explicitly and purposively invoke the reduction. It may be methodologically possible to take that for granted, *if I have a methodology that prevents me from sliding into empiricism or idealism*. The task of the methodological scholars called for earlier would be to articulate such a methodology, one that makes explicit its philosophical assumptions regarding the subject's relation to the world so as to explicitly justify the appeal to the first-person perspective.[35] In our current situation, such a methodology would need to explicitly justify its rejection of an empiricist or idealist view, as one of these remains the dominant (or at least a strongly plausible) view in most research in the natural and social sciences. Such a rejection is an enactment of the *epoché*, whether that terminology is invoked or not. It would also need to explicate what method it is using, if not an empiricist or idealist one; assuming the method articulated in some way relates to the expressive relation between self, world, and flesh, such an explication would be an enacting of the reduction, whether that terminology is invoked or not. Without an explicit justification of this type, the method invoked would fail to be persuasive, and its results or insights would remain theoretically suspect.

Hence, if we construe phenomenology primarily as a mode of engaging the world (i.e., of understanding "the matters themselves" *qua* phenomena) or as a method (i.e., the means by which we can best understand "the matters themselves"), we can see that some appeal to transcendental processes is *always* made as part of scientific theorizing.[36] If we want to be rigorous in our scientific theorizing, we must make these transcendental processes—and the effect they have on our theorizing—as explicit as possible. This, precisely, is the task of transcendental phenomenology (as a rigorous science), and it cannot be divorced, in this sense, from the task of phenomenology more broadly (to get back to the "things themselves"). While not every piece of phenomenological research will make these transcendental processes explicit (since we all need to limit the scope of our theoretical projects in various ways), every piece of phenomenological research will make use of those transcendental processes implicitly in its theorizing, and therefore, I think, the more explicit those processes can be made, the better the resulting theorizing will be. This is just to say, if we agree that phenomena are an intertwining or entanglement of, at least, spirit, *Stiftung*, materiality, and individuality, then the better account we can give of the relevant spirit(s) and *Stiftung(en)* (as discussed in Chapters 2 and 3), and of the processes of materialization and individuation (as discussed in Chapters 3 and 4), the stronger our account of that phenomenon will be. And insofar as spirit and *Stiftung* are transcendental empiricals, leaving the transcendental entirely out of our phenomenological investigations will leave us with less satisfying results than if we do account for that axis of our experience.

And the strength or normative force of these accounts is not merely descriptive but also transformative. Insofar as expressing those transcendental processes itself alters those processes, drawing our attention to them, as we saw in the last chapter, has critical and political weight: it gives us not only a more accurate account of the phenomena in question (as we have seen) but also an account that can be more personally transformative and existentially and socially meaningful. In that regard, the reduction is not simply a methodological tool for describing the transcendental; it is also "a personal transformation or an existential imperative" (FE, 82), for it "is ultimately I who must read these investigations, and it is only in relation to my experience that they can reveal something previously hidden about its constitution" (FE, 106). That is, uncovering the entanglement of this particular phenomenon with subjectivity helps me better understand both the phenomenon and myself as a subject who is entangled with this phenomenon. And better understanding my entanglement with this phenomenon also helps me better understand the entanglements (and entanglings) I have with other phenomena, and with the world. And because those entanglements with (empirical) phenomena are themselves partially constitutive of the transcendental processes by which I "make sense" of everything in my experience, better understanding them does not simply alter some (empirical) thoughts I have, or give me new (empirical) insights about the world—it changes and transforms (perhaps infinitesimally, perhaps more seriously) the very engagements I have with everything else in the world.

Losing sight of the transcendental processes at work in the entangling of phenomena, therefore, causes us to lose sight of "what makes an experience—whether individual or collective—transformative of how one thinks about one's self or the world" and so causes us to miss how experience might "not only motivate politics but also itself act as a medium of political change" (AE, 29). Accounting for the transcendental is therefore a methodological necessity, but one with political (in the dually constitutive sense we are using that term in this book) resonances and implications: failing to adequately account for transcendental processes—failing to account for phenomenology as a distinct sensing of the world—is to lose the social, existential, and political impact that theorizing can have as a mode of (personal, cultural, and political) transformation. And if we look at our current cultural and political climate, we might see that it was not only 1930s Germany that faced a *Crisis* that, perhaps, better phenomenological attunement could help to mollify.

6

Toward a Phenomenological Politics
The Political Implications of Expressivity

We are now in position, finally, to return most explicitly to some of the political themes outlined in the Introduction. Most notably, we are now in position to clarify the relation between our previous discussions of subjectivity (as a process or expressive function of flesh) and the individual subjects that are the presumed bedrock of much contemporary political conversation. We could not address this concern in a satisfactory manner earlier, insofar as we first had to address a significant misunderstanding of the phenomenological nature of our analyses so far. Many people assume that phenomenology's emphasis on subjectivity renders it unhelpful for addressing social or political issues.[1] As a philosophy of subjectivity, the thinking goes, it is constrained to talking only about individual subjects and their experience, and therefore has little to contribute to talk about collective action, societal struggles, communal concerns, structural issues, and so on.

But our analyses from previous chapters have shown this supposition to be doubly incorrect. First, a philosophy of subjectivity need not be constrained to talking about individual subjects, insofar as subjectivity names a process or a particular way of sensing the world and not a concrete, individual substance (i.e., a subject). Certainly, there is a relationship between subjectivity and subjects, but that relationship does not restrict an interest in the former to only studying the latter, for it is in the nature of subjectivity itself to be intersubjective or "suprasubjective" (Hua 6, 270), that is, "suprapersonal" (Hua 14, 199).

Second, we saw in Chapter 5 that phenomenology's methodological origin in subjective experience does not mean that it is restricted to studying subjectivity as its sole object of inquiry. Once the sharp subject/object distinction is done away with, either methodologically (via the *epoché*) or philosophically (via the phenomenological understanding of intentionality), subjectivity is no longer isolated from other things in the world, and therefore a focus on subjectivity need not imply the lack of insight into anything nonsubjective. Rather, as we have seen already, a focus on subjectivity as expressive provides us a way of accessing all kinds of questions about the world and our various ways of relating to it. Indeed, focusing on subjectivity might be the *only* way to truly understand the "matters themselves" we encounter in our lives, as we argued in the last chapter. A focus on subjectivity does not, therefore, *prima facie* restrict us only to talking about individual subjects and their experience.

This connects directly to the concerns raised in the Introduction about how to simultaneously account for the personal, lived component of experience (*Erlebnis*) and the communal or shared component. We have seen that *Erlebnis*, as a product of subjectivity, is already caught up in a communal, interpretive framework that is internally constitutive of individual subjects while also, simultaneously, putting them in contact with the world. Our focus on subjectivity, understood in light of expressivity, therefore allows us to articulate a distinctly communal (i.e., suprasubjective or suprapersonal) mode of sensing the world, one that carries its own unique sense: a communal orientation that directs individual subjects "toward the other" (Hua 11, 343) and toward the world in particular ways.

This, in turn, implies that there is a twofold notion of the political at work within the account of experiencing (the phenomeno-logic) that we have been developing here: a principle of communal orientation (an internal makeup that structures the community in particular ways) and a principle of communal action (a force that is expressed in and through that makeup). The relation between these principles, we will see, is expressive, and therefore generative. It is also transcendental. As such, clarifying the relationship between subjectivity and subjects requires accounting for the transcendental and empirical influences of the political on the human and natural worlds. In light of this, our analyses call for the articulation of a "phenomenological politics," akin to the "phenomenological psychology" of the early period of phenomenology's development. The task of such a phenomenological politics would be to explore and explain, clearly and rigorously, the various means and processes by which individual subjects are constituted by the suprasubjective forces at work in a community and, conversely, the various means and processes by which communities (as suprasubjective forces) are constituted by the activities of subjects, both individually and collectively. Such a phenomenological politics is therefore not simply a matter of the *polis* but of *politeia* (constitution), a move that opens us to new understandings of both phenomenology and politics.

The Intersubjectivity of Subjectivity: Spiritual Communities

Let us begin, then, by examining the particular type of communal nature at work in subjectivity. Initially, this move seems to maintain a certain privileging of subjects vis-à-vis subjectivity. Husserl, for example, is first able to move beyond a concern solely with individual monads only by showing the necessity of other subjects for our engagement with the world. To do this, he locates the necessity of other subjects within the experience of any subject in two ways: we encounter things in the world that give themselves to us as other subjects (and not simply as objects), and we encounter things in the world that can be explicable only by recourse to other subjects. These two are not entirely distinct, of course, but are related: insofar as we see words arranged in a meaningful fashion, or hear musical notes in a certain order, we cannot help but be convinced that these things must have been produced by another subject, like myself. There are even times when we encounter something that cannot be explained by any one other subject, but by a collection of subjects: the performance of a piece of music by an orchestra, the execution of a particular play by a sports team, or the enacting of broad and sweeping social distancing measures during a pandemic "are all examples of interpersonal accomplishments that cannot really be attributed to any particular agent. They are created and shared together, based on a common resolution or a common goal."[2]

In these regards, we cannot help but posit the existence of other subjects. But how, then, can phenomenology understand or make sense of these "other subjects"? Husserl's initial attempt, rather famously, is via the notion of empathy. Empathy, in this phenomenological sense, is not primarily an emotion or a feeling-with others, a compassionate affection for other people, as in the traditional sense of the term (Hua 37, 194). Rather, empathy is here taken in a peculiar phenomenological sense: I see, in the movements and actions of this other thing I encounter in the world, movements and actions that are like me, like my own ego. Hence, I posit this other thing as an *alter ego*, another ego that is like me in the sense that it is not just an object but also a subject. This identification with other people as other *people*, that is, as things with which I share a world (Hua 14, 477), is understood in terms of association or "pairing" in which I see the other "as if I were there" (Hua 15, 427), and in which "I receive this character of being 'my' self by virtue of the contrastive pairing that necessarily takes place" (Hua 1, 144; see also Hua 14, 244; Hua 4, 96). Empathy is the condition, then, not only of my experience of others *qua* other subjects, but also of myself *qua* subject.[3]

But such an account, at least on the surface, seems problematic. For one thing, we do not seem to have an experience of inferring the existence of other people in this fashion: we do not come to a conclusion about the subjectivity of other people, but rather we take them simply as subjects. Indeed, we must precisely presume the subjectivity of others if we are to take their actions as intentional, either individually or collectively. As we discussed in Chapter 2, it is only if I take the other person as already expressive that I can come to understand what they say. For this reason, Husserl suggests that his account of empathy must be taken as a "fictive genesis" (Hua 14, 477): fictive, insofar as it may not be something we actually experience, and a genesis insofar as it is an attempt to account for our acquisition of the ability to identity other subjects as subjects with whom we share a common world.

Qua genesis, we see a second problem with the account of empathy outlined before: it seems overly cognitive, theoretical, and purposive. There is too much awareness and purposeful thought to account for what is, it seems, a fairly ready and immediate identification: as discussed already in Chapter 2, we "*intuitively*" take a speaker to be a person who is expressing something; we do not reason to his being a subject, we "*perceive* him as such" (LI I, 189). Insofar as our construal of other people as subjects is intuitive and perceptual, it seems that it cannot be the result of a judgment or series of judgments as seemingly described in the account of empathy.

And indeed, when Husserl himself develops more fully his genetic and generative phenomenological investigations, his account of the primal relation to other subjects is altered, though in ways that he may not have always fully realized. When he begins to develop his account of passivity (at various levels), for example, Husserl comes to posit the relation to others, not primarily as one of intellectual assent or theoretical judgment but of a certain kind of passivity that Robert Pfaller calls "interpassivity,"[4] in which we recognize in our engagements with the world an unconscious or unwilled relation to others. On such an account, we simply find ourselves always already in relation with others, not due to a subjective choice, but due to the conditions or nature of subjectivity itself (TSO, 152–53).[5]

It is not simply the subject, then, that requires recourse to other subjects, but subjectivity itself, as a transcendental process. We saw in the last chapter how subjectivity is generated out of the expressive unity of flesh as a particular kind of sensing the world. Just as all visible things share in visibility or are part of the same visible "world," so, too, do subjective things share in subjectivity (or consciousness, sentience, etc.), not in the sense of all sharing the same mind (in a type of panpsychism), but in the sense of all sharing in the same world of sentience, that is, in the world as sensible, as knowable. The presumption of such a common world is necessary for us to think the primal relation between subjects: "We could not be persons for others if a common surrounding world did not stand there for us in a community, in an intentional linkage of our lives. Correlatively spoken, the one is constituted essentially with the other" (Hua 14, 191). In this regard, it is not just a common world that is the necessary prerequisite for subjectivity, but also a common community: we share not only the "material" conditions of the world, but also the "spiritual" conditions of subjectivities constituted within the flesh of the world. Out of this shared world and this shared community, the possibility of communication between subjects arises (Hua 1, 149), and from communication comes the possibility of giving a specific (ideal) permanence to objective reality (Hua 14, 202; see also IOG). As such, the "life" of the community and the "worldliness" of the world are both generated out of the expressive unity of flesh.

This situation is made explicit in Husserl's concept of the lifeworld, where it opens us to a certain duality at work in this communal generation. The concept of lifeworld has "a *necessary* and at the same time *dangerous* double meaning" (Hua 6, 460): it refers both to the "realm of original self-evidences" that functions as the universal ground of all meaning, and to the world of spiritual accomplishments (Hua 6, 130–32, 294–313).[6] This ambiguity is reinforced by Husserl's use of lifeworld to refer both to one shared lifeworld (*the* lifeworld) and to different "types" of lifeworld (e.g., the "Indian" lifeworld or that of "Chinese peasants"; Hua 6, 141; see also Hua 29, 313; TSO, 157). It is clear, then, that lifeworld refers both to the transcendental foundation of sense and to its individual actualizations in "particular worlds" (Hua 6, 460; see also TSO, 158). This double meaning is necessary precisely because the lifeworld is always pregiven as a horizon (Hua 6, 141–46; Hua 39, 99–105) that is necessarily both the "universal horizon" (Hua 6, 147), what Merleau-Ponty will call the "horizon of all horizons" (PhP, 381), and is actualized in particular ways by particular spiritual communities.[7] As such, the lifeworld functions as a transcendental empirical, as we discussed in Chapter 4: *qua* transcendental, it shows the necessity for any subject to draw on the work of other subjects via its use of (suprasubjectively constituted) spirit in the shaping of its horizons and lifeworld, and therefore in all of its engagements with the world, including its engagements with other concrete, individual subjects. As empirical, it shows us that this drawing on spirit always happens within particular spiritual communities that are both expressed in concrete cultural activities and constitutive of the way that subjects within that community intuit the world.

We should expect to find, therefore, similarities among subjectivities sharing a spiritual community, that is, those sharing a particular, empirically constituted, lifeworld. These similarities will be both in *how* those subjects enact or express their subjectivity and in *what* those subjective performances produce. These similarities are not the result of conscious thought and reflection by individual subjects, but rather are first revealed as "social habitualities" (Hua 15, 208) or "styles" (Hua 14, 205; TSO, 159) that work passively, pretheoretically, to shape the entirety of any subject's engagement with the world.[8] In this regard, Husserl's claim that "everything worldly is intersubjectively constituted" (Hua 15, 45) is not a statement about the necessity of purposive agreement between subjects (akin to the "collective intentionalities" of Searle's social ontology),[9] but about the transcendental connection between subjects that is inherent to subjectivity itself. This connection is not, first and foremost, a connection between already established, discrete individuals, but is rather a certain "anonymous" function (VI, 142) that coordinates subjectivity's orientation toward the world and, because distinct subjects share the functions of subjectivity, also coordinates individual subjects' orientations toward the world and toward other subjects.[10] As such, the coordination of subjectivity's passive connection to the world entails a "connection with the passivity of all other [subjects]" such that "my life and the life of another do not merely exist, each for themselves; rather, one is 'directed' toward the other" (Hua 11, 343) in and through each of our individual engagements with subjectivity and the world. Intentionality is therefore *always* "collective intentionality," insofar as subjectivity is always communally (i.e., spiritually, politically, etc.) constituted.[11]

As we have seen with the notions of spirit (in Chapter 2) and of sensings (in Chapter 3), the very directedness of subjectivity is therefore always dual (to the world and to others).[12] This duality is not a simple duality, but a coordinated duality, held in tension and mutually co-determining: my orientation to the world shapes my orientation to others (e.g., through the cultural products I produce, the "spiritual meaning" they express, etc.), even as my orientation to others shapes my orientation to the world (e.g., through the habits and styles inculcated in me as a member of my spiritual community). This co-determining relation of tension should by now be recognizable as an expressive relation, one that can be discussed under the title of "spirit."

From Intersubjectivity to Political Constitution:
The Transcendental We

With his notion of a spiritual community, Husserl suggests something like a "transcendental we,"[13] rather than simply a transcendental I. But to truly appreciate the political implications of this "transcendental we," and hence of the expressive account of phenomenality, we must maintain our focus on the primacy of subjectivity (as process) over subjects. To do this, we must avoid two potential misunderstandings: first, that the "we" is just a collection of individual I's somehow working together; and second, that the "we," the community, becomes simply another individual, hypostatized into a subject of its own rather than being a relation or web of relationships.

The first potential misunderstanding, then, is to treat the transcendental we as a voluntary association of individual subjects. Doing so fails to acknowledge the role of communal relations as transcendental processes and overemphasizes the distinctness of individuals: it fails to account for the differentiated nature of subjectivity itself as a process generated in the expressive unity of flesh. Many contemporary social ontologies take voluntary interaction as the basis of social relationships, and so they evidence this problematic way of understanding social groups on the model of an individual subject. Such voluntary interaction is characterized by "active and reciprocal cooperation between individual agents" (TSO, 150), and leads to a "collective intentionality" in which a certain directedness is shared within a social body. This idea of collective intentionality likely finds its roots in Sellars's notion of a "we-intention."[14] However, this we-intention does not function like a group mind,[15] and so we are left to wonder whether the we-intention is anything other than a collection of "I-intentions." While Searle, at least, seems adamant that collective intentionality is irreducibly collective and not simply a combination of individual intentionalities, it is widely assumed by many in the "collective intentionality" discussions that intentionality is about minds, that minds are individual (no group minds), and that each individual has his or her own mind.[16] Given these assumptions, it seems that it must be individuals, and not a group, that intend a joint action, which is just to say that the "joint" action is the coming together of individuals in voluntary association.[17] This is not to say collective intentions are *simply* a series or collection of individual intentions: what is at stake in much of the contemporary debate is precisely the relation that must hold between the individual intentions to make them sufficiently collective to constitute a collective intention. But there is an inherent individuality to this account that both starts with individual subjects and presumes the radical individuality of individual subjects: the collective or the communal is the coming-together of individuals in some way.[18]

This view is rooted in a substantial account of the subject that privileges the individual substance (a "subject," a "mind") over a process (subjectivity). *Qua* substance, it must be the case that either I am the subject or that there is a collective substance ("we," the nation, etc.) of which each individual is a local instantiation. If one does not want to hypostatize the group or community into its own subjective entity, the only other option seems to be radically distinct individual subjects, whose connection must then be explained *post facto*. But with the process-based account of subjectivity discussed in Chapter 5, we can see that, for phenomenology, subjectivity is a function (of knowing the world) that is actualized in various localized nexuses of sensings. The account of the transcendental outlined in Chapter 4, then, would help us see that individual nexuses of sensings (i.e., individual subjects) necessarily draw on a shared function (subjectivity), which in turn produces, within various *Stiftungen* or transcendentally empirical "spiritual communities," certain shared actions (habits, styles) and contents (we "sense" the world in similar ways) that provide the context for the localized actualizations of the shared function. This transcendental subjectivity necessarily precedes, phenomenologically speaking, any voluntary interaction between subjects, insofar as the very subjectivity of individual subjects actualizes, within particular transcendentally empirical contexts, the process(es) of transcendental subjectivity. While there may also be things individual subjects purposefully do together as a group and for a shared purpose (e.g., an orchestra playing a piece of music together, a sports team playing a game together), that is not the *primary* mode of subjective interaction.

The primary mode—and that which perhaps enables the other modes—of subjective interaction, of intersubjective action, is subjectivity itself. And to speak of the social or the political, then, it is not necessary to speak only of the later, voluntary social groupings, but we can speak already of subjectivity itself as inherently social or political, even before it is intersubjective: before it is a relation between distinct subjects, subjectivity already expresses a relation to others and to one's social situation (e.g., one's "spiritual" community) that is both constitutive and constituting.[19] This "before" is not a temporal or logical priority, but a phenomenological one: this transcendentally necessary sociality, the transcendental we, like "the spatial form" in nature (Hua 8, 317), provides "the 'social space' which allows the temporal simultaneity and succession of individual subjects" (TSO, 166n6). That is to say, it provides the internal makeup that makes subjects what they are, even as it continues to unfold that internal makeup via transcendental processes (of differentiation, actualization, generation, etc.). In light of earlier analyses in this book, we might say that the "transcendental we" is a differentiated process (subjectivity) that allows for differentiation into distinct subjects, or that individual subjects *express* spiritual communities. But in whatever terminology one chooses to use, the point is that sociality precedes individuation when it comes to subjectivity.[20]

If we see the transcendental necessity of something like a "transcendental we," then, we cannot conceive of that "we" primarily in terms of an association of preexisting individuals. But we should also not misconstrue the transcendental nature of this sociality by turning the collective into its own reified subject or substance: while the "we" is not a collection of individuals, we must also not understand it as a different (kind of) individual. Husserl seems to make this mistake himself at times: in *Ideas II*, for example, he speaks of communities as *"personal unities of a higher order"* that *"have their own lives,* [and] preserve themselves by lasting through time *despite the joining or leaving of individuals"* (Hua 4, 182). This is not an isolated incident,[21] but a purposeful statement of a certain type of "life," "unity," or "consciousness" that adheres to the community *qua* community (see Hua 27, 21). How are we to make sense of this phenomenologically? It seems, on its surface, to be a substantializing of the community, and therefore unphenomenological.[22] But, while it is clear that Husserl attributes certain subjective elements to the community as a whole, this need not mean that he understands the community as a subject. It could simply mean that Husserl believes that certain subjective *functions*, including intentionality, can happen at the communal as well as at the personal level. That voluntary association of individuals is not the primary mode of intersubjective relations does not entail that it is not a *distinct* (and legitimate) mode of intersubjective relations, one that requires its own unique phenomenological analyses. Husserl himself saw this, describing how social relations between individuals have their own two-sided character, their own sense of reciprocity and of objectivity, unique forms of intentionality, and different kinds of anticipations and responsibilities (see Hua 13, 98–104; TSO, 149).

In this regard, we could say that Husserl does treat the community, at times, as a localized nexus of (at least some types of) subjective functions. But this is not yet to hypostatize the community in a problematic way. For the problematic element of the hypostatization would be to treat the community *primarily* as an individual. Doing that would lose the transcendental nature of subjectivity as process (rendering it instead simply a property of the subject) and the transcendental nature of the political (leaving it simply the interaction between individual subjects). This, in turn, would lose the generative nature of the relation between subjectivity and the subject, thereby significantly altering our understanding of the political subject. For once we take the subject to precede (and constitute) subjectivity, then the subject is necessarily the producer (and not the product) of any and all subjective acts or activities: the subject can be what expresses itself, but it can never be an expression. This fails to acknowledge the differential and autopoietic nature of expressing which, in turn, causes us to fail to adequately understand the ongoing unfolding of expression: we come to think that it is the subject that primarily combines meaning, being, and doing rather than see that those three are necessarily intertwined in phenomenality itself. And if it is the subject that combines those things, and subjects are each individual and discrete, then it remains difficult to see how one can take phenomena as giving us access to anything more than the will, desire, or idiosyncrasies of individual subjects. Indeed, all we can learn about subjects, it seems, is what they do and produce, and nothing about how or why they do it. As such, questions of why they do what they do must also be answered only by recourse to the will, desire, or idiosyncrasies of individual subjects: there are no laws, principles, and the like explaining subjective functioning except that which subjects give to themselves.

This account of the autonomous subject—the subject who gives its law to itself—is a central tenet of modern social and political philosophies. Once this account of the political subject is granted, any kind of social or political interaction must be explained by recourse to subjective will: political subjects can only be legitimately subjected to a (political) law if they have some hand in crafting the law, either directly or indirectly (through some kind of representative that they have willfully given their individual power of law-making to, be that a democratically elected representative or, as in *Leviathan*, some other kind of leader to whom the subject gives its (tacit or explicit) consent). The *polis*, then, is construed as a voluntary association of individuals, rather than as a given, constitutive power of individual formation: the *polis* is understood as a *res* (*publica*), and not as the site or product of *politeia*.[23] As such it loses any transcendental function (e.g., as *Stiftung*) and can be understood only empirically (as historical tradition, social institution, etc.). While individual persons might be shaped by their community in certain empirical ways, as political subjects they are not transcendentally constituted but only constituting, and "politics" then comes to name the (empirical) processes by which individuals voluntarily come together (by subjective choice) in various ways for various purposes, communal or individual.[24]

But, as I said, the various types of ways that people can interact with each other is not *all* that there is to learn, phenomenologically, from the political nature of subjectivity. For while we can learn things about communities and some of their unique modes of functioning, we can also learn things about the constitution of unique subjects within particular communities. Once we grant the phenomenological primacy of subjectivity (as process) over subjects (as individuals), we can see that even the very exercise of our subjectivity is itself an expressive and therefore political (in the sense of the constitution of subjectivity and subjects) issue. It is not the case that individual subjects simply choose how to engage with other individual subjects in ways that best fit their individual personalities, characters, and such; rather, things like personalities, characters, etc. are themselves already politically constituted. While individual persons have their own "personal style," and so, too, may communities, these two are not simply analogically related, but actually related (Hua 27, 21): a person's character is, in part, "given" to them by the spirit at work in their community (Hua 1, 135; Hua 6, 270). That is, while the communal we is transcendentally necessary in the constitution of subjectivity, it is also, in its transcendental empirical form as *this* or *that* particular community, necessary in the constitution of individuals as subjects and as persons.

This is significant insofar as it relativizes subjectivity, including political subjectivity (in the narrower sense of voluntary association), to the context of its expression. It is not the case that politics is simply a matter of setting the laws that would allow people to exercise their own autonomy free from various encumbrances. Rather, politics is also (and perhaps foremost) about generating particular kinds of political subjects. It should be clear that such generation is not, on the expressive account, something to be controlled by particular individual subjects, be they governing authorities or anyone else. This is not, in that sense, an apology for government controlled social construction. Rather, generation is part of the autopoietic unfolding of the phenomenal world, and, as such, is the result of processes that are not primarily controlled by autonomous subjects, but that generate subjects in particular ways. Politics is therefore not primarily about the voluntary acts of subjects within the *polis*, but about the *politeia* that constitute both the *polis* and the people who are its constituent parts. *Qua* expressions, these constitutive "political" forces necessarily alter their context with every expression, such that it becomes necessary to determine both the ideal goal—the "expressed"—and its expressions, to see how the goal's expression in its various expressions have functioned to alter the goal, its expressions, and the entire contextual process of expressing.[25] Eventually, it seems inevitable that the infinitesimal alterations caused by our expression(s) of those political ideals will lead to singular points at which the expression will be transformed into a "new" expression.

Let me use an example to help illustrate the political implications of privileging subjectivity over subjects that I am arguing for here. One of the big breakthroughs of modern political theory was the notion of universal human rights. This notion had tremendous liberational potential and has been used for centuries to help people gain more political rights. But there are at least two limitations to this liberational potential: first, as we have already discussed, is the narrowed notion of politics at work in this understanding of "political rights." By focusing only on the voluntary association of individual subjects, political rights came to be equated solely with the laws that were (or weren't) in place and how they prevented (or did not prevent) people from exercising their autonomy. Suffrage was one essential element of this within democracies, but it also included the presumption that democracy (or at least democratic elements) was necessary for legitimate governance. With this often came the requirement of access to education (so as to equip people to make good democratic choices); the right to live and act in accordance with one's conscience (one's moral autonomy) in issues relating to religion, free speech, free assembly; and so on. In this way, a certain account of (neoliberal) subjectivity was presumed, and the task of political rights was to preserve the autonomy of these subjects.

This presumed account of subjects is contained in the claim of "universal" human rights. The presumption, clearly, is that all people are political subjects of the autonomous kind: everyone *is* an autonomous subject, so everyone deserves to be able to enter into whatever types of voluntary associations they want to, provided doing so doesn't infringe on the rights of others. But is everyone actually an autonomous subject, in this sense? The invocation of actuality is significant here: it is not a question of whether or not everyone *really* is an autonomous subject, but whether or not they *actually* are. The difference has to do with whether subjectivity is a question of essence (possibility and its realization) or of generation (transcendental structures and their means of actualization). Clearly, we have been arguing in this book that subjectivity is generated, not realized. *Qua* generated, it emerges out of particular transcendental structures that are coordinated in particular ways to particular actual (empirical) conditions. If this is true—if particular accounts of subjectivity emerge out of particular actual conditions—then the notion that any one account of subjectivity would be "universal" is highly unlikely, almost impossible once we grant that actual conditions vary in different times, places, cultures, and the like. Rather, "universal" human rights are actually very localized: they are the conceptual product of a particular time and place in human history, and are generated out of a particular set of historical and social conditions.[26]

Their historical emergence does not, in and of itself, invalidate the notion of universal human rights. They could remain helpful as an ideal, even if we wonder about the account of subjectivity presumed in them. But even as an ideal, they are not unproblematic. If we say, for example, that the universality of autonomous subjectivity is a goal, and not a presumption— that this account of autonomous subjectivity *should be* universal[27]—then the problem of the differing actual conditions of actual people names the problem to be solved. In such a case, the task would be to analyze the conditions under which autonomous subjectivity emerged, and then figure out how to replicate those conditions everywhere else, to produce the conditions in which autonomous subjectivity could become universal. Such analysis and replication would then become the "political" project, and the implementation of certain "political rights," or certain sets of laws and judicial structures might be put in place precisely as necessary contextual factors for the emergence of autonomous subjectivity.

This project would seem problematic in two ways. First, given the continuous or unfolding nature of generativity, it seems unlikely that one set of conditions could be imported to a different set of conditions and produce similar results. Indeed, both of those suppositions seem dubious: that one *could* import a set of conditions into a different set of conditions (since they would not grow organically out of the conditions already in place, they would not be the same conditions, with the same continuities, etc.), and that, were it possible to do so, doing so would yield similar results (since, again, the conditions would not be continuous in the same way, it is unlikely they would generate the same results). If nothing else, the involvement of subjects purposefully trying to bring about a certain set of conditions or certain results would itself be a difference within the conditions that would, almost necessarily, alter the conditions and what they could generate. In that regard, such a project seems impossible: subjects simply don't have that kind of control over the autopoietic unfolding of expressing, especially regarding the generation of subjectivity (a point we will return to in the next section).

A second problem, though, would be whether such a project would be *desirable*. The attempt to take a set of generative conditions from one cultural context and impose it on a different cultural context is the project of colonialism. It is the attempt to make "others" like "us," even (or perhaps especially) "for their own good." If a necessary prerequisite of autonomous subjectivity is a certain set of democratic conditions that require the broad dissemination of literacy, for example, then it isn't obvious that democracy would be well suited to cultures that are primarily oral. Instituting democracy there, under those conditions, might produce "autonomous subjectivity" (though, again, we have good reason to doubt whether it would, in fact, have that outcome), but it would do so at the cost of significantly altering the culture in which it would be enacted, and perhaps destroying an element (oral transmission) that it holds as central. Granted, since any culture is autopoietically unfolding and generated/generative, the alteration of a culture is inevitable, and therefore its being altered is not, in and of itself, bad. But if it is being altered by some particular subjects to make that culture more like the culture of those subjects, then (and especially if those subjects are not themselves part of the culture being altered) I think it is fair to ask by what justification those subjects should be able to alter the culture for others. The principles of autonomy (valued by the subjects trying to alter the culture) would seem to suggest that the alteration should occur only with the volition and consent of the culture being changed—though it isn't clear what form that consent would take, or which subjects from the culture being altered would have to agree to it (all of them? a majority? those with traditional authority?), or what would constitute "acceptable" reasons for them doing so (if some small portion consents to it because they will benefit personally from it, is that sufficient?).

My point here is not to rehash the critiques of democracy and the spreading of democracy as a colonialist enterprise.[28] Rather, my point is that the shift to a generative account of subjectivity, and the resulting shift in the account of the political subject, calls into question the very possibility of the "universal" when it comes to politics. If we take politics in the sense of *politeia*, as I am arguing we should, the most we could say about the "universal" would be to treat it something like the transcendental, that is, a universality of form or approach and not of content, since the difference between the transcendental and the (transcendental) empirical is not a difference of content, but of focus or axis. We could say, perhaps, as a matter of transcendental politics, that every subject is shaped, in its subjectivity, by a "transcendental we," but any attempt to give content to that transcendental we will necessarily be a transcendental empirical content which, *qua* transcendental *empirical*, cannot be universal across communities but only (perhaps) within a particular community.[29] Any attempt to universalize the content of my transcendental we is, by necessity, a colonial enterprise, which would need to be justified, as colonial enterprise, to be morally permissible. And insofar as subjective activities are indexed to the lifeworld or communal spiritual horizons operative for that subject, it is unclear precisely what kind of justification would be necessary, or possible, to justify the imposition of one lifeworld on another lifeworld: certainly, such a move could be justified within the confines of the imposing (colonial) lifeworld, but it seems that the move would have to be justified also within the confines of the imposed (colonized) lifeworld, and perhaps even by people within that lifeworld, and not simply by those constituted within a different lifeworld. This would have its own set of problems.[30]

My point, then, is simply that political subjectivity is necessarily a matter of how subjects are generated within a particular set of conditions before it can be a matter of how subjects act within a *polis*. This point is not necessarily new. It has already been explored or discussed by many theorists of race, gender, and sexuality,[31] some of whom (especially Sara Heinämaa) have also highlighted the importance of expression in making this connection. What I hope has come clear here is that these conclusions are not merely accidental to phenomenology—one way that phenomenology can be applied; rather, they signal something essential about a phenomenological understanding of subjectivity that is rooted in the knot at the core of experience itself. That is, the idea that everything about our engagement with ourselves, others, and the world is premised on our spiritual/cultural situation is a fundamental phenomenological notion. Denying the influence of our spiritual situation on our individual constitution is as much the product of cultural/spiritual circumstances as is affirming it. So, if one wants to contend that people see these connections only because they are women or Black or queer, it would be equally true to say that people fail to see these connections only because they are men and white and straight.[32] This is not to play "identity politics" or to "make everything political" (in the narrower sense of the political described above); it is simply to acknowledge the necessity of the generation of subjectivity within some "transcendental we" or other.

A Phenomenological Politics

This kind of relativizing of subjectivity to its spiritual context threatens to devolve into a dangerous kind of moral and epistemological relativism ("That's true for you, but not true for me") as long as our alternatives are only "subjective autonomy" ("I can do whatever I want") or "causal determinism" ("I can do only what is dictated by my context"). To combat this threat, we need a philosophical field or subdiscipline whose task is to articulate precisely *how* communities, societal institutions, and the like are constitutive of individual persons, not purely transcendentally or purely empirically (as may, e.g., be done in sociology), but in a transcendental empirical fashion. This field would seek a precise account of·how subjects are generated, not just transcendentally out of *some* community, or simply empirically within this or that community (via statistical likelihoods, demographic generalities, and so on: "a woman in the United States is *x* percent more likely to . . ."), but transcendentally within this or that community.

Given the necessary tie to "this or that" community, it may not be possible to see how subjects are generated in a transcendental empirical factor, but only how certain (types of?) subjects are generated there (e.g., how is a Black man constituted in twenty-first-century America?). But even this may be problematic: insofar as we presume certain types to be constitutionally or generatively pertinent, both the presumption of which types might be pertinent (racial? gendered? sexual? economic?) and the determination of who fits those types (who counts as, e.g., Black or queer? who decides that?) would themselves be political and phenomenological questions within a particular context. To account for this, the researcher in such a field would have to be able to reflect back upon on their own research and its presuppositions as part of what is being studied. For this reason, perhaps the most promising line of research for such a field would be to examine the constitution, not of subjects in this or that community, or even of some types of subjects in this or that community, but of *this particular subject* in this particular community: What are the conditions that shape this subject's constitution in this community? What are the transcendental elements of those conditions, and what are simply empirical (and localized) conditions? Insofar as the researcher's own work must inevitably be part of the investigation itself (they and their research are part of the expressive and generative conditions they are examining), it would seem that the best particular subject to investigate would be the researcher themselves. Such an investigation—into the conditions of my own generation within this or that particular community (for even the selection of which community I am generated within is itself telling: Is it my political community? My religious community? My familial community? My ethnic or economic or sexual community?)—would require a certain kind of reflection into my own experiences, a reflection that, to be able to access the transcendental nature of my "empirical" community, would need to employ the reduction. That is to say, such an investigation must be phenomenological.

Qua phenomenological, such an investigation must avoid hypostatizing the community itself, as if it were either simply an empirical phenomenon or a static thing that is not constantly being altered by its various expressions. To do this, it would need to be attuned, not just to how I am constituted within this community, but also how this community is (transcendentally) constituted in and by the activities of subjects within it. Thinking in terms of expression and differential relations, tracing the various infinitesimal alterations that happen to the community via its expressions in various subjects and objects reminds us that the community is not a transcendent point of reference that simply generates subjects, but is itself being altered by its generations. A community, phenomenologically understood, would be an autopoietic unfolding that is constantly generating new expressions of itself—new relationships and new relata—even as it itself is being constantly (re)generated by those expressions. And some of those relata would needs be subjective, given both the ongoing alteration of subjectivity and the generation of distinct subjects.

This would be an essential difference between a community, in the sense we are talking about it here, and a *Stiftung* as we have talked about in previous chapters. While a *Stiftung* necessarily has subjective elements to it (the *Stiftung* of geometry, for example, required both insights from an original geometer and the communication of those insights for other geometers), a community of the sense we are talking about here necessarily has subjects. These subjects are both a product of the subjective elements within the *Stiftung* and a mode of enacting those subjective elements,[33] and our concern is primarily with those subjects: how they are generated, how their generation affects the community as a whole and its further generations, how they relate to other such generations and expressions, and so forth. This is just to say that such a community must, necessarily, be *political*.

We have arrived, then, at the necessity of an investigation that must be at once phenomenological and political: we have arrived at the need for a phenomenological politics. Such a need emerges out of the focus on expressivity, and all that has opened up. But without precisely clarifying the mechanisms of subjective generation (the generation of subjects and the ways subjects generate), the claim of the constitutive or generative necessity of the "transcendental we," of some spiritual community or other, remains too vague to be helpful. Indeed, it threatens to be harmful, if it is misconstrued in ways that are overly idealistic/autonomous or overly empirical/deterministic. It is therefore essential that these investigations maintain their distinctive *transcendental empirical* focus, if we are to advance past sophomoric relativism and properly understand the influence of various communal identities on political constitution.

In the current social climate of the West, this task is not merely academic. Every day, it seems, some new issue or flashpoint arises that brings our attention again to the various ways that communal identities shape individuals and are shaped by the political realities of our time: #MeToo, Black Lives Matter, Trump, and Brexit name but a few recent movements that have implications for the narrow sense of politics we are working with, but that find their impulse and motivation in the broader notion of political constitution we are trying to indicate, and whose further elaboration we are here calling for. Understanding these complex movements is beset by a "both siderism" that, like the relativism that concerned us in previous paragraphs, claims to seek to understand "both sides" of the issue but in fact properly understands neither, insofar as it fails to account for the generativity wrought by the expressive nature of the phenomenalization at stake. This generativity, you will recall, is necessarily asymmetrical: we "live through" one element to "live in" the other; we engage with the "alien" always from the (normative) position of "home." Anthony Steinbock talks about two types of violence that can arise when this generative relationship is not properly understood: hierarchical domination, which "denies the uniqueness of the alien and attempts to subsume the alien under the rule of the 'first'" (HB, 250); and the reversibility of perspectives, which "presupposes that home and alien are now interchangeable and mutually accessible, that is, symmetrically accessible to the same degree" (HB, 252).

The first is the problem of colonization outlined before and is widely (though perhaps not universally) understood to be problematic. The second is less obviously violent, and so it bears a bit more discussion here. For on its surface, the reversibility of perspectives seems like an admirable, perhaps even necessary, ethical move, in keeping with Husserl's early invocation of empathy discussed above: to better understand the other, I must seek to understand it the same way I understand my own perspective. But this move is "futile and naïve at best" (HB, 253), because it presumes a static account in which we are arrayed before a series of perspectival possibilities that we can choose from, rather than acknowledge that we are actually always already embedded in a generative context full of generative force that we can never escape or opt out of. As such, it denies the "generative dimension of the home in its phenomenologically privileged status" and so "it violates the limit-claims of the alien whose generative density resists such an assumption of mutual accessibility" (HB, 252). Both siderism is problematic, then, because it fails to account for our own generation, as subjects and as individuals, within differing communities that exercise a normative power over us that is simultaneously epistemological, ontological, and practical or poeitic: both sides can never be treated as equal, neutral possibilities, because neither side is constituted as a neutral possibility, but always as an asymmetrical, normative, expressive and transcendental structure that constitutes and generates us in its actual autopoietic unfolding.

But this does not leave us trapped in our own perspective, precisely because our "home" is never simply a static perspective. *Qua* generative force, "home" is always unfolding and refolding itself—transforming itself—in its relation with the "alien," as we discussed in Chapter 1. We are not, therefore, being asked to choose sides, but to take up, critique, and transform our generative structure in relation to that which we encounter or experience.

Yet even then, our own "personal and historical past" is not fully accessible to us (HB, 254)—the structures that generate subjectivity and us as individual subjects are never fully reducible to our individual selves, even as they are obviously significant in our constitution, and we in theirs.

As such, there is a relation between the critical transformation of these transcendental and communal structures and the critical transformation of ourselves, a relation that is essentially political, in the dual sense, and tied to experience. All our experience is necessarily transformative (as we have established in previous chapters), and since our selves and our subjectivity are both generated out of that phenomenal experience, that means the critical transformation of experience also works to transform ourselves.[34] As such, we must understand that "radical political movements necessarily imply practices of the self" (FE, 49). Johanna Oksala casts this in terms of feminism, but I am arguing that the point is applicable more broadly:

> the political importance of experience is connected to the broader question of what feminist politics is and what its goals are. It is my contention that feminism as a radical political project must aim at profound social transformation, not merely at some quantitative gain such as increase in women's power, political rights, or social benefits. It has to aim to change who we are—both as men and as women. In other words, it has to assume that our experience of the world could be qualitatively transformed if our society operated along different kinds of cultural and political practices and was governed by different norms. Such transformation requires politics that is able to question and transform the cultural representations and values that shape and structure our experiences, but it also requires self-transformation—political practices that aim to change our singular experiences. (FE, 49)

Radical political action, that which would get to the root (*radix*) of the problem, seeks nothing else than a fundamental transformation of society *and the individuals within it*, precisely because those two things are not distinct from each other. But they are not equivalent with each other either. They are, as we have seen, tied together in a differential and expressive relationship that functions transcendentally via processes of phenomenalization.

While these processes are affected by the actions of subjects, it is not clear that any subjects can control those processes or their unfolding. Whether this is simply a matter of ignorance that could be corrected by further study or is a matter of necessity (given our finite nature as subjects and our own generative histories within particular homeworlds), we are not yet in a position to say. But this (potentially necessary) lack of control over transcendental processes implies that the role of political movements, transcendentally speaking, is, perhaps, more critical than prescriptive. This, of course, is different from what that role might be empirically speaking, that is, within the confines of particular empirical conditions. Certain conditions might (or perhaps must) include prescriptive empirical claims: "this type of behavior must stop," or "these rules and laws must be abandoned." But the transcendental effect of such empirical claims—the rate of change they will institute, *qua* transcendental—is not, perhaps, knowable in advance or controllable by any subject or group of subjects. This does not mean we should do nothing, however: "The idea that practices engender [or express?] reality does not eliminate the role of the individual, but it does limit it. The web of practices in which we are embedded necessarily shapes our thought and understanding. Nothing I do can change the totality of it, but equally nothing I do is politically insignificant either" (FE, 35). Everything we do alters, however infinitesimally, the contexts and structures that constitute us. As such, we begin to see how "experience [might] not only motivate politics but also itself act as a medium of political change" (AE, 29).

And if we cannot control the forces that constitute us, we should, at least, learn to pay attention to our constitution, to understand both how we came to be as we are and how we might become otherwise. Hence, there is an ongoing, critical character to our experience (as discussed in previous chapters) and to radical political movements. But this critical character, as I said in Chapter 5, is also necessary for phenomenology itself. As such, a phenomenological politics is not simply one way that phenomenology is applied in a particular discipline, but it speaks to the heart of phenomenology's self-understanding at this moment, much the way phenomenological psychology did in the early years of phenomenology's unfolding. For this to be the case, and for this politics to remain robustly phenomenological, *it must maintain a transcendental dimension* if it is to explore the various relationships of constitution, institution, and expression that exist between (communal) subjectivity and individual subjects. It must maintain a dual focus on the ways in which subjects and subjectivity are constituted within the community, and the ways in which the community is constituted by the actions of subjects.

For Husserl, this dual focus manifested itself in the need to distinguish between community and culture. Community is the name for the habits and styles—the manner of subjectivity—inculcated within people who share that community. Culture, on the other hand, names "the objective accomplishments of this community" (TSO, 161),[35] including, perhaps, individual persons as subjects. For a community is expressed only in and through the individuals that make up that community, individuals with certain kinds of traits, habits, characteristics—with a certain "style." Hence, we can say that we only learn of the community via an analysis of the individual people within it, much like we only learn of transcendental structures via an analysis of empirical phenomena. To construe such individuals as cultural objects, we would have to take them as "spiritual products" expressing a "spiritual meaningfulness," since culture, as we saw already in Chapter 2, is accomplished in and through the "things" it produces (pieces of writing, scientific theorems, artistic creations, "houses, bridges, tools, works of art, and so on"; Hua 8, 151), things that have a "spiritual" meaningfulness (Hua 9, 111; 118; 384; Hua 4, 236) that is necessarily expressed in and through them (Hua 9, 112). Insofar as an individual person's "character" or "style" is "given to them" by their spiritual community (Hua 1, 135; Hua 6, 270), we can, I think, take that individual to be a "spiritual product," expressing the "spiritual meaningfulness" found in its character or style in and through itself as an individual subject.

Expressivity is therefore central to both community and culture. The significance of this should not be lost on us now. It helps us see that, *qua* expression, culture is both constituted by the community (that it expresses) and constitutive of that community (as the alterations wrought by its expressions alter the community that is expressed). Maintaining this relationship between community and culture—a relationship that parallels the relationship between subjectivity and subjects—is essential both to getting a properly transcendental account of phenomenological politics and to differentiating Husserl's account of spiritual community from Hegel's (see TSO, 161–62): whereas Hegel sees communities being transformed or changed primarily through the activity of remarkable individuals "who appear to draw the impulse of their life from themselves," but who are actually following some secret demands of the world-spirit,[36] Husserl sees communal change happening through the activities of the community as a whole (Hua 27, 22), that is to say, from the community in its subjective orientations and activities or from how the community constitutes its subjects to be subjective. For Husserl, this account of communal renewal requires the clarification of a *social ethics*, which he defines as "the ethics of communities *as* communities" (Hua 27, 22). But, *qua* community, this ethics applies to the habits and styles it inculcates in people. That is, it applies as much, or more, to its constitution of a certain manner of subjectivity as it does to its cultural productions. Social ethics are, then, about how a community sets up subjectivity in its relation to the world; it is about sensings and intentionality itself, and not simply about collective productions (like an orchestra or a sports team) or "collective intentionality."

Social ethics, then, becomes a division or subdiscipline of phenomenological politics. Its object of study would include what we call "social conditioning" and not simply "social agreement."[37] That is, it would pertain to "collective behavior[s] which do not rely, at least explicitly, on active acceptance or common agreement" but which still "define and structure our common life" (TSO, 151) through "passive habituation, through our entanglement with all sorts of habits and conventions"[38] of which we may or may not be consciously aware. Thinking this social conditioning in a phenomenological manner allows us to focus on the dual constitution inherent in the expressive relations between individual subjects and communal subjectivity or between cultural objects and the community, rather than see them as wholly one-sided (the imposition of a "cultural ideology" or "political unconscious"[39] on subjects, for example). This helps us avoid the problem of cultural determinism, and hence it opens a way of investigating subjective generation that avoids the dilemma of subjective autonomy or causal determinism.

This new mode of phenomenological political investigation, in turn, can help us approach contemporary sociopolitical questions in a new way: structural oppression, for example, must be understood as a type of intrasubjective habit or "style" that is constitutive of individuals within certain communities even as it shapes both the cultural accomplishments and the ongoing unfolding of that community.[40] Racism or sexism, therefore, are not simply matters either of social structures that must be reorganized (for example, juridically or legally) or of individual, volitional choices or decisions. Rather, both individual choices and social structures are themselves expressive of a deeper "spirit" at work in the community, shaping that community in a myriad of ways that cannot be fixed simply by changing the political or legal frameworks in which we operate or by encouraging changes in people's thought processes or decision making. Of course, changing the political and legal frameworks and/or altering people's decision making could both be important steps in the process of altering the spiritual community, but they are not sufficient to tackling the problem of structural oppression, insofar as they don't get to its (phenomenological) "root." As mentioned, to fight against oppression at its root, we must "transform the cultural representations and values that shape and structure our experiences" (FE, 49). The struggle against oppression is a struggle not simply against culture (i.e., against particular "objective accomplishments") but against certain types of community itself—not simply against certain phenomena, but against certain "styles" of phenomenalization—because oppression, phenomenologically understood, is not primarily a structural problem or an individual problem but a spiritual problem, shaping the very constitution of individual habits and styles within a community.[41]

Judith Butler arguably comes to a similar conclusion, albeit in less phenomenological language, in *The Force of Nonviolence*.[42] There, she calls for a "new political imaginary" (FNV, 11) or "social imaginary" (FNV, 14) that acknowledges that "the self is constituted through its relations with others" such that the self is "defined" by its "social ties" (FNV, 9): "whoever I am will be steadily sustained and transformed by my connections with others" (FNV, 200). This is a profound reorientation of politics, calling us to come to terms with our "reliance on social and material structures and on the environment" (FNV, 41) in a way that challenges the autonomous subject and, perhaps, the whole neoliberal political economy that goes with it. But to truly appreciate this, we must understand the depth of the problem: violence is not merely an empirical problem but functions as "an attack on the structure of being" (FNV, 138),[43] an "attack on [social] 'bonds'" or "interdependency" that is "more fundamental" than the "attack on persons," precisely because "Singularity and distinctness . . . constitute differentiating characteristics of beings who are defined and sustained by virtue of their interrelationality" (FNV, 16).

It is that interrelationality—occurring at a (phenomenological?) level prior to individuation—that is being threatened, and that we must, in turn, protect. Hence, Butler calls us to think of nonviolence also on this "deeper" (or transcendental) level, as a positive account of "what obligations we have to preserve the life of the other or others" (FNV, 104). We are then encouraged not simply to "preserve" or "secure the life that already is," but to "safeguard" the "conditions for the possibility of a life to become livable, perhaps even to flourish" by securing and reproducing "the conditions of becoming, of living, of futurity, where the content of that life, that living, can be neither prescribed nor predicted, and where self-determination emerges" (FNV, 94). In the phenomenological vocabulary we have been developing in this work, we can read this as a call to preserve the (transcendental) conditions that enable the flourishing of all forms of life—that makes all lives "grievable," in Butler's language.[44] For if subjects are the products of culture in the way outlined earlier, they are necessarily constituted in relations to others (via subjectivity and spirit) and necessarily caught up with cultural "infrastructures" that they rely on, for both biological and subjective life. Hence, safeguarding those conditions and infrastructures for all forms of life is necessary for true social equality, "a version of social equality that does not rely on the reproduction of individualism" (FNV, 147) or other neoliberal presuppositions, but which can account for the generation of subjectivity and subjects in various actual conditions.

All of this seems to resonate with the expressive account of individual subjects as the expression of particular spiritual communities that are actualized within the differentiating processes of expressive flesh that we are outlining here. The relation between community and culture therefore helps explain the relationship between subjectivity and subjects, and its clarification may prove helpful for the type of radical political movements that Butler encourages.[45] But for phenomenological politics to be helpful in approaching such issues, it must necessarily be focused on the transcendental function of the "transcendental we." Doing so will help us better understand the relation between subjectivity, communities (transcendental and social/empirical), and individual subjects. For if it is, in fact, the case that "my life and the life of another do not merely exist, each for themselves; rather, one is 'directed' toward the other" (Hua 11, 343), then the nature of subjectivity itself is inherently political. But this sense of politics is itself a matter of sense, of a sensing (Chapter 2) that provides a direction or orientation in the world before it is differentiated into distinct meanings (Chapter 3). This orientation, in turn, actualizes phenomena (including, perhaps, individual subjects as phenomena) that necessarily express a transcendental axis (Chapter 4) that we can access via phenomenological reflection on our first-person perspective (Chapter 5).

The "phenomenological knot" at the core of subjectivity therefore is not primarily individual but political. In a use of the phrase that threatens to undermine our entire understanding of "monad," Husserl claims that "in their absolute being, the monads *are dependent*" (Hua 14, 268). But we can now see that this mode of dependence is, perhaps, akin to the "pre-established harmony" of Merleau-Ponty and of Leibniz (at least of De-leuze's Leibniz), a harmony that is indexed to the differential relation of expressivity. It is only, then, through an understanding of expressivity as a phenomeno-logic that we can make sense of the (political) nature of subjectivity and the (political) processes whereby that (political) subjectivity generates subjects.

Conclusion
The Logic of Phenomenality

The foregoing analysis of expressivity in phenomenology has shown us that the core of experience is a tangled knot of knowing, being, doing, and *politeia*, and that phenomenology provides us a unique way of untangling that knot by articulating differentiations that are initially experienced as a unity. This knot is constantly weaving, unweaving, and reweaving itself as it is expressed in experience, and both subjects and subjectivity are caught up in this autopoietic unfolding of experience, relativized to a spiritual sense that they constitute even as they are constituted by it.

We have therefore addressed the two major theses of the book: that expressivity is central to the (political) core of experience and to phenomenology as the best way to explain and clarify that core. This, in turn, enabled us to prove three major claims: first, political questions can never be entirely separated from our understanding of (human) experience; second, phenomenology remains an essential methodological tool for understanding "political" questions as they pertain to experience; and third, every transcendental claim concerning "human experience" is never fully separable from particular empirical circumstances. Insofar as experience necessarily requires recourse to subjective processes (the seer who sees the seen in visibility, the toucher who touches the touched in tactility, etc.) and insofar as subjectivity—as a mode of sensing the world—is necessarily constituted (*politeia*) within communities that are simultaneously empirically situated and transcendentally operative, experience is necessarily political. And because the true (expressive) nature of *politeia* can only be brought to light via the phenomenological reduction that alone reveals the transcendental dimension of experiencing, phenomenology is necessary to understand the full range of "political" significance. Finally, because descriptions of that transcendental dimension are performed by subjects that have been constituted within particular empirical circumstances that shape their very subjectivity, those descriptions always "make sense" within particular *Stiftungen* that they simultaneously reinforce and reinscribe or reform.

The preceding chapter's call for a "phenomenological politics," then, was a call to both phenomenology and politics and an argument for their necessary intertwining: radical politics requires the kind of acknowledgment and transformation of the transcendental conditions of experiencing that phenomenology makes possible, even as phenomenology requires certain accounts of the relation between subjectivity and world that come to light most explicitly (in our current contexts) in the type of work that is often called "political" (e.g., critical race theory, feminism, queer theory, disability studies, etc.). It should also be clear that such discourses are not actually any more "political" than, say, formal epistemology or modal logic, which also presume certain understandings of subjectivity, its relationship to individual subjects and to communities, the relationship between transcendental functions and empirical conditions, and so on. Phenomenology does not become political when it engages the issues of critical phenomenology; rather, engaging the issues of critical phenomenology has enabled phenomenologists to recognize the political nature of experience that was always already operative in experiencing itself.

If I have accomplished the aims of the book as set out in the Introduction, it may be beneficial to clarify briefly here, in the Conclusion, one final element of the analysis. In this work, I was endeavoring to show that the political nature of subjectivity is a transcendental necessity of experience itself when experience is understood as operating according to a logic of expression. For all we have accomplished so far, I have still not adequately thematized the "logic" of expression. Granted, in clarifying the account of expressivity, I have tried to articulate the logic of phenomenality itself: that phenomenality drives itself forward by way of an expressive force that pushes it into ever-new expressions while simultaneously opening it to a particular kind of reflection that enables us to understand all phenomena better by clarifying their nature as (entangled) phenomena. This is a particular kind of logic (one I have described as generative rather than static or genetic), and its central mechanism is an autopoietic differentiating movement that must necessarily coordinate two things within a (particular kind of) unity.

But this logic holds a tension necessarily at work in its heart, a tension that can manifest as an apparent contradiction leading to a number of problems if we are not careful in how we "make sense" of this logic. It is the tension between the simultaneous necessity of differentiation and unity within the "auto" of phenomenality's autopoietic unfolding, and properly understanding this tension is crucial for all we have established so far. For if we fail to appreciate *how* (and not simply *that*) experience can be at once both individual and communal, both prereflectively "lived-through" and reflectively "understood," we threaten to misunderstand both the entire relationship between transcendental and empirical that emerged here with our emphasis on expressivity, and the relation between identity and difference when it comes to "selves," which we should now understand as applying not just to subjects but to any and all individual phenomena (as "things themselves").

At stake in this difficulty in understanding both elements of experience, therefore, is an issue that is at once both practical and theoretical. Practically, it manifests itself in several methodological issues we have already highlighted, issues that make it hard for (transcendental) phenomenology to be understood by those working outside of that tradition. While this is often taken to be simply a problem of linguistic or conceptual expression, whereby it is claimed that those working in the phenomenological (or post-phenomenological; see FE, 105–8) tradition of philosophy simply use— some might say abuse—language in a way that is unnecessarily vague in their articulation of claims, and so render their claims difficult to understand, our analysis of expressivity as the logic of phenomenality helps us situate the problem of clear linguistic or conceptual expression in a broader (phenomeno) logical context—one that requires us to pay further attention to the distinction between a logic of predication and a logic of sensings mentioned briefly in Chapter 4. For if sense is primarily a differentiated sensing, then its clear articulation requires an articulation of that differentiated nature in a way that may not fit well with the subject-predicate structure common to most Western grammars. That is to say, clearly articulating the "things themselves" is (logically) complicated when the "auto," the "self" of those selves, is not simply self-identical but is generatively and differentially constituted. By relativizing phenomena to sense/sensing, expressivity roots phenomena (including both subjects and objects) in experience itself, rather than root experience in subjects. But making sense of such experience requires recourse to some unity (e.g., flesh) that precedes differentiation (e.g., into subject and object or self and other). Therefore, the autopoiesis of the "logic" of phenomenality requires an "auto" that is a unity preceding differentiation, even as it also seems to require a differentiation that goes "all the way down."

To avoid this becoming an outright contradiction, we must highlight the importance of an expressive account of "logical" relationships: expressivity is a differential relating (i.e., express*ing*) rather than a means simply of translating one relata (e.g., a thought or idea as the "expressed") into the medium of another relata (e.g., linguistic communication as the "expression"). I have tried to articulate such an account of expressivity in the present work: expressivity as the force forming a phenomenal unity (that is not a unity of identity) between asymmetrical elements and not simply expression as another (proto)phenomenon. But we need precise clarification on the nature of the "logic" of phenomenality that I am laying out here: without careful attention to how we are "making sense" of expressivity as a logic, we risk confusions that will have ontological, epistemological, practical, and political implications.

Expressivity as Phenomeno-logic: The How of Phenomenality

Let us begin by outlining the "logic of phenomenality" at work in our account of expressivity thus far. In short, I have been arguing that expressivity is the "logic," the operative "how," by which phenomenality works: phenomenality simply is the coordinated and generative unity of asymmetrical elements such that what happens with one element necessarily affects the other. This logic, as I hope I have made clear, is not accomplished or performed by something outside itself but functions as a self-unfolding process of autopoiesis. One significant outcome of this has been the clarification that phenomenality (or experiencing) precedes subjectivity: subjectivity is a phenomenon before and so that it can be an instrument constituting phenomenality. This is just to say that the logic of phenomenality is not something wholly controlled or performed by subjects, but rather subjects are performances of phenomenality: we are instruments of this logic before we are its practitioners.

In this regard, we can see that the "logic" of phenomenality must necessarily explain how subjects are able to constitute phenomena (as Husserl tries to explain), but also how subjectivity is constituted (as Merleau-Ponty explains) and how subjects are generated (both actualized and individuated) in relation to subjectivity. All of these remain, essentially, questions relevant to the logic of phenomenality.

Beginning to answer these questions requires a clarification of the type of unity this generative logic forms. I have called this unity a phenomenal unity, rather than an ontological, identical, or substantial one, and have discussed "flesh" as a prototypical example of this unity. This unity is best understood as a certain kind of innate movement that is inherently productive or generative: an unfolding or process that in Greek is referred to as *poiesis*. Such a poietic movement can necessarily be looked at in two different ways. Internally differentiated in and through its differentiations into various individual (though entangled) phenomena, this unity, when looked at in one way, is seen as a process or movement that *qualifies* the whole (in the case of flesh, qualifies it as expressive, that is, as held in differential relationship and not simply as identical); looked at in another way, it is seen as distinct things that can be *quantified*, sorted, distinguished, compared, and so forth. Its self-unfolding is precisely its act(s) of differentiation, which simultaneously make it itself and a collection of different things. We saw this dual (though unified) movement already in Chapter 1 with its discussion of expressivity as an express*ing* of express*ions*: the movement of expressing is internally characterized (or qualified) as expressive insofar as it produces (quantitatively distinct) expressions, each of which (we saw in Chapter 4) can be understood both as itself (on its own terms as a distinct phenomenon) and insofar as it is part of the (same) expressive movement. The two are not wholly separable: an expression is an expression only insofar as it expresses, that is, is part of the movement of expressing, and expressing is only expressing insofar as it generates expressions. It is only in our reflection that we can distinguish between these: distinguish, for instance, a particular phenomenon from the alterations it makes to the entire context and structures by which I "make sense" of the world. That is, it is only in subjective experience that the two movements, the two types of processes at work in the phenomenal unity, can be distinguished.

Saying that subjectivity is not primary for phenomenality is not to say, therefore, that it is not necessary or not significant. Subjectivity is crucial for phenomenality, insofar as subjectivity is the type of differentiation within flesh that allows for the type of thinking (reflection) that enables us to distinguish between the two movements of experience's unfolding, between a quality (as subjective, as objective, as touched, as visible, etc.) and the various quantitative individuals or things that express that quality (e.g., subjects, objects, things touched, things seen, etc.). *Qua* expression of flesh, subjectivity is therefore necessarily doubly coordinated with flesh: on the one hand, it is able to access flesh—in all its qualitative and quantitative differentiations—in the unique (reflective) mode characteristic of subjectivity; on the other hand, it remains part of the unfolding of flesh such that the very expressing of subjectivity in its various expressions is necessarily an alteration within flesh (both qualitatively and quantitatively: expressions of subjectivity affect both the other qualities of flesh, such as objectivity, tactility, visibility, etc., and the other quantities of flesh, such as discrete objects, tactile or visible things, etc.). Because subjectivity is both a unique (and significant) mode of accessing flesh and is itself an unfolding of flesh, we can say that there is a "subjectivity" to objectivity, to tactility, to visibility, and so on. That is, objects are necessarily given to be understood objectively, the tactile is able to be touched, the visible able to be seen, and the like, just as subjectivity is necessarily also objective, tactile, visible, and so forth—that is, subjectivity is always embodied subjectivity.

This last point is crucial to our understanding of subjectivity (and of Merleau-Ponty's work in general). It is not the case simply that *subjects* are embodied (i.e., that any particular nexus of subjectivity is necessarily individualized in a body), but that *subjectivity* itself is a particular embodiment of flesh, a way of engaging the world that has emerged as a unique expression of flesh. *Qua* expression of flesh, subjectivity operates in both movements of flesh, simultaneously the means by which flesh is able to reflect, in various ways (perception, imagination, idealization, etc.), on the qualities and quantities of itself-as-flesh, and a distinct quality (as opposed to visibility, tactility, etc.) that can also itself be differentiated (into this subject or that subject, in this *Stiftung* or that one, etc.).

We can see, then, a rapid multiplying of expressivity at work in the logic of phenomenality: subjectivity is an expression of flesh, in and as it is itself expressed in subjects; those subjects in turn can express themselves in various acts that are also expressions of the various qualitative expressions of flesh (e.g., visibility, tactility, etc.), each of which is implicated in and by all the other qualitative expressions (e.g., there is subjectivity and tactility to visibility, etc.).[1] This interimplication of the qualitative expressions ensures that each quality of flesh is expressed in and by *Stiftungen* that, *qua* modes of communal living, are necessarily expressions (of the spiritual communities in which they emerge) that shape the habits and tendencies— the "spiritual life"—of subjects generated within those communities, and *qua* modes of culture, are expressed in concrete, individual instances. In this regard, subjectivity expresses itself, not only in concrete subjects, but also in "cultural expressions," (both *Stiftungen* and concrete phenomena) that are themselves essentially subjective (i.e., tied to subjectivity) without being subjects.[2]

The relation between a quality and its quantitative individuation is therefore expressive in this account of the logic of phenomenality. This opens us to see individuals as the expressive coordinates of qualities, and not as the ontological products of qualities and some other metaphysical attribute (e.g., form and matter, substance and accidents), the "owners" of various properties (color, texture, etc.), or the "subjects" of various predicates. In this regard, what we take to be "individuals" can be understood as particular nexuses of various qualitative expressions: we may choose to speak, not of the individual tree that happens to be green and hard and biotic, but rather of various qualities—of greening (or coloring or visibility) and hardening (or tactility) and biotizing (or growing)—that happen to have come together, in this particular moment, in and as that individual tree.[3] When quantities express qualities rather than qualities qualifying individuals, we move to a logic of sensing from a logic of predication.[4]

This "logic of sensing" names something essential to the expressive logic of phenomenality: that subjectivity neither precedes and conditions the world it engages, nor is entirely distinct from it, but rather is in a kind of mutually coordinating contact with the world. In Chapter 3, I discussed this in terms of the mutual reversibility of sensings: I touch the world even as I am touched by the world. My "touching" of the world is inseparable from my being-touched, insofar as both are expressive of the "world" of tactility. And that world, as we saw in the discussion of *The Visible and the Invisible* in Chapter 5, is itself inseparable from the "world" of vision, of sensibility, of linguisticality, and so on. That is, sensings are mutually reversible in precisely the double sense just articulated for the logic of phenomenality: the reversibility of distinct quantities (e.g., touching-touched) and also the reversibility of qualities (tactility-visibility, visibility-linguisticality, etc.). This double reversibility then leads to a fourfold series of interactions that the logic of sensing tries to account for: how qualities (or sensings as modes of phenomenality) affect other qualities, how qualities affect quantities (or phenomena), how quantities affect other quantities, and how quantities affect qualities.

This fourfold series of interactions was considered under the language of "affectivity" in Chapters 2 and 3. There, affectivity referred to the subject's being touched by the world both passively, as a being-affected by things in the world (i.e., as intentionality, in its broadest phenomenological sense as discussed in Chapter 5), and quasi-actively, as the "feelings" or "tendencies" (Hua 11, 149–50) by which subjects engage the world primordially (i.e., I am affected this way or that way by this thing). These "tendencies" are pregiven to subjects within social horizons and spiritual communities, via the "spiritual meaning" (Hua 39, 427; see also Hua 9, 111, 118, 384, 408; Hua 4, 236) given to phenomena produced as "spiritual products" (Hua 6, 270) and via the "character" that marks the spirit at work in a particular community (Hua 1, 135; Hua 6, 270). As such, these affective tendencies are the expression of subjectivity unique to a particular spiritual community, and so are always already political (Chapter 6). Affectivity, as our primordial engagement with the world, is therefore necessarily political (in the sense of *politeia*) and generative (i.e., generating and generated): it was not simply the case that communities shape subjectivity, but also that subjective activities (and their cultural products) shape spirit and spiritual communities. As such, this affectivity, *qua* spiritual expression, is not only a being-affected, but also an affecting: sensings do not simply "take in" the world, but genuinely engage subjectivity with the world in an engagement that ultimately alters the entire expressive context. That is, the "affecting" of affectivity is not simply a property of subjects that affects the conditions of appearing for those subjects, but it is an affecting of what appears. The generative nature of expressivity therefore renders phenomenality, which operates by this expressive logic, an essential coordination of appearing and appearances: phenomenality is not simply a "making manifest" or "letting show up" that which is otherwise unaffected by its appearing,[5] but is an ongoing affection that affects both the (transcendental) conditions of appearing and the (empirical) actuality of appearances. This affective functioning is not simply a collection of two distinct movements or elements (a being-affected and an affecting)—a combination of two distinct properties that accrue to the same subject—but is the essential coordination or intertwining (*Verflechtung*) of those two movements such that the being-affected is itself always already an affecting, and vice versa.

The logic of sensing, therefore, is necessarily concerned with affecting as a being-affected and vice versa. Insofar as the being-affected is itself an affecting, such that the affecting necessarily alters the conditions of the being-affected, causing new affections that, in turn, alter the conditions again, thereby causing new affections, and so forth, the dual nature of the logic of phenomenality cannot be separated from its ongoing force of generativity. As such, there is a necessarily self-altering character to phenomenality's generativity: it is not simply the case that phenomena can be generative of other things, given the right conditions, but that phenomenality itself is driven, by its own logic (which, again, is not a set of rational principles but the fundamental "how" of its operation), to new affections, new coordinations of being-affected and affecting. In this regard, phenomenality is the self-affection by which phenomena generate new phenomena by and within the logic of phenomenality. Subjectivity is a crucial and necessary element of that generativity—but it remains part of the generative movement of phenomenality itself, and not something distinct from it. This is crucial to the very nature of subjectivity itself.

Language and the Difficulties in Expressing Expression

Having outlined the logic of phenomenality, we can see why we must think more clearly about what it means to "make sense." Given the generative nature of phenomenality, the logic of phenomenality yields a notion of sense—as sensings—that is necessarily both productive and a product, both generating and generated, both constituting and constituted.[6] To "make sense" in this fashion is, therefore, not simply to create something (i.e., "sense" or an idea) that is distinct from the process of its creation (as an idea is thought to be distinct from the act of thinking which creates it), but rather to engage in a particular way of altering phenomenality (ideally, linguistically, conceptually, etc.).

The significance of this for how we "make sense" of things philosophically quickly becomes clear: because of the duality of its generative nature, "making sense" never merely describes the world "as it is," but always (at least infinitesimally) alters the world, in and through the very process of "making sense" of it. This is doubly true when we begin to try to "make sense" of how we make sense: the way that we linguistically account for (i.e., talk about) sense/sensings, and perhaps especially the way we talk about the particular sensing of linguisticality, necessarily affects our understanding of all the other sensings and of the logic that governs them, and so the way we linguistically account for sense/sensings alters how we are (how we live, what we do, etc.) in the world.[7] *Qua* sensing, linguisticality is coordinated with all the other sensings, as (qualitative) expressions of flesh.[8] This coordination implies that alterations to linguisticality will necessarily alter its relation to those other sensings, and therefore alter those other sensings themselves. And since any particular linguistic expression (any determinate phrase or article by which we try to explain how we "make sense") will, *qua* expression, necessarily alter the linguistic conditions of its own expression (alter the linguistic conventions within a particular academic *Stiftung*, but also alter the conventions of the language it is written in, the social settings it is written in, etc.), the words we say and the language we use will necessarily change and alter the world we inhabit. The expressive logic of phenomenality therefore helps us see that how we talk changes what we talk about at least as much as what we talk about changes how we talk.

The question of "making sense" of the logic of phenomenality is, therefore, both a practical and theoretical question: How do we articulate the logic of phenomenality adequately,[9] if every articulation will necessarily alter both the expressed and its expressions? This question does not arise (at least with anywhere near the same force) if I think of "making sense" and linguistic expression according to the logic of predication: if I assume I can linguistically express my sense, Y, straightforwardly in a proposition, Z, then there is no theoretical problem of linguistic expression to consider, and the only thing to worry about is expressing Y clearly enough that everyone who hears Z will know Y. If, however, I assume that my articulation of Y as Z will necessarily alter the expressive conditions, X, in a way that does not simply add Z to X but alters all the relationships within X, and, as such, perhaps even alters the "meaning" of Y itself in X, then the problem of linguistic expression becomes a theoretical problem, and not simply the more practical problem of being clear. For if it is not simply my expression of Y as Z that might be unclear, but rather the very position or sense of Y itself within X, given my expression of it as Z, then the question of clarity becomes tied quite closely to the articulation of the differential equation that measures the rate of change caused by the differential relation. That is, the only way to be clear about what I want to express (Y) is to attempt to express the precise ways in which my expressing Y necessarily alters Y and its future expressions: I can only be clear about Y by articulating Y's generativity and not simply its "meaning."

Perhaps an example will help clarify this point further. In Chapter 1, I articulated a related point in terms of my friendliness (the expressed, Y) being expressed via the act of smiling at a coworker as we pass in the hallway (Z) within a particular context (X, which includes contemporary social mores, rules about workplace behavior, the feelings I have for my coworker and other people, things going on in my life and my coworker's life, etc.). The point being made here, then, is that in smiling at my coworker I'm not only hoping that my act of smiling is properly expressing my friendliness toward them (the only issue at work in a logic of predication), but I am also concerned with the way that friendliness and the broader social context (X) are altered by my act of smiling at a coworker: I must be clear not just about how my smile expresses my friendliness but also how that friendliness is altered, within the broader social context, by my smiling at my coworker. Expressing my friendliness doesn't *just* express my friendliness, it also changes it and, with it, the whole context I share with my coworker. Hence, I must be clear on both how my smiling expresses my friendliness and how my friendliness is being altered within that particular context by that smiling. Both are essential to "understanding" the situation; my action cannot be evaluated (for its clarity) simply based on what my smile means in the context of expressing my friendliness, it must also be evaluated for how that friendliness is situated in the various parts of my life. And this can be addressed only if we look not simply at my friendliness but at friendship as the differential relationship that generates and determines both my friendliness and the particular acts by which I express it.

This example perhaps takes on a more recognizable urgency if we change the particular means of expressing my friendliness (Z) from "smiling at a coworker" to "speaking appreciatively of their appearance" or "giving a hug." The latter are, no doubt, appropriate expressions of friendliness *within certain friendships*—but not within all. So, if I am very good friends with my coworker and we have known each other for a long time, perhaps I could express that friendliness by saying I think he looks good in those pants or giving him a hug. But if I have only recently met my coworker, and we are, at this stage, more "work friends" than "friend friends," then both of those are almost certainly inappropriate expressions of friendliness within the confines of the rate of change that is marked by the term "friendship." Simply looking at whether a particular action is an expression of friendliness ("but I often hug my friends") fails to account for the generativity that comes with expressivity, and which measures the relationship that is always unfolding and changing as the actions by which I express my friendliness change that friendliness, and so open up new and different possibilities of expressing it.

Accounting for the relationship that this relationship (friendship) itself has with other possible expressive relationships within my experiencing of the world further complicates the issue. For my friendship is not the only relevant relationship at work in our example. Since it is precisely a coworker I am smiling at, in the context of the workplace, my friendliness and its expressions are also marked by other conditions in the broader context of that exchange: social mores for workplace settings ("professionalism"), for example, are also a relevant force determining the relationship between my friendliness and its expressions. Hence, it is also possible that a certain expression (e.g., commenting on their appearance) that might clearly express my friendliness—even within the confines of my friendship with that particular coworker (let's say someone I've known and been good friends with for years)—might nevertheless be inappropriate insofar as our friendship is here deployed in the contexts of workplace professionalism and cultural diversity that also alter that friendship and its expressions: our friendship is here differentially related to the professionalism that creates a positive working environment for *all* coworkers, and not just the two of us. Making sense of my comment, therefore, cannot look solely at what it "means"; it must account also for its expression within the differential relationship of our friendship, and for our friendship's intertwining with other differential relationships at play in the expressive power of that particular action.[10]

This reassessment of "sense" (as generative sensing) therefore moves us beyond an equation of sense with what a subject "means to say," insofar as our conscious intention (which we saw in Chapters 5 and 6 must be distinguished from the broader notion of intentionality as an openness on to the world) is only one part of subjectivity (a part that is itself an expression in several ways: of my subjectivity, of the spiritual community in which I was generated as a subject with particular habits and tendencies, of the life-world in which I function as this particular subject, etc.), and subjective intention is only one part of language's expressiveness (language expresses what the subject "means to say," but it also expresses the linguistic context of the subject, the styles and habits constitutive of the subject's spiritual community, etc.). Because expressivity is rapidly multiplying, via various types and levels of expressive relationships, sense, like phenomenality in general, can no longer be governed by the will of a subject,[11] but by the expressive logic that we are trying to articulate via a logic of sensing.

This alteration of sense (as sensing) is difficult to note or explain within a linguistic logic that, like those of most Western languages, presumes a subject-predicate structure in which certain claims are predicated of stable subjects. For if expressivity requires a logic of sensing that is distinct from a logic of predication, but the very linguistic structure available to articulate phenomenality itself presumes a predicate structure, then it may not be possible to articulate expressive claims properly within that language.[12] But then it would seem that the claims of an expressive logic could never be adequately articulated within the languages of the phenomenological tradition. Indeed, such articulations would seem doomed to be nonsense or absurdity: is "the tree greens"[13] any less absurd than "green is or" (LI, 201)?

Phenomenology—but also, perhaps, the "radical political movements" that operate according to the same logic, as we noted in the last chapter—then find itself in a certain linguistic or linguistically expressive bind: does it try to articulate itself in a language consistent with a logic of sensing, a language that would be more adequate to its subject matter, perhaps, and therefore to what it "wants" to express, but that threatens to be entirely misunderstood given the different logic at work in the linguistic structure available to it for "normal" statements of sense?[14] Or does phenomenology seek to translate its findings into a logic of predication, so as to be more easily understood, even if what is "understood" thereby is no longer adequate to the phenomena, or consistent with the phenomenal logic that phenomenology is trying to express?

The double bind of expressivity's linguistic expression therefore seems to leave those attuned to expressivity's phenomenal logic with two choices: either articulate claims clearly, in which case, they will not quite be adequate to the expressive claims they want to make; or, articulate those expressive claims adequately via nonpredicative language, which, given our current linguistic possibilities, often means poetically, through means of literature or even the purposeful use of nonsense,[15] in which case they will not be recognized as philosophically serious. In the former case, one's claims appear either trite, uninteresting, or miscast: "a psychological observation made to pass for logic,"[16] for example, or "assertions [that] are either false or trivial."[17] In the latter case, one appears to no longer be interested in philosophy as the pursuit of truth, but rather seems to be simply engaging in rhetoric, sophistry, or linguistic manipulation: a series of "semi-intelligible attacks upon the values of reason, truth and scholarship."[18]

This book has tried to articulate a "third way" that has sometimes been used historically to try to get out of this linguistic double bind. Chapter 4 talked about a method of "reading" or rereading the tradition, the *Stiftung*, in a critically transformative way. In this way, a person can attempt to trace the impacts of various means and modes of expression, in and across the contexts in which they are expressed. Via this method, sense is both "actualized in the present" and "continuously reborn in the transcendental field . . . thereby giving way to future actualizations."[19] We can call this method a differential approach, one rooted in calculus rather than poetry or literature, insofar as it seeks to show how expressing an expressive claim is not done primarily through a singular proposition or any one predication, but by tracing the alterations to the *Stiftung* made in and by any one expression.[20] By tracing the series of changes made through a *Stiftung* by one expression (be it the notion of expression in *Voice and Phenomenon* or the notions of "male" and "female" in Genevieve Lloyd's *The Man of Reason*) we can at least bring to light the "differential equation" governing the "sense" of that expression and its coordination to the expressed and to expressing, though it remains unclear whether we can articulate or express the equation itself, as such. Still, it is, perhaps, only in bringing attention to this equation that we can properly situate the "sense" of any one moment along the curve, precisely by seeing that it is not simply an individual point, but a moment (*this* particular moment) on a curve (*this* particular curve). Regardless, this method of critically transformative "reading" as a mode of expressing sense/sensing is methodologically rooted in the expressive logic of phenomenality, which is necessarily a genetic logic that operates by bringing to light the very relation that motivates or drives that generativity. We have said that this relation—expressivity—cannot be articulated simply in terms of a constant relationship between relata because it differentially determines its relata in and through its relation. As such, this is a logic premised on the calculus rather than on set theory, algebraic semantics, or other forms of mathematics, but it is a (mathematical) logic nonetheless.[21]

And this logic, we saw, underscores a new account of the relation between epistemology, ontology, qualities, and quantities. For whereas the logic of predication seems to deal with quantities as ontological (things have existence) and qualities as epistemological (they are conditions by which we know those things, whether or not those things "have" those qualities as ontological properties or not), the expressive logic of sensings at issue here does not simply reverse the relationships between quality, quantity, epistemology, and ontology but ties (or reties) them together in a particular way. Via the notion of coordinated sensings and their expression in a *Stiftung*, the logic of sensings necessarily intertwines knowing, being, and doing at the heart of phenomenality: phenomenality is an unfolding (doing) of the actualization of genetic conditions (both ontological and epistemological) that are altered (both ontologically and epistemologically) in their actualization in a way that necessarily leads to further unfolding. The concept of expressivity, therefore, is nothing short of a "recreating of logic and ontology" and epistemology, such that "being, knowing and acting or producing are measured and systematized by this concept."[22]

This recreation of the relation between logic, ontology, and epistemology is essential to phenomenality's expressive logic: "Being, knowing, and [doing] are the three forms of expression."[23] We encountered this already in Chapter 1, where we saw that expressivity, in its broadest form, simply is the coordination of expressed and expression via expressing (we could say, too: the coordination of knowing and being via doing). This need for a structural coordination of phenomenality is not new, but the mode of its coordination is: it was long presumed that the subject coordinated knowing and being via its own activities, be that transcendentally (in Kant), or by bringing its knowing in line with being (empiricism), or bringing being in line with its knowing (idealism). But in those explanations the coordination requires transcendence (of the subject) and distinction (between subject and world, between knowing and being, between phenomenal and noumenal). In expressivity, we have seen, the coordination is generative and differential, and therefore autopoietic.

And this autopoietic coordination of knowing, being, and doing manifests itself, we said, in sensings. Each sensing is a certain coordination of knowing, being, and doing: seer, seen, and seeing; toucher, touched, and touching; speaker, speech, and speaking; etc. This coordination, like all expressive coordinations, is not between fully distinct parts, but a coordinated relationship producing or generating its relata: the "act" of vision simply is a seer seeing a seen; the act of language simply is a speaker speaking speech (or a reader reading a read); the act of thinking simply is a thinker thinking thoughts. Each sensing is, therefore, to its core, the coordination of these three forms of expression, such that, in reflection, each sensing can be looked at in any one of these three ways, though in the sensing itself we experience only the unity of the three in the sensing. That is, each sensing is necessarily woven of the three strands of knowing, being, and doing, and the weaving of these three strands through all the sensings necessarily weaves the sensings themselves together into a kind of cloth or tapestry of human experience. Like Penelope's burial shroud, this tapestry is always being woven and rewoven, and the constant weaving ensures that not only the strands but also the distinct sensings are inherently connected and generative of each other.[24] This does not diminish the difference between them (tactility is still a distinct sensing from visibility, since each gives the world in a different way), but rather constitutes that difference: visibility is what it is, "in itself" so to speak, only in relation to the other sensings.

In this regard, the expressive logic necessarily entails that the "auto" of its autopoiesis is necessarily a differentiated "auto." If it is a "self," it is a self that is necessarily constituted or generated by its internal relations to its other: there is always an other "in" me (Derrida), a relation to an Other that is constitutive of any "me" (Levinas), an alterity that precedes and conditions the same.[25] The "things themselves" of phenomenology can only ever be an "in itself" after (and because) they are first constituted as "for each other," and all phenomena are necessarily entangled phenomena, including conscious subjects. This is necessary to the "logic" of phenomenality.[26]

Hence, the practical problem of the linguistic and conceptual expression of a logic of expressivity leads us necessarily to the theoretical problem of the differential nature of the conditions of phenomenality itself. This, in turn, helps us clarify that the phenomenological knot at the core of human experience is always tying, untying, and retying the strands of knowing, being, and doing in and as phenomenality itself. Any logic that would adequately articulate this must itself operate by a logic of sensing, attuned to the alteration and differentiation at stake in phenomena. Simple predication, relying as it does on stable and self-identical subjects, will not do.

Experience and the Relativization of Subjectivity and Objectivity

We have seen, then, that the individual cannot be strictly self-identical, even if it can be (reflectively) differentiated into the unique being that it is. In the logic of phenomenality, every "self" is always for-others and for the world, and so is "in itself" only tertiarily: announcing itself as distinct via sensings that are each internally differentiated and together are mutually differentiated and delimiting. This follows from our understanding of the core of experience as a constantly knotting tapestry.

But this constantly weaving core is a feature of experience itself, and not simply human or subjective experience. To understand that, we must understand more clearly the relationship between individual human beings, subjects, and subjectivity. This requires returning our attention (yet again) to the generation of the subject and of subjectivity and the corresponding triple relativization of the subject to sense.

The first step of attending to the generation of the subject is to remove its status as an absolute ground. *Qua* phenomenon, the subject can no longer be seen as that which creates or sustains phenomenality, as discussed in the first section of this chapter (and in Chapter 2). The subject is a phenomenon, insofar as it is doubly generated (as subjective and as *this* subject) within the expressive logic of phenomenality. But this does not entail that it is simply an object like other objects or a thing like other things. This should be obvious already in our characterization of it as a phenomenon: as a phenomenon, it is fundamentally entangled. And anything that is fundamentally entangled is, by necessity, not an object, if by "object" we mean something like a thing-in-itself (*Ding-an-sich*) that is what it is distinct from any essential relation to subjects or subjective actions. Yet, to posit something as a phenomenon is not, necessarily, to define it as a non-object. Quite the contrary: an object is a particular way of understanding or construing a phenomenon. As such, objectivity is a product of phenomenality and necessarily relativized to subjectivity, insofar as the processes of abstraction, idealization, and so on that are necessary to generate a phenomenon as an object are subjective processes that must be enacted by subjects. Objectivity is generated by subjective processes, themselves generated within the autopoietic unfolding of phenomenality.

This is not simply an epistemological claim that only subjects can know or understand objects as objects. Rather, it is a phenomenological claim that something's being an object is founded upon its first being a phenomenon encountered or "sensed" in a particular way by subjectivity: in actual experiential circumstances, objects are objects, strictly speaking, only as a subjective achievement, that is, as an actual achievement of actual beings within "what actually is." It is not the case, therefore, that a mountain or a molecule is really there *only* in its physical form or chemical composition. While the geological constitution of a mountain (its being made of particular elements formed together in particular ways) is "actual," so, too, is the mountain's offering beautiful views, its being a source of economic

activity for people living in the area, its status as a habitat for various spe-
cies and therefore its inclusion within a biosphere, and so on. All of this is
"actually" there in "what actually is," and therefore taking it *only* in its
chemical composition or its physical form is to abstract that one actual element from other actual elements for some purpose or other. This can be a
legitimate undertaking, done well and for good reasons. But it is, precisely,
an undertaking and an abstraction: something done or performed via various subjective functions acted out within, and according to, the logic of
phenomenality. To construe the mountain fundamentally as an object—
that is, as something distinct in its essence from subjects and subjective
activity—is something that is actually done by subjects performing subjective processes.[27]

What is true of objects is true also of subjects: construing "the subject"
as an individual entity—engaging with the world around it according to
its own whims, desires, volitions, and will—is also an abstraction of a certain kind, performed via subjective processes. This does not threaten the
actuality of the subject any more than it did the actuality of the object:
subjects actually do exist as individual entities with whims, desires, volitions, and will, but they also "actually" are expressions of a spiritual community, localized nexuses of sensings, and so on. Like with waves and
particles in physics, it is no more (nor any less) actual to talk of subjects as
distinct individuals than it is to talk of subjectivity as widely distributed
processes. The difference is a matter of perspective, of how they are taken.
In this regard, subjects are phenomena like any other phenomena in the
multifaceted nature of their actuality, equally qualitative and quantitative,
transcendental and empirical, expressed and expression. As such, they are
necessarily indexed, or relativized, to the sensing(s) by which they are engaged: engaging the subject or the mountain via visibility will yield a much
different experience (seeing the mountain) than engaging the subject or
the mountain via linguisticality (talking about the mountain), ideality
(thinking conceptually about the mountain), or any other sensing. And
given the way that experience is necessarily self-altering (an expression alters its conditions of expression, etc.) and composed of the knot of knowing, being, doing, and *politeia*, the different experiences yielded by the
various sensings not only offer a different epistemological exposure to the
"thing itself" but also fundamentally alter the subject, the phenomena, and
the relation between them in different ways: epistemologically, ontologically, praxically, and politically.

This, of course, is true of all phenomena. And though subjects are
phenomenal, they are nonetheless unique phenomena (as, perhaps, are all
phenomena, always generated in this context with these conditions, etc.).

Their uniqueness comes, we can see now, not in their engagement with subjective processes, but in the type of engagement they have with those processes: they can function as the subject, and not simply the object, of the various sensings (they can see, and not just be seen; they can speak, and not simply be spoken about).[28] As such, a subject can equally well be seen as a distinct individual, "possessing" its own traits, desires, whims, and the like, and as an accidental nexus of a series of processes (the subject function of subjective processes). Similarly, an object can equally well be seen as a distinct individual, "possessing" its own essential traits, and as an accidental nexus of a series of processes (the object function of subjective processes: the thing seen, the thing spoken about, etc.). Taking it one step further, a human being can be seen as a distinct individual with its own traits or as an accidental nexus of a series of processes, in which it sometimes actualizes the subjective function of subjective processes (it sees, it speaks, etc.), and sometimes actualizes the objective function of subjective processes (it is seen, it is spoken about, etc.).

Hence, the human subject is triply relativized: along with objects, it is necessarily indexed to subjectivity; subjectivity is necessarily indexed to sensings; and sensings are ultimately indexed to the expressive unity of flesh. This relativization to subjectivity, to sensings, and to flesh is the ultimate explanation of the relation between subjective conceptions and "objective" referents. It is accomplished via sensings, which necessarily engage the world in processes that are simultaneously subjective and objective (a seer and a seen) in a way that must be considered expressive: the seer sees the seen, the speaker speaks the spoken, and so on. The relativization of the subject to sense, therefore, fulfills the founding promise of the phenomenological *Stiftung*.

In doing so, it explains a phenomenality that necessarily encompasses subjectivity and is not merely created by it. As such, this phenomenality exceeds subjectivity.[29] Experience is not primarily the experience of a subject, or even subjective experience, but a kind of generative experiencing that exceeds both subject and object, subjective and objective functions. The phenomenological knot at the core of experience necessarily exceeds the human and the subjective: we do not tie the knot ourselves, but we ourselves are woven into its tapestry. The auto-affective or autopoietic nature of phenomenality does not refer to the "auto" or the "self" of the subject, or of subjectivity, or even of individual phenomena, but to the "auto" of phenomenality itself. It is not, therefore, a substantial auto-affection, the affection of a self-same substance, but a processual or poeitic auto-affection of affecting affects, of being-affected by and as affecting. It is, precisely, an auto-affection that precedes (and generates) the distinction between affected and affecting, between affects and their effects. To understand that auto-affection, then, we must study the relation of affectivity in itself and not primarily as the relation between a subject and its object. In this regard, auto-affectivity must be understood, in its primary sense, in a manner that does not require the genitive: it is not an affecting *of* something *by* something, but simply affectivity itself, prior to the distinction between the subject and object of affection, and generating that distinction out of its self-relation.[30]

In exceeding these things, auto-affective experience exceeds even the ability to distinguish or make distinctions: there can be no hetero-affectivity within auto-affectivity itself because the nature of its "auto" is such that there can be no "hetero." This necessarily follows from the excessive character of phenomenality itself. But there *can* be "hetero-"affection when it comes to subjectivity, and perhaps more specifically to consciousness as a process of subjectivity that enables the (reflective) distinction between self and other, subject and world. Hence, the type of affectivity by which something is affected by something else arises only with the generation of subjectivity, and once subjectivity is generated, it enables this new type of affectivity. But this type of (hetero-)affectivity is not true of experience as such, but only of subjective experience. Experience as such—experiencing as the constant (re)weaving of knowing, being, doing, and *politeia*—remains unified, not substantially nor ontologically but phenomenally.

The (Political) Logic of Phenomenality

We can now return to the problem announced at the beginning of this Conclusion, a problem that threatened to become an outright contradiction if we were not careful in how we "made sense" of the logic of phenomenality. Our analysis of expressivity in phenomenology has highlighted the "logic" that governs phenomenality and constantly generates it in an auto-poietic movement that is nothing other than phenomenality itself. Yet this very movement must be simultaneously differentiated and a unity that precedes distinction: it must necessarily be the "other in me" and the affectivity that precedes the distinction between self and other. We have marked the precise manner by which these two accounts can be held together as expressivity, that is, the phenomenal unity of coordinated and generative asymmetrical elements that are experienced as a unity but which can, upon later reflection, be differentiated. The two accounts are therefore held together within and as experiencing itself, and not by some act of the subject. We do not make this differentiated unity work—we "work" (as subjects) because of this differentiated unity.

We can understand this according to the logic of phenomenality if we are willing to conceive of that logic not as a conceptual logic (a logic that would govern simply the conceptual, linguistic, or ideal modes of sensing), but as a phenomeno-logic, a logic of phenomenality itself. The nature of such a logic can, perhaps, best be described as a logic of how things unfold in a way that is stable and self-altering, a way that is generative. In this sense, calling it the "logic of phenomenality" means both that it is the logic that pertains to phenomenality and that phenomenality is its mode of logicizing: it is phenomenal in both its mode of functioning and its realm of application. But these are, precisely, not two wholly distinct movements; they are tied together in the unity particular to phenomenality as the tying together of knowing, being, and doing. This unity, as the expressive coordination of the two movements, is what entails phenomenality's generativity: the unity of process, of an unfolding that leads to a quantitative unity of distinct individuals. These two unities are joined in and by the "logic of phenomenality."

This unity—a process that produces individuals that are not fully distinguishable from the processes that produce them—is simply the unity of experience, as I have said. But we can also now see that is thoroughly political. For in defining politics via *politeia* and not simply via the *polis*, the political is understood as that which is constitutive for a social body (what makes a particular community what it is) while also being that which is constituting that body (as a constituting force). It is the self-same movement that is simultaneously a constituting force and the "body" constituted by that force.

The fundamentally political nature of the logic of phenomenality appears especially clearly in regard to subjectivity as one of the processes generated within the phenomenal unity. Subjectivity is necessary for the unfolding of experience, insofar as it puts into play the full ramifications of the fourfold relations of influence between qualities and quantities. But subjectivity nevertheless remains part of that unfolding. That is to say, subjectivity is necessarily both transcendentally constitutive of particular conditions (i.e., those conditions would not be the same without the role that subjectivity plays) even as it is constituted within particular conditions (i.e., subjectivity is generated in particular ways within particular situations). These are not two distinct movements of subjectivity but rather constitute the phenomenal unity at the core of subjectivity itself: subjectivity is the generation within flesh that allows flesh to reflect upon itself transcendentally.

The "lived" component of subjectivity (as a unique quality of experience) is therefore necessary to a proper understanding of experience, for it is *qua* lived experience (*Erlebnis*) that the coordination of transcendental processes and individual phenomena is enacted or experienced by individual subjects: the logic of phenomenality is experienced subjectively as the lived character of experiencing, insofar as the "lived language of life itself" is the mode of accessing the "spontaneous self-expression" inherent to life (FE, 85). Paying attention to subjectivity in this way enables us to see new relations of influence between empirical conditions and particular quantities (i.e., distinct subjects, distinct phenomena) and between empirical conditions and particular qualities (i.e., how subjectivity, visibility, linguisticality, etc., work). This reveals that the "interpretive frame" that functions as the shared component of experience is also necessary to a proper understanding of experience—even as it cannot be wholly separated from the "lived" component of subjectivity (given the role of spiritual communities in the constitution of subjectivity). As such, both *Erlebnis* and *Erfahrung* are necessary for a full and robust understanding of experience.

When we pay attention to both of these elements in their fundamental intertwining in phenomenality itself, we see that experience is fundamentally altered, not simply by empirical conditions, but by the type of political constitution (*politeia*) that happens within the autopoietic unfolding of flesh (understood as expressive generativity). Since only phenomenology opens us to see and understand the transcendental dimension of that *politeia*, phenomenology is necessary to appreciating the political dimension of experience, not simply epistemologically (i.e., by understanding it) but also ontologically (i.e., by helping constitute the conditions—and hence also what they condition—as what they are through our critically transformative articulation of them) and practically, that is, by changing particular phenomena within particular contexts (subjects, laws, social institutions, etc.).

This is just to say, phenomenology is both necessarily (i.e., inherently, qualitatively) political and necessary for politics. But this is true only because experience itself is necessarily political and necessary for politics. The fundamental relation between experience and politics, therefore, must be articulated if we are to properly understand experience and politics. And this relation can only be articulated clearly by being attuned to the dynamic of expressivity that functions as the very logic propelling phenomenality itself. This dynamic is difficult to articulate clearly, but it is imperative—epistemologically, ontologically, practically, and politically—that we try.

Acknowledgments

There are many people who played roles in seeing this book written and published, many more than I will be able to mention here.

The students in my Foundations of Phenomenology class in Winter 2020 were very patient in working through an early (and very rough) draft of this book with me. The political ramifications of expressivity really emerged out of the conversations in that class. I'd like to thank Ian Admiraal, Anna Boessenkool, Amanda Ciezki, Erica Kath, Dawson Strand, Abigail Hofstede, Jueun Moon, Mark Standish, and Theoren Tolsma for those conversations and for their feedback and helpful suggestions. I'd also like to thank participants of all the conferences that have provided feedback on various elements of this project over the years, especially the Society for Phenomenology and the Human Sciences, the Society for the Phenomenology of Religious Experience, the Society for Existential and Phenomenological Theory and Culture, and the Back to the Things Themselves! workshop. All have put up with my talking about expression for the last several years. Thanks especially to Michael Barber, Olga Louchakova-Schwartz, and Nina Belmonte for their ongoing encouragement of my work.

Academically, I'd like to thank Gayle Solomon, for very helpful and enlightening feedback on an earlier draft of this book, and for (gently) pushing me in a direction I needed to go; Thomas Nail, for helping me see a bit of the bigger picture of what I was on to and for encouraging me to chase after it; Aaron Simmons, for encouraging me to speak with my own voice; Marie-Eve Morin, Christine Daigle, and Antonio Calcagno, for our summer reading group, and helping me work through Butler; Jay Worthy, for his dissertation on Merleau-Ponty; Richard Kearney, for all his support, encouragement, and advice over the years—and for the walks; Brian Treanor, for his friendship; Leonard Lawlor, for his constant support of this project, from its early infancy to now—and for dinner in Calgary; Ellie Anderson, for challenging me to think more about how Derrida fits into this project; and Crina Gschwandtner, for all the conversations and helpful clarifications.

Practically, I would not have been able to finish the book without the help of Anna Boessenkool and Erica Kath, who both worked as research assistants for this book at various stages. The book is immeasurably clearer and better than it would have been without their work, and I am very grateful for all they've done. I'm also very thankful for the knowledgeable assistance of Tom Lay, Katie Sweeney, Gregory McNamee, Eric Newman, and everyone at Fordham University Press for bringing this project to fruition. I also want to acknowledge the Social Sciences and Humanities Research Council of Canada (SSHRC), which supported my work (and phenomenology in Canada) through the Canada Research Chair in Phenomenology and Philosophy of Religion. I could not have written this book without the tangible support of the King's University, especially the department of philosophy, the faculty of arts, my deans (Arlette Zinck and William Van Arragon) and the VPARs (Hank Bestman and Kris Ooms), who provided me with teaching releases and dedicated research time so that I could finish this project.

Personally, this book was one of the hardest things I have ever written. Most of it was written during the COVID-19 pandemic, which was difficult on me, as it was on so many others. I would not have made it through without several friends and their support. Thank you to Jon Zeyl, Rebecca Warren, Jennifer Braun, Elizabeth Willson Gordon, Marie-Eve Morin, Nathan and Carrie Knysh, Sam and Stephanie Hofmeyer, Mark and Pauline Gurnett, Wes and Hazel Tovell, Gord and Laura Falk, Doug and Kari Siewert, Mark Troast, Scott Kreider, Jon Faber, and all the others who kept me (relatively) okay with their conversations, emails, texts, and Zoom calls. And, of course, thanks to Tanya, Hendrik, and Frankie, who had to put up with a distracted and cranky housemate these last two months as I finished revisions.

Finally, this book is dedicated to Mark Tazelaar, for helping me when I most needed it, and always pushing me and my career forward, often at his own expense. While I may be out of my element, I'd just like to say: "You're not wrong, Walter . . ."

Notes

Introduction: Experience and the Problem of Expression

1. For more on de Beauvoir as a phenomenological figure, cf. Sara Heinämaa, *Toward a Phenomenology of Sexual Difference: Husserl, Merleau-Ponty, Beauvoir* (Lanham, MD: Rowman & Littlefield, 2003).

2. Maurice Merleau-Ponty, *The Sensible World and the World of Expression: Course Notes from the Collège de France, 1953*, trans. Bryan Smyth (Evanston, IL: Northwestern University Press, 2020), cited in text as SWWE.

3. We can call this "asymmetrical" insofar as, while both elements are present, one is taken to be more worthy of our interest and attention, not simply accidentally, but by the nature of the expression itself: the expression functions, *qua* expressive, only by directing our attention through itself toward the expressed, thereby subordinating its own importance to that of the expressed. Marion's phenomenological analyses of the icon (as opposed to the idol) may prove relevant in this regard. See Jean-Luc Marion, *The Idol and Distance: Five Studies*, trans. Thomas A. Carlson (New York: Fordham University Press, 2001).

4. Donald A. Landes, *Merleau-Ponty and the Paradoxes of Expression* (London: Bloomsbury Academic, 2013), 10.

5. Cressida J. Heyes, *Anaesthetics of Existence: Essays on Experience at the Edge* (Durham, NC: Duke University Press, 2020), 29, cited in text as AE.

6. Johanna Oksala, *Feminist Experiences: Foucauldian and Phenomenological Investigations* (Evanston, IL: Northwestern University Press, 2016), 14, cited in text as FE. See also AE, 20.

7. Joan W. Scott, "The Evidence of Experience," in *Critical Inquiry* 17, no. 4 (1991): 773–97, at 777.

8. See Linda Martín Alcoff, "Dangerous Pleasures: Foucault and the Politics of Pedophilia," in *Feminist Interpretations of Michel Foucault,* ed. Susan J. Hekman (University Park: Pennsylvania State University Press, 1996), 99–135; and AE, 36.

9. Scott's "The Evidence of Experience" is an archetypical example here.

10. Though Oksala does at times seem to maintain a sharp distinction between embodiment and "normative cultural practices and structures of meaning" (FE, 14), this threatens, I would argue, to reinstate the "prediscursive" or "immediate" nature of lived experience, simply locating it in the body rather than in consciousness. Expression, as we will see, can help us avoid this by making sense of the lived body as already expressive of "normative cultural practices and structures of meaning." I will discuss this further in Chapter 2.

11. For a thorough explanation of these terms and how they arise in Husserl's thought, see Anthony Steinbock, *Home and Beyond: Generative Phenomenology After Husserl* (Evanston, IL: Northwestern University Press, 1995), cited in text as HB.

12. Gottlob Frege, "Sense and Reference," *The Philosophical Review* 57, no. 3 (1948): 209–30, at 214.

13. Ibid., 213. The point is made clearer if we change to a nonmathematical example: the referent of "the author of *Futurity in Phenomenology*" is identical to the referent of "Hendrik and Frankie's dad," though the sense of the two is very different, and remains somewhat "dependent" insofar as it is possible that there is more than one family with children named Hendrik and Frankie, and so the sense of this particular phrase is tied to my family.

14. See Gottlob Frege, *The Foundations of Arithmetic*, where he claims that one of the "fundamental principles" guiding his work is to seek "always to separate sharply the psychological from the logical, the subjective from the objective." Frege, *The Foundations of Arithmetic: A Logico-Mathematical Enquiry into the Concept of Number*, trans. J. L. Austin (Evanston, IL: Northwestern University Press, 1950), x.

15. I make this case in some detail in "Spiritual Expression and the Promise of Phenomenology," in *The Subject(s) of Phenomenology: New Approaches to Husserl*, ed. Iulian Apostelescu, Verdran Grahovac, and Patrick Flack (New York: Springer, 2020), 245–69.

16. We will return to the notion of *Stiftung*, normally translated as "institution." It is important to distinguish this German notion of institution from the political understanding of institution as social organizations. The German notion of *Stiftung* includes both that organizational sense and a sense of something begun with a purpose that then perdures through time. Hence, it has connotations in English also of tradition and initiation. It thereby captures the dual sense of constitution (as both an active force and an internal makeup) that I am seeking with the word "political" in ways that are not well connoted by the political understanding of "institution." I will, generally speaking, leave *Stiftung* untranslated so that this dual connotation is not lost.

17. We will return to this notion and its significance for expressivity in Chapter 1.

18. See Joshua Kates, *Essential History: Jacques Derrida and the Development of Deconstruction* (Evanston, IL: Northwestern University Press, 2005).

19. See Charles Taylor, *A Secular Age* (Cambridge, MA: Harvard University Press, 2007).

20. See Oksala, *Feminist Experiences*, 82, and Eugen Fink, *Sixth Cartesian Meditation: The Idea of a Transcendental Theory of Method*, trans. R. Bruzina (Bloomington: Indiana University Press, 1995), 88–89.

21. Neal DeRoo, *Futurity in Phenomenology: Promise and Method in Husserl, Levinas, and Derrida*. (New York: Fordham University Press, 2013), 141.

22. Russell's infamous—and unfortunately influential—reading of Heidegger is one noteworthy example of this reception of transcendental phenomenology by philosophers beyond phenomenology; the "Cambridge Affair" with Derrida is another. On Russell's reading of Heidegger, see Bertrand Russell, *Wisdom of the West: A Historical Survey of Western Philosophy in Its Social and Political Setting* (London: Bloomsbury Books, 1989), 303: "Martin Heidegger's philosophy is extremely obscure and highly eccentric in its terminology. One cannot help suspecting that language is here running riot." On the "Cambridge Affair," see Barry Smith, "Letter to the Editor," *The Times* (London), May 9, 1992.

23. Derrida touches on this in *The Problem of Genesis in Husserl's Philosophy*, trans. Geoffrey Bennington and Rachel Bowlby (Chicago: University of Chicago Press, 1989), but the discussion there seems very abstract and theoretical and is therefore not well cited or discussed among "applied" phenomenologists.

24. This is most notable in Dan Zahavi's "Applied Phenomenology," in which he argues that knowledge of transcendental or philosophical phenomenology is not necessary for "applied" uses of phenomenology. Zahavi, "Applied Phenomenology: Why It Is Safe to Ignore the Epoché," *Continental Philosophy Review* (2019): 1–15. This is especially notable in that Zahavi himself is one of the world's best commentators on Husserl and his transcendental phenomenology.

25. In sitting on a committee that evaluates grant applications in philosophy, I was struck by how strongly a "problem-based" approach to scholarship was assumed in both the application itself and in the adjudication of applications, and how this affected the ability of applications by those in the "Continental" school to be understood by non-Continental thinkers.

26. There are, of course, other factors at play in these issues of exploitation and oppression, both structurally and individually. In suggesting expressivity as a way to help alleviate the larger philosophical issue—that of the nature of the connection between the phenomenal elements of experience—I do not mean to suggest that the problems of exploitation and oppression will somehow disappear. However, I think that the figure-based approach to philosophy is an exacerbating tendency whose amelioration may in part help fight against some of these other issues.

27. See David Macey, "Fanon, Phenomenology, Race," *Radical Philosophy* 95 (1999): 8–14; Linda Martín Alcoff, "Towards a Phenomenology of Racial Embodiment," *Radical Philosophy* 95 (1999): 15–26; Lewis R. Gordon, *Bad Faith and Antiblack Racism* (Atlantic Highlands, NJ: Humanities Press, 1995); and Lewis R. Gordon, "Fanon, Philosophy, Racism," in *Racism and Philosophy*, ed. Susan E. Babbitt and Sue Campbell (Ithaca, NY: Cornell University Press, 1999), 32–49.

28. On the "classical" transcendental side, see Dan Zahavi, "Transcendental Subjectivity and Metaphysics," *Human Studies* 25 (2002): 103–16.

29. See Lisa Guenther, "Critical Phenomenology," in *50 Concepts for a Critical Phenomenology*, ed. Gayle Weiss, Gayle Salamon, and Ann V. Murphy (Evanston, IL: Northwestern University Press, 2020), 11–16, where she describes critical phenomenology as "both a way of doing philosophy and a way of approaching political activism" (15).

30. HB, 268.

31. Guenther, "Critical Phenomenology," 15; see also Frantz Fanon, *Black Skin, White Masks* trans. Charles Lam Markmann (New York: Grove Press, 1967), 82.

32. HB, 266.

33. Also, critical phenomenology is trying "to generate new and liberatory possibilities for meaningful experience and existence"; Guenther, "Critical Phenomenology," 15. Again, though, it is not obvious that Husserl's work in the *Crisis* is trying to do something different, even if the way it does it and some of its foundational assumptions (e.g., about what is more liberatory, about who should lead that charge, etc.) are quite different.

34. See, for example, Renaud Barbaras, *The Being of the Phenomenon: Merleau-Ponty's Ontology.* trans. Leonard Lawlor and Ted Toadvine (Bloomington: Indiana University Press, 2004); Donald A. Landes, *Merleau-Ponty and the Paradoxes of Expression* (London: Bloomsbury Academic, 2013); Véronique Fóti, *Tracing Expression in Merleau-Ponty* (Evanston, IL: Northwestern University Press, 2013); Leonard Lawlor, "The End of Phenomenology: Expressionism in Deleuze and Merleau-Ponty," *Continental Philosophy Review* 31 (1998): 15–34.

35. See, for example, Audrey Wasser, "Deleuze's Expressionism," *Angelaki: Journal of Theoretical Humanities* 12, no. 2 (2007): 49–66; Sean Bowden, "The Intensive Expression of the Virtual: Revisiting the Relation of Expression in *Difference and Repetition*," *Deleuze Studies* 11, no. 2 (2017): 216–39; Thomas Nail, "Expression, Immanence and Constructivism: 'Spinozism' and Gilles Deleuze," *Deleuze Studies* 2, no. 2 (2008), 201–19.

36. There are two notable exceptions to this, one historical and one contemporary. Historically, Remy Kwant's book *Phenomenology of Expression*, trans. Henry J. Koren (Pittsburgh: Duquesne University Press, 1969), though that is mainly an extrapolation from Merleau-Ponty, does, at least, try to offer a broader phenomenology of expression. In the contemporary setting, the research groups in Finland centered around the work of Sara Heinämaa are

doing very interesting work on the application of phenomenological accounts of expression, though these tend to focus mainly on Husserl's work.

37. For example, at the 2017 annual meeting of SPEP, after Andrew Dunstall gave a paper trying to recover or reassess the value of expression as a concept in Derrida's thought, a prominent Derrida scholar in the audience remarked: "But Derrida went through so much trouble to get rid of the concept of expression—why would you want to bring it back?"

38. This view is examined in more detail in Kates, *Essential History*. Both Derrida and Michel Henry criticize this view of expression in Husserl; see Derrida, *Voice and Phenomenon: Introduction to the Problem of the Sign in Husserl's Phenomenology,* trans. Leonard Lawlor (Evanston, IL: Northwestern University Press, 2010), 32, cited in text as VP, and Michel Henry, *The Essence of Manifestation*, trans. G. Etzkor (The Hague: Martinus Nijhoff, 1973), cited in text as EM.

39. VP, 15.

40. I think there are also continuities to establish to Deleuze, Derrida, and Henry as well. Such a task will be alluded to in various places throughout the present book, but its full realization must be put off for the time being.

41. Heidegger already sees this point and opens the door to our reading of this relationship in terms of expression, in § 7 of *Being and Time*, trans. Joan Stambaugh (Albany: State University of New York Press, 1996), cited in text as BT. There, he distinguishes the "phenomenological concept of phenomenon" (27/31) from appearance (among other possible equivocal uses of the term "phenomenon") and equates appearance with "a referential relation in being themselves such that what does the referring (the making-known) can fulfill its possible function only if it shows itself in itself—only if it is a 'phenomenon'" (27/31). Not only is the latter reminiscent of Husserl's description of indications in *Logical Investigations*, trans. J. N. Findlay (New York: Routledge, 2000), but Heidegger even mentions indications specifically (though not exclusively) as having the "fundamental formal structure of appearing" (26/29). This equation of a nonphenomenological understanding with indication is only one step of affirming the fundamental phenomenality of phenomenon as expressive, however. He also equates *logos* with "*relation* and *relationship*" (30/34), but in such a way that the relata must be synthesized in a particular (and particularly phenomenological) understanding of synthesis as a "let[ting] something be seen in its *togetherness* with something, to let something be seen *as* something" (29/33), a synthesis that seems very similar to Husserl's notion of expression as a phenomenal unity. A full elaboration of expression in Heidegger would also have to examine the way the concept is used in later parts of *Being and Time*, not to mention other works, and we have no time for such an elaboration in the current work. Hence, I leave it here merely as a suggestion, a call for future research.

42. A student compared an earlier draft of this chapter to the book *Salt, Fat, Acid, Heat: Mastering the Elements of Good Cooking*, which is not a cookbook

per se but a guide to how cooking works. It does not give you recipes to follow to make "good food" but rather explains the chemistry behind cooking, so you can not only make food but also learn how to cook. Similarly, this chapter does not give a step-by-step guide on how to perform a "phenomenology of X" but rather articulates the "chemistry" of phenomenology, so that one will not simply come up with phenomenological results but will, I hope, learn how to phenomenologize.

1. A Phenomenological Account of Expressivity

1. I mean "function" here in the mathematical sense as that which defines the relationship between variables. As we will see, focusing on how expression functions as a function is in a sense consistent with expressivity, which operates as a kind of differential relation that is akin to the role of functions in calculus, a point that emerges most clearly in Deleuze's account of expression, e.g., in *Expressionism in Philosophy: Spinoza*, trans. Martin Joughin (New York: Zone Books, 1992), cited in text as EiP. It is eminently significant for situating Deleuze's project both philosophically, noting the preference for Leibniz over Spinoza when it comes to "expressive individuation" (EiP, 11), and mathematically (Deleuze's preference for "differential calculus and Riemannian manifolds" as compared to the "algebra and sets" preferred by Alain Badiou. See Badiou, *Deleuze: The Clamor of Being*, trans. Louise Burchill (Minneapolis: University of Minnesota Press, 2000), 1. See also Daniel Smith, "Mathematics and the Theory of Multiplicities: Deleuze and Badiou Revisited," in his *Essays on Deleuze*, 287–311 (Edinburgh: Edinburgh University Press, 2012). This method of thinking of expressivity in terms of "functions" will be further justified in Chapter 4 in a discussion of "reading" the *Stiftung* as a key component of transcendental phenomenological method. At this stage, then, I must apologize for using some of the methodological tools that have not yet been fully developed or explained.

2. For that type of analysis, consult Neal DeRoo, "Spiritual Expression and the Promise of Phenomenology," in *The Subject(s) of Phenomenology: Rereading Husserl*, ed. Iulian Apostelescu, Verdran Grahovac, and Patrick Flack (New York: Springer, 2020), and "Merleau-Ponty and Ab/Normal Phenomenology: The Husserlian Roots of Merleau-Ponty's Account of Expression," in *Normality, Abnormality, and Pathology in Merleau-Ponty*, ed. Talia Walsh and Susan Bredlau (Albany: State University of New York Press, 2022).

3. In the following, I will use "expression" to remain consistent with that term's use in the figures being discussed, even when they mean what we would now mean by "expressivity." The conflation of expression and expressivity is a significant factor in the function expression plays in Husserl's work in *Logical Investigations*, and so we cannot simply cover over that conflation, even if not doing so risks some possible misunderstandings in the context of the distinctions we have laid out in the Introduction, and will establish further as the book unfolds.

4. For more on the relation between Husserl's account of expression and the dialogue between Husserl and Frege, see my "Spiritual Expression and the Promise of Phenomenology."

5. Vernon W. Cisney, *Derrida's Voice and Phenomenon* (Edinburgh: Edinburgh University Press, 2014), 59.

6. Here, one could argue, is the entirety of Husserl's difference from Frege, in a nutshell. For Frege, sense is merely a "vehicle," a way of presenting the *Bedeutung*, the referent (SR, 210), which remains essentially distinct from both the referent and the sign. Husserl, on the other hand, is interested in the "phenomenal unity" that makes the "vehicle" metaphor no longer tenable.

7. An ambiguity that he seems to inherit from Frege, who uses "expression" to mean both a broader category that could include propositions, predicates, etc. within it, and, in a more precise way, to speak specifically of the relation between a name and its sense (as opposed to its referent). Both uses of expression are captured in the following quotation: "A proper name (word, sign, sign combination, expression) expresses its sense, refers to or designates its referent. By means of a sign we express its sense and designate its referent." Gottlob Frege, "Sense and Reference," *The Philosophical Review* 57, no. 3 (1948): 209–30, at 214.

8. See Joshua Kates, *Essential History: Jacques Derrida and the Development of Deconstruction* (Evanston, IL: Northwestern University Press, 2005).

9. It can be argued that, in later works (perhaps starting already in *Ideas II*), Husserl himself also goes a long way in offering such an account. We will return to this suggestion in our discussion of generativity later in this chapter and of the "material-spiritual" in the function of subjectivity in Chapter 2.

10. This point is made in great detail by Donald Landes in *Merleau-Ponty and the Paradoxes of Expression* (London: Bloomsbury Academic, 2013). See 16–22.

11. This translation is slightly modified: I have removed the translator's insertion of "phenomenon" after "another" to maintain the possibility (which I think is essential to Merleau-Ponty) that expressivity functions in phenomenality, and not merely with already constituted phenomena.

12. See Landes, *Merleau-Ponty and the Paradoxes of Expression*; Véronique Fóti, *Tracing Expression in Merleau-Ponty* (Evanston, IL: Northwestern University Press, 2013); Remigius Kwant, *The Phenomenology of Expression*, trans. Henry J. Koren (Pittsburgh, PA: Duquesne University Press, 1969); and Renaud Barbaras, *The Being of the Phenomenon: Merleau-Ponty's Ontology*, trans. Leonard Lawlor and Ted Toadvine (Bloomington: Indiana University Press, 2004).

13. Establishing this point is the major theme of Barbaras, *The Being of the Phenomenon*.

14. We will return to this claim in more detail in Chapters 2 and 5.

15. We can articulate this dilemma this way: if the unity is not asymmetrical, it is not clear that it remains the "phenomenal unity" that Husserl's account of expression is concerned with and which is so important to a phenomenological

understanding of the world. But if the unity is asymmetrical, we seem to slide back toward either essentialism/idealism/psychologism (if we privilege "living in" the "subjective" realm of sense and meaning) or naïve realism/empiricism (if we privilege the "living in" the "objective" realm of "facts" and beings). As such, it is either not expression or, if it is, it is no longer phenomenological.

16. As David Morris articulates it, sense is "inseparable from the directedness of being" itself. David Morris, "The Chirality of Being: Exploring a Merleau-Pontian Ontology of Sense," *Chiasmi International* 12 (2011): 165–82, at 170. See Maurice Merleau-Ponty, *The Visible and the Invisible*, trans. Alphonso Lingis (Evanston, IL: Northwestern University Press, 1968), 107: "a Being that therefore is sense and sense of sense" (translation modified), cited in text as VI.

17. For more on the asymmetry of Merleau-Ponty's relation between being and sense, see Morris, "The Chirality of Being."

18. On sense as a movement of self-differentiation and autoproduction, see Martina Ferrari, "Poietic Transpatiality: Merleau-Ponty and the Sense of Nature," *Chiasmi International* 20 (2018): 385–401, cited in text as PT.

19. Maurice Merleau-Ponty, *Nature: Course Notes from the College de France*, ed. Dominique Seglard, trans. Robert Vallier (Evanston, IL: Northwestern University Press, 2003), 3, cited in text as N.

20. See Maurice Merleau-Ponty, *L'institution / La passivité: Notes de cours au Collège de France (1954–1955)* (Paris: Editions Belin, 2003). For *Stiftung*, See Barbaras, *The Being of the Phenomenon*, 58. The notion of *Stiftung* has great complexity in Merleau-Ponty's later work. In its German provenance (Merleau-Ponty takes the term over from Husserl), *Stiftung* refers to an institution, foundation, or tradition that pursues a purpose determined by its founder or "initiator." For a summary of this term and its significance for Merleau-Ponty, see Robert Vallier, "Institution: The Significance of Merleau-Ponty's 1954 Course at the Collège de France," *Chiasmi International* 7 (2005): 281–302. *Stiftung* is usually translated as institution, but it also has resonances of foundation, tradition, even initiation. In the context of the current book, however, the notion of "institution" has too many connotations in politics (i.e., as pertaining to distinct social organizations) that do not fit well with the range of connotations found in *Stiftung*. This is why some critical phenomenologists choose to translate the term differently. Keith Whitmoyer, for example, translates it as "initiations" (alongside "institutions"), in keeping with Merleau-Ponty's own translation of *Stiftung* in VI, 243; see Keith Whitmoyer, "Sens/Sense," in *50 Concepts for a Critical Phenomenology*, ed. Gayle Weiss, Gayle Salamon, and Ann V. Murphy (Evanston, IL: Northwestern University Press, 2020), 303–7, at 305; see also 307n12. I will leave the word *Stiftung* largely untranslated to avoid ambiguity and misconception.

21. See Leonard Lawlor, *Thinking through French Philosophy: The Being of the Question* (Bloomington: Indiana University Press, 2003), 1–2.

22. Landes speaks of this in terms of "metastable equilibriums" and "transduction" throughout *The Paradoxes of Expression*; see also Maurice Merleau-Ponty,

"Themes from the Lectures at the College de France, 1952–1960," in *In Praise of Philosophy and Other Essays*, trans. John O'Neill (Evanston, IL: Northwestern University Press, 1988), 22–27, cited in text as LCF.

23. It may strike some as odd to include Deleuze here in a discussion of a "phenomenological" account of expression, given Deleuze's own criticisms of phenomenology. While arguing for Deleuze's inclusion here would take us too far afield, it is worth nothing that phenomenology remains a significant "landmark" for Deleuze's thought. See Alain Beaulieu, "Edmund Husserl," in *Deleuze's Philosophical Lineage*, ed. Graham Jones and Jon Roffe (Edinburgh: Edinburgh University Press, 2009), 262). Some Deleuze scholars openly wonder whether Deleuze's philosophy could be considered phenomenological. See, for example, Stephan Günzel, "Deleuze and Phenomenology," *Metodo: International Studies in Phenomenology and Philosophy* 2 no. 3 (2014): 31. Regardless of that question, however, I agree with Beaulieu's analysis that "phenomenological themes remain omnipresent in Deleuze's development" ("Edmund Husserl," 261); for a more detailed treatment, see Beaulieu, *Gilles Deleuze et la phénoménologie* (Paris: Vrin, 2004). The focus on expressivity that we are highlighting in phenomenology in this work therefore opens a new door for making such a connection between Deleuze and phenomenology, given the focus on expression in Deleuze's early works, such as *Expressionism in Philosophy: Spinoza* and *Difference and Repetition*. Some of these connections have already been noted, for example by Leonard Lawlor in *Thinking through French Philosophy* and "The End of Phenomenology: Expressionism in Deleuze and Merleau-Ponty," *Continental Philosophy Review* 31 (1998): 15–34, and by Jack Reynolds and Jon Roffe, "Deleuze and Merleau-Ponty: Immanence, Univocity and Phenomenology," *Journal of the British Society for Phenomenology* 37, no. 3 (2006): 228–51. For these reasons, I hope the invocation of Deleuze in a "phenomenological" account of expression will be permitted by the reader.

24. These might actually be one and the same metaphysical account, if Deleuze is right that "the oneness and identity of the divine substance are in truth the only guarantee of a unique and identical self, and God is retained so long as the self is preserved." *Difference and Repetition*, trans. Paul Patton (London: Athlone Press, 1994), 58.

25. Insofar as the expressed "does not exist outside of the expression"; see Deleuze, *Expressionism in Philosophy*, 333.

26. Leibniz's development of the infinitesimal calculus is an essential element in Deleuze's account of the genetic operation of expression. This should not surprise us, given that *Expressionism in Philosophy* is, contrary to what the subtitle suggests, as much about Leibniz as it is about Spinoza (see EiP, 335). Some of the Leibnizian elements are developed more strongly in *Difference and Repetition* and *The Fold: Leibniz and the Baroque*, trans. Tom Conley (Minneapolis: University of Minnesota Press, 1993). For more on the relation between Deleuze and the Leibnizian calculus, see Daniel Smith, "Deleuze on Leibniz: Difference, Continuity and the Calculus," in *Current Continental Theory and*

Modern Philosophy (Evanston, IL: Northwestern University Press, 2006), 127–47; and Daniel Smith, "The Conditions of the New," in *Essays on Deleuze* (Edinburgh: Edinburgh University Press, 2012), 247.

27. See, for example, his discussion of ontogenesis in VI, 14, 102, 213.

28. See Landes's definition of expression as "any enduring response to the weight of the past, the weight of the ideal, and the weight of the present situation, broadly construed," in *Merleau-Ponty and the Paradoxes of Expression*, 10.

29. See also MS B 3 III (1931), 41b; discussed by Anthony Steinbock in *Home and Beyond: Generative Phenomenology after Husserl* (Evanston, IL: Northwestern University Press, 1995), 188 and 303n5. Compare this to our earlier discussion of our life as an interrogation of *Stiftungen* as "those events which sediment in me a sense, not just as survivals or residues [of the past], but as the invitation to a sequel, the requirement of a future" (LCF, 108–9).

30. See *Home and Beyond*, 194–96, for Steinbock's discussion of homeworld in relation to the German term *Stamm* with its various connotations; manuscript C 17 84 b.

31. In this regard, home functions somewhat similarly to *Stiftung*. However, home is more primordial or "deeper" than *Stiftung*—closer to an ultratranscendental than the more transcendentally empirical nature of *Stiftungen*, to anticipate some distinctions we will not make until Chapter 4. One could say, therefore, that "home" perhaps names how *Stiftungen* function generatively. We must be careful, though: Husserl famously speaks of geometry as a *Stiftung*, but it is unlikely that this *Stiftung* ever functions as the primary phenomenological "home" for anyone. However, we can say that geometry functions as home, or in a homely (*heimlich*) way, when I'm doing geometry; that is, something is marked as "geometrical" insofar as geometry is the normatively relevant "home" within which its sense is constituted. This, I think, is somewhat different from Steinbock's use of "homeworld," which seems to be more akin to a distinct individual "thing" or "phenomenon" (perhaps a "transcendental empirical"?) that is necessarily indexed to a particular subject, rather than a process (homeliness or *heimlichkeit*) that is perhaps relevant to all phenomena.

32. See also Bernhard Waldenfels, "Experience of the Alien in Husserl's Phenomenology," trans. Anthony J. Steinbock, *Research in Phenomenology* 20 (1990): 19–33.

33. Compare also Merleau-Ponty's "hyper-dialectic" as a "dialectic without synthesis" (VI, 95).

34. Husserl is not necessarily "later": he begins to speak of generativity in some manuscripts dated as early as 1920, which is certainly later than *Logical Investigations* but still quite far from the *Crisis* era.

2. Material-Spiritual Flesh: The Subjective Implications of Expressivity

1. Sara Heinämaa, "Embodiment and Expressivity in Husserl's Phenomenology: From Logical Investigations to Cartesian Meditations," *SATS: Northern European Journal of Philosophy* 11 (2010): 6, cited in text as EE.

2. For example: "The spiritual life . . . of persons is expressed in . . . countenance and gestures" (Hua 4, 246).

3. "With" might not be the best word to describe the person-body relationship at this point. We will return to this question of the expressive relation between the person and the body below.

4. I follow Heinämaa in altering the translation of Leibkörper from "Corporeal Body," in the English translation of *Ideas II* to "body." See EE, 7. I do not use the language of the "living body" yet at this stage because, as we will see, the relation between "living body" and the primal expressive unity remains an open question at this point.

5. The intensive interest in modern philosophy at work in other parts of the *Crisis* suggests that "entelechy" should here likely be read more in its Leibnizian than in a strictly Aristotelian sense. Such a reading further reinforces the vitality and relation to life that are characteristic of spirit, in its Husserlian sense.

6. For more on the use of the Kantian Idea in the work of the later Husserl, see Jacques Derrida, *Of Spirit: Heidegger and the Question* (Chicago: University of Chicago Press, 1989).

7. There are clear resonances here with the Heideggerian notion of "concealment" elaborated in *Being and Time*; see also Jean-Luc Marion, *Reduction and Givenness: Investigations of Husserl, Heidegger, and Phenomenology* (Evanston, IL: Northwestern University Press, 1998).

8. In this regard, it is similar to "home" as discussed Chapter 1. However, the two cannot be entirely conflated: "home" names a process that explains generative functioning itself; "spirit" names that process as constituted within a particular "spiritual community" (as will be discussed in Chapter 6). As such, "spirit" perhaps names a transcendental process, while "home" names the ultra-transcendental process of generativity that enables "spirit" to function transcendentally, to anticipate a distinction we will not make explicitly until Chapter 4. We might also say that "spirit" names the sense of "home" that is operative within a particular context, and which therefore affects how *Stiftungen* are "made sense of" within that context. Hence, home, spirit, and *Stiftung* are related, but not equivalent, concepts.

9. This is doubly true when we account for the temporal nature of my experience: I do not encounter this thing only as a desk, but as a desk that I come across after having walked into my office and before I pull out my computer and place it upon the desk. Husserl's essential breakthrough was in explaining that temporality is not added on to my experience proper: I have an experience ("desk") and then work that experience into the stream of my temporal life ("I encounter the desk after I enter my office"), nor is my experience secondary upon the "form" of my temporal life (I am just a temporal stream into which some experience or other must come into and occupy). Rather, Husserl's notion of double intentionality (as both transverse and horizontal) gives him the means to explain how my experience is always already inherently constituted as temporal. This double intentionality is

essential to Husserl's notion of "absolute consciousness," and hence to his entire phenomenological approach to philosophy (see Hua 10, 380–81); see also Toine Kortooms, *Phenomenology of Time: Edmund Husserl's Analysis of Time-Consciousness* (Dordrecht: Kluwer Academic, 2002). The notion of fulfillment is what makes possible that double intentionality: in fulfillment, what I expect is simultaneously experienced as itself and as what was expected (or what disappointed the expectation, etc.), thereby uniting the stream of experienced objects with the stream of temporal experience. This fulfillment is possible only with the two modes of bringing to intuition discussed earlier: the clarifying and the confirming. See Neal DeRoo, "A Positive Account of Protention and Its Implications for Internal Time-Consciousness," in *Epistemology, Archaeology, Ethics: Current Investigations of Husserl's Corpus*, ed. Pol Vandevelde and Sebastian Luft (London: Continuum, 2010), 102–19.

10. Presentiments are the preobjectively functioning expectations that function as an "intentional guide for seeing . . . significant interconnections" (Hua 6, 275–76). By pursuing these expected connections, we are able to confirm for ourselves these presentiments, and so establish "confirmed certainty" (Hua 6, 276). As such, presentiment is a crucial element in the expectation-fulfillment structure of Husserl's account of our intuitive engagement with the world.

11. This theme is examined at much greater length than I can do here in Simo Pulkkinen, "Lifeworld as an Embodiment of Spiritual Meaning: The Constitutive Dynamics of Activity and Passivity in Husserl," in *The Phenomenology of Embodied Subjectivity: Contributions to Phenomenology* 71, ed. R. T. Jensen and Dermot Moran (Cham, Switzerland: Springer, 2013), cited in text as LE. I think the notion of expression would be a helpful addition to Pulkkinen's analysis. I draw heavily on Pulkkinen's translations of material from Hua 39; unless otherwise cited, all translations from that volume are Pulkkinen's.

12. For an extended discussion of this "spirit" of barbarism, see Michel Henry, *Barbarism*, trans. Scott Davidson (London: Continuum, 2013), cited in text as BR.

13. Sara Heinämaa, "On the Transcendental Undercurrents of Phenomenology: The Case of the Living Body," *Continental Philosophy Review* 54, no. 2 (2021): 237–57, cited in text as OTU.

14. We will see in Chapter 6 that the fact that both the "meaning" and the "objects" are considered spiritual and expressive becomes important in clarifying the relation between community and culture in Husserl, and therefore differentiating his account of spiritual expression from Hegel's. See also TSO, 17–18.

15. Sara Heinämaa, *Toward a Phenomenology of Sexual Difference: Husserl, Merleau-Ponty, Beauvoir* (Lanham: Rowman & Littlefield, 2003), 32.

16. Alia Al-Saji, "Bodies and Sensings: On the Uses of Husserlian Phenomenology for Feminist Theory," *Continental Philosophy Review* 43, no. 1 (2010): 13–37, at 18, cited in text as BaS.

17. Heinämaa, *Toward a Phenomenology of Sexual Difference*, 29.

18. There are resonances here with the Levinasian project as described, for example, in John Drabinski, *Sensibility and Singularity: The Problem of Phenomenology in Levinas* (Albany: State University of New York Press, 2001).

19. This reflection also opens up the distinction between my body as a living body (*Leib*), capable of touching, as opposed to other, merely objective bodies (*Körper*) that can be touched. And we are starting to see more clearly the implications of Heinämaa's earlier claim that the body must be understood as an expressive unity before it can be distinguished into the distinct elements of interest to the empirical and psychological sciences.

20. Henry, *Barbarism*, 45–46.

21. I am here assuming a certain subjectivity, an ownness, to the *Leib*, which therefore requires me to distinguish between *Leib* and *Empfindnisse*. Al-Saji does not make this distinction, instead equating the living body with the "field of sensings," and therefore considering the lived body as presubjective (see BaS, 23). There are other times where she seems to distinguish a "tactile body" as "a subject not defined in opposition to an object" (BaS, 24), though it is not immediately clear whether the "tactile body" is distinct from the living body, or if "the lived body is constituted as a tactile field" (BaS, 25) in a way that equates it with the living body. For purposes of clarity and ease of reference, I have distinguished the living body from the field of sensings, though this distinction is, again, a question of attitude rather than an ontological distinction. Put otherwise, I might want to say that the living body is an expression of a localized field of sensings, and hence a distinction can be made between them, though the distinction is not experienced as two distinct things in our phenomenal experience: it is only reflection that enables us to distinguish them.

22. This is precisely the mistake that Alia Al-Saji argues Merleau-Ponty makes in his account of the touching-touched relationship in *Phenomenology of Perception*. There, Merleau-Ponty claims that we can only alternate between subject-positions (touching) and object-positions (touched): "insofar as it sees or touches the world, my body can therefore be neither seen nor touched" (PhP, 92), and so "what was meant by talking about 'double sensations' is that, in passing from one role to the other, I can identify the hand touched as the same one which will in a moment be touching" (PhP 93). It is significant, Al-Saji argues, that Merleau-Ponty is only able to move beyond this understanding of the touching-touched relationship when he "shifts from the framework of a philosophy of consciousness to a philosophy of the flesh" (BaS, 20n24).

23. It is also what Husserl refers to as "Earth" when he says, "The Earth does not move" (FI, 313).

24. See, for example, David Abram, "In the Depths of a Breathing Planet: Gaia and the Transformation of Experience," in *Gaia in Turmoil: Climate Change, Biodepletion, and Earth Ethics in an Age of Crisis*, ed. Eileen Crist and H. Bruce Rinker (Cambridge, MA: MIT Press, 2010), 221–42.

25. See Edward Casey, "Taking a Glance at the Environment: Preliminary Thoughts on a Promising Topic," in *Eco-Phenomenology: Back to the Earth Itself,*

ed. Charles S. Brown and Ted Toadvine (Albany: State University of New York Press, 2003), 187–210; and William Edelglass, James Hatley, and Christian Diehm, *Facing Nature: Levinas and Environmental Thought* (Pittsburgh, PA: Duquesne University Press, 2012).

26. See Michel Henry, *Incarnation: A Philosophy of Flesh*, trans. Karl Kefty (Evanston, IL: Northwestern University Press, 2015).

27. There are obvious resonances here to Merleau-Ponty's work, for example his claim that "the world is made of the same stuff as the body" (EaM, 163). See also Merleau-Ponty, "Eye and Mind," in *The Primacy of Perception*, ed. James M. Edie, trans. Carleton Dallery (Evanston, IL: Northwestern University Press, 1964), 163, cited in text as EaM. We will return to these resonances explicitly in the next chapter, when we turn to the epistemological and onto-logical implications of expressivity. Heinämaa discusses the relation between Merleau-Ponty's and Husserl's accounts of the lived body in its relation to expressivity in *Toward a Phenomenology of Sexual Difference*, 37–44.

28. Oksala describes this as "an attitude where our ontological preunder-standing of the world is not visible to us at all" (FE, 108). We will return to this in Chapter 5.

29. Emmanuel Levinas, *Discovering Existence with Husserl*, ed. and trans. Richard A. Cohen and Michael B. Smith (Evanston, IL: Northwestern University Press, 1998), 147.

30. Henry makes the ultimate equation between spirituality and affectivity in *Words of Christ*, but fully explaining his position would require, I think, too far a detour into the concept of "life" to be helpful at this stage. Those interested in his account of spirituality as affectivity are asked to consult Neal DeRoo, "Spiritual Life and Cultural Discernment: Renewing Spirituality through Henry," in *The Practical Philosophy of Michel Henry*, ed. Brian Harding and Michael R. Kelly (Bloomsbury, 2022), 45–65.

31. See also Christina Schües, "Conflicting Apprehensions and the Question of Sensations," in *Alterity and Facticity*, ed. Natalie Depraz and Dan Zahavi (Dordrecht: Kluwer, 1998), 139–62; and Sara Ahmed, *Queer Phenomenology: Orientations, Objects, Others* (Durham, NC: Duke University Press, 2006).

32. We will return to the question of how it is that we "feel" or experience the phenomenal conditions of our experiencing in Chapter 4.

33. Which is a variant of "en-" done before *b*, *m*, *p*, or *ph*.

34. Or, more technically still: the subject embodies the Earth, the sensuous-spiritual precedent of the world. In this regard, both the subject and the world are necessarily expressions or embodiments of the spiritual-material.

35. Heinämaa argues "living body" is better English nomenclature than "lived body" as a translation of the German *Leib* insofar as the latter (at least in English and French) implies that the power of living is a secondary attribute of some particular bodies as opposed to others (i.e., "lived bodies" as opposed to "nonlived bodies"), an attribute that is not generated within or by the bodies

themselves, but must come from somewhere else (OTU, 5). See also *Toward a Phenomenology of Sexual Difference*, xx n9 and xxi n12.

36. Simone de Beauvoir, *The Second Sex*, trans. and ed. H. M. Parshley (Harmondsworth: Penguin, 1953), 66. The phenomenological provenance of de Beauvoir's use of "body" is argued at length in Heinämaa, *Toward a Phenomenology of Sexual Difference*.

37. For more on the expressive nature of movement in the world, see SWWE, 32–86.

38. One could try to equate spirit with a second-person perspective, insofar as it involves some kind of intimate relationship or community with the others, and not merely "objective distance." However, the personal element of the second-person perspective is clearly missing, a point that distinguishes Levinas (and his Buberian influence) from Merleau-Ponty. For Levinas, the appeal to others, even in the face-to-face encounter with an Other, is always already an invocation of "the third." Hence, it is no longer a second-person perspective. Emmanuel Levinas, *Totality and Infinity: An Essay on Exteriority* (Pittsburgh, PA: Duquesne University Press, 1969), 213.

39. This is not to say that the distinction cannot prove helpful in other, later moments of our experience, as we will see shortly. In this regard, I do not mean to dismiss all discourses or understandings of embodiment that focus on this first-person versus third-person perspective. I only mean to suggest that those understandings are not helpful to the primal layer of embodiment, the expressive unity that precedes the distinction between subject and object.

40. Discussed by Heinämaa in OTU, 10–12.

41. Earlier, I suggested making the distinction between the tactile body/ body as tactility and the living body as a way of marking the difference between the nonegoic and the egoic bodies. This is only a suggestion for ease of reference; to make the case more compellingly, I would have to explore in more detail whether "life" has a necessarily personal component to it, or whether life can remain impersonal, prepersonal, or suprapersonal. Derrida seems to argue that life is impersonal (depending on your view of the relation between différance and khora in Derrida's work). Henry seems to argue for something like the suprapersonal view, at least in his later work. I will return to this question of "life" and its relation to the questions of expression and indication in the Conclusion.

42. See Steven Crowell, "Transcendental Phenomenology and the Seductions of Naturalism: Subjectivity, Consciousness, and Meaning," in *The Oxford Handbook of Contemporary Phenomenology*, ed. Dan Zahavi (Oxford: Oxford University Press, 2012), 25–47.

43. Al-Saji makes this argument convincingly in BaS in her criticism of Merleau-Ponty's reading of the touching-touched passage in *Phenomenology of Perception*.

44. Crowell, "Transcendental Phenomenology," 44, as discussed in OTU, 11.

45. There are interesting—and as far as I know unexplored—resonances here with Emmanuelle Falque's notion of the "spread body." Falque, "The Discarnate Madman," trans. Sarah Horton, *Journal for Continental Philosophy of Religion* 1, no. 1 (2019): 90–117. See George Yancy, "Confiscated Bodies," in *50 Concepts for a Critical Phenomenology*, ed. Gayle Weiss, Gayle Salamon, and Ann V. Murphy (Evanston, IL: Northwestern University Press, 2020), 69–75, at 73.

46. Frantz Fanon, *Black Skin, White Masks*, trans. Charles Lam Markmann (New York: Grove Press, 1967); Cornel West with David Ritz, *Brother West, Living and Loving Out Loud: A Memoir* (New York: Smiley Books, 2009), 124; W. E. B. Du Bois, "The Souls of White Folk," in *W. E. B. Du Bois: A Reader*, ed. David Levering Lewis (New York: Henry Holt, 1995); Sara Ahmed, "A Phenomenology of Whiteness," *Feminist Theory* 8, no. 2 (2007): 149–68; Gayle Salamon, "'The Place Where Life Hides Away': Merleau-Ponty, Fanon, and the Location of Bodily Being" *Differences* 17:2 [2006], 96–112, and *Assuming a Body: Transgender and Rhetorics of Materiality* (New York: Columbia University Press, 2010); Judith Butler, "Endangered/Endangering: Schematic Racism and White Paranoia," in *Reading Rodney King, Reading Urban Uprising*, ed. Robert Gooding-Williams (New York: Routledge, 1993).

47. Judith Butler, *Precarious Life: The Powers of Mourning and Violence* (New York: Verso, 2006), 26.

48. This is something that Heinämaa highlights in her distinctly phenomenological reading of de Beauvoir in *Toward a Phenomenology of Sexual Difference*; see, for example, her claim that "for Beauvoir, women and men are two different variations of the human way of relating to the world . . . the principal difference is the experiential difference between two types of living bodies, women's bodies and men's bodies" (84).

49. Such as, for example, in phenomenological psychology, or in applications of phenomenology in fields such as nursing studies or psychopathology where, for methodological reasons, the researcher may choose to focus on the individual's self-experiences and the meaning they have for that individual. We will return to some of these methodological concerns in Chapter 5.

50. It remains to be seen—though it lies outside the scope of the present inquiry—whether Husserl's own uses of "monad" (for example, in *Cartesian Meditations*) are the result of such purposeful methodological decisions or are simply the result of him not yet fully appreciating the implications of some of the insights he has made (as was the case, I suggested, with his account of the inner mental life of the subject in §8 of *Logical Investigations*).

51. On the social constitution of subjective life, see also Butler, *Precarious Life*.

3. From Sense to Sensings:
The Epistemological Implications of Expressivity

1. This term was made famous by Karen Barad, who we will discuss later in the chapter.

2. I have alluded to this point earlier in this book; in my "Spiritual Expression and the Promise of Phenomenology," I argue at some length that clarifying and elaborating "sense" is in fact the promissory force driving the entire phenomenological enterprise. Neal DeRoo, "Spiritual Expression and the Promise of Phenomenology," in *The Subject(s) of Phenomenology: Rereading Husserl*, ed. Iulian Apostelescu, Verdran Grahovac, and Patrick Flack (New York: Springer, 2020), 245–69.

3. See R. E. Aquila, "Husserl and Frege on Meaning," *Journal of the History of Philosophy* 12, no. 3 (1974): 377–83.

4. This remains asymmetrical insofar as, *qua* touching, the body as touched is effaced or diminishes itself so as to "live in" the body as touching. This is not to say that the body as touched disappears; it is still there, but its importance or value is minimized vis-à-vis its status as touching. That the roles can be reversed (that, *qua* touched, the body as touching is effaced or diminishes itself so as to "live in" the body as touched) does not imply that the two are fully symmetrical insofar as the *function* of each remains asymmetrical, even if the things fulfilling that function can be reversed.

5. Is it possible to "notice" myself as both touched and touching simultaneously? That is, can I directly experience the "double touching" at play here? With sufficient attention paid to the reduction, I think one can bracket the question of "subject" or "object" and experience simply touch, though I'm not yet sure we can reflect on both at the same time. Rather, we can reflect either on touching-the-world, on being-touched, or on touch, and can shift between these three in our reflection precisely because we experience all three, together, in the phenomenal unity of the original experience.

6. I will examine this claim in greater detail in Chapter 5, when I discuss how subjectivity (as process) is generated out of flesh, and in the Conclusion, when I clarify the relation between subjects, objects, and subjectivity. This examination must be postponed for now, insofar as we have not yet clarified the notion of the transcendental that must be in place to properly understand the expressive relationship at work in subjectivity (Chapter 4).

7. The Dutch phenomenologist Herman Dooyeweerd may have realized this already in the 1930s, when he claimed that "meaning is the being of creaturely beings"; see *A New Critique of Theoretical Thought*, trans. David H. Freeman and William S. Young (Philadelphia: Presbyterian and Reformed Publishing, 1953), 1:4 (translation modified). For more on Dooyeweerd and his significance for phenomenology, see Neal DeRoo, "Meaning, Being and Time: The Phenomenological Significance of Dooyeweerd's Thought," in *Phenomenology for the Twenty-First Century*, ed. J. Aaron Simmons and James E. Hackett (Palgrave Macmillan, 2016), 77–96.

8. For the relation between these three texts on the question of elaborating an ontology of flesh, see Renaud Barbaras, *The Being of the Phenomenon: Merleau-Ponty's Ontology*, trans. Leonard Lawlor and Ted Toadvine (Bloomington: Indiana University Press, 2004), 148–51.

9. Maurice Merleau-Ponty, "Eye and Mind," in *The Primacy of Perception*, ed. James M. Edie, trans. Carleton Dallery (Evanston, IL: Northwestern University Press, 1964), 163, cited in text as EaM.

10. The reference to Heidegger is to *Introduction to Metaphysics*, trans. Ralph Manheim (New York: Doubleday, 1961), 27–28.

11. For more on this notion, see Miguel de Beistegui, *Truth and Genesis: Philosophy as Differential Ontology* (Bloomington: Indiana University Press, 2004).

12. There is an extensive argument against Sartre and his conception of consciousness as a nothingness, a non-Being, in *The Visible and the Invisible*.

13. For an analysis (and critique) of Merleau-Ponty on the "folds" of being, see Luce Irigaray, *An Ethics of Sexual Difference* (Ithaca, NY: Cornell University Press, 1993). This notion of "folds" is crucial to Deleuze's development of a differential or generative ontology. See Deleuze, *The Fold: Leibniz and the Baroque* (Minneapolis: University of Minnesota Press, 1993), and de Beistegui, *Truth and Genesis*. Unfortunately, working Deleuze's account into the present study would require too much background explication and, as such, would be more trouble than it is worth for the purposes of the present book. For now we must leave it simply as an unpursued path opened up by our analysis of expression and expressivity.

14. For more on the complexity of *Stiftung* as a German term, its usage in Merleau-Ponty, and why I leave it untranslated here, see the relevant footnotes in the Introduction and Chapter 1.

15. See Barbaras, *The Being of the Phenomenon*, 58.

16. In the hermeneutic mode, we could translate this as: "Every seeing is a seeing-as."

17. We must be careful here, for certainly the *geistig* indicates a certain "cultural achievement," yet one that, *qua* spiritual, precedes the culture/nature distinction. We will not be able to fully clarify this relation until we have properly explained the relation between the transcendental and the empirical elements of our experience (Chapter 4), and so we will return to this question of the relationship between culture and spirit in Chapter 6. My thanks to Mark Standish for bringing the quotation to my attention.

18. It must be noted that the distinction between nature as noninstituted and other things as "instituted" is not maintained by Merleau-Ponty as a firm and sharp distinction: in *The Visible and the Invisible*, for example, Merleau-Ponty talks about subjectivity or consciousness as a "natural negativity" that is also a "first institution, always already there" (VI, 216).

19. Yet, some senses and *Stiftungen* do seem to be inaugurated by individual people in a particular historical circumstance, as Husserl famously discusses in the "Origin of Geometry," in *The Crisis of European Sciences and Transcendental Phenomenology*, trans. David Carr (Evanston, IL: Northwestern University Press, 1970), 353–78. Insofar as individual subjects are themselves generated out of nature, even this can be considered, in one way, an unfolding of the latent sense of nature: the geometer does not create triangles or the relations

between the sides within them, she simply is given insight into them in a way that she is able to articulate and communicate conceptually and linguistically, thereby opening a new *Stiftung* (geometry) within the linguistic or conceptual sensings. Whether ideality is itself a distinct mode of sensing or simply a *Stiftung* within, say, linguisticality, is difficult to discern, especially in light of Husserl's "Vienna Lecture," which seems to accord an inaugurating moment to the rise of ideality while simultaneously suggesting that this type of ideality offers a type of novelty that is different, in kind, from other conceptual or practical approaches.

20. Martina Ferrari, "Poetic Transpatiality: Merleau-Ponty and the Sense of Nature," *Chiasmi International* 20 (2018): 390, cited in text as PT.

21. The term "ultratranscendental" refers to processes that produce the (transcendental) processes that produce phenomena. I will explain this term in more detail in Chapter 4.

22. For more on this transcendental conception of the "earth," see EJ, §38; Edmund Husserl, "Fundamental Investigations on the Phenomenological Origin of the Spatiality of Nature," in *Shorter Works*, trans. Fred Kersten, ed. Peter McCormick and Frederick A. Elleston (South Bend, IN: University of Notre Dame Press, 1981), 222–33; and Jacques Derrida, *Edmund Husserl's Origin of Geometry: An Introduction*, trans. John P. Leavey (Lincoln: University of Nebraska Press, 1989), 83–86.

23. For more on the nature-culture distinction, especially as it functions in the early Merleau-Ponty (and in Judith Butler), but not anymore in the later Merleau-Ponty precisely because of the emergence of "flesh" as what I am calling an "expressive" ontology, see PT, 390–91; and David Morris, "The Chirality of Being: Exploring a Merleau-Pontian Ontology of Sense," *Chiasmi International* 12 (2011): 165–82.

24. Both implications can be found in a working note from *The Visible and the Invisible,* where Merleau-Ponty says that the process of differentiation, this "*separation (écart)* which . . . forms meaning," is not something "I affect myself with," not something "I constitute as a lack by the upsurge of an end which I give myself—it is [rather] a natural negativity, a first institution, always already there." Maurice Merleau-Ponty, *The Visible and the Invisible*, trans. Alphonso Lingis (Evanston, IL: Northwestern University Press, 1968), VI, 216.

25. Morris, "Chirality of Being," 171.

26. Though both Merleau-Ponty (e.g., VI, 216) and Husserl (throughout the *Crisis* and the "Origin of Geometry") give in to the temptation to refer to it as an "end" or "telos," the connotations of that language imply too much (agential) control, too strong a sense of predetermination, to be proper for the generativity at work in phenomenalization. We would do better to maintain the use of "spirit" or even "spiritual sense" in Chapter 2 to name this directedness, a directedness that is not guided or controlled by an agent, though it certainly is "guided" (by spirit, by sense).

27. Morris, "Chirality of Being," 175n4.

28. *Qua* differentiating "pulp" (VI, 114), flesh is the differentiation of differentiations, a differential field that is differenciated all the way down. For more on the difference (and relation) between differentiation and differenciation, see Gilles Deleuze, *Difference and Repetition,* trans. Paul Patton (London: Athlone Press, 1994), 246.

29. In philosophy, poiesis is one of the traditional Greek categories for ways of engaging the world, alongside praxis, techne, and the like. It refers to the activity in which something is brought into being that did not exist before. See Donald Polkinghorne, *Practice and the Human Sciences: The Case for a Judgment-Based Practice of Care* (Albany: State University of New York Press, 2004), 115.

30. Merleau-Ponty's articulation of differentiation in terms of right and left is discussed by both Ferrari, "Poetic Transpatiality," 394, and Morris, "Chirality of Being." It points to some larger problems in "handedness" that some phenomenologists have taken up. See, for example, Holger Lyre, "Handedness, Self-Models and Embodied Cognitive Content," *Phenomenology and the Cognitive Sciences* 7 (2008): 529–38.

31. See James van Cleve and Robert E. Frederick, eds., *The Philosophy of Right and Left: Incongruent Counterparts and the Nature of Space* (Dordrecht: Springer, 1991), especially the article by Graham Nerlich, "Hands, Knees, and Absolute Space." See also Morris's extensive discussions of the issues of "chirality" in "The Chirality of Being."

32. One might be tempted to say "action" here in place of doing, but "action" perhaps implies an "actor" and an "agent" and therefore is not helpful language at this point.

33. In his *New Critique of Theoretical Thought*, Dooyeweerd discusses at length the particular type of objectivity found in Western philosophy's conception of "theoretical thought," and encapsulated, for him, in the German word for object (*Gegenstand*), which can be literally translated as "stand-against." In this view, there is an antithetical or oppositional structure inherent to this account of objectivity, though this antithetical structure is merely intentional, not ontic (I, 38–39). While for Dooyeweerd this antithetical structure is properly speaking between the logical aspect of our thought and the nonlogical aspects of our temporal experience (I, 18; 38–39), he argues that in much of Western epistemology, the subject-object relation has come to be identified with the *Gegenstand* relation (I, 43), thereby leading to the presupposition of an antithetical relationship also between subject and object. The phenomenological method is an important step in overcoming this problematic identification in order to recover a proper understanding of the *Gegenstand* relation, and therefore of theoretical thought more generally. For an elaboration of Dooyeweerd's view of the "*Gegenstand* relation," see Hendrik Hart, "Dooyeweerd's Gegenstand Theory of Theory," in *The Legacy of Herman Dooyeweerd: Reflections on Critical Philosophy in the Christian Tradition*, ed. C.T. McIntire, (Lanham, MD: University Press of America, 1985), 143–66.

34. This is not all cosmetic surgery is, as the performance artist ORLAN shows in her own engagements with cosmetic surgery. This remains a somewhat controversial talking point in feminist discourses. See Cressida J. Heyes, *Anaesthetics of Existence: Essays on Experience at the Edge* (Durham, NC: Duke University Press, 2020), 10–11; and Meredith Jones, *Skintight: An Anatomy of Cosmetic Surgery* (Oxford: Berg, 2008).

35. Karen M. Barad, *Meeting the Universe Halfway: Quantum Physics and the Entanglement of Matter and Meaning* (Durham, NC: Duke University Press, 2007), 333.

36. Ibid.

37. Gina Zavota, "A Feminist Approach to The Visible and the Invisible through Karen Barad's Agential Realism," *Acta Structuralica Special Issue* 2 (2018): 164.

38. Barad, *Meeting the Universe Halfway*, 333.

39. Ibid., 44–45.

40. To be clear, Barad clearly construes "agents" well beyond anthropomorphic or even subjective terms. As Zavota points out, Barad is clear that individual agents "only emerge through their "intra-action" or entanglement" (148), therefore "emphasizing the fact that they are not independent agencies existing outside the process of which they are a part" (164). My claim is not so much that Barad's position is incompatible with the phenomenological one as that phenomenology's emphasis differs from Barad's in a way that makes the term "agential realism" helpful for Barad in a way it may not be helpful for phenomenology.

41. Barad, *Meeting the Universe Halfway*, 44–45.

42. Going from suggestion to demonstration will have to wait until Chapter 5, when we return to the question of the generation of subjectivity out of the expressive unity of flesh.

43. Gilles Deleuze, "The Method of Dramatization," *Bulletin de la Société Française de Philosophie* 62 (1967): 89–118, at 95.

44. See Anthony Steinbock, *Home and Beyond: Generative Phenomenology after Husserl* (Evanston, IL: Northwestern University Press, 1995); Anthony Steinbock, "Husserl's Static and Genetic Phenomenology: Translator's Introduction to Two Essays," in *Continental Philosophy Review* 31, no. 2 (1998): 127–34; Janet Donohoe, *Husserl on Ethics and Intersubjectivity: From Static and Genetic Phenomenology* (New York: Humanity Books, 2004).

45. Deleuze, "Method of Dramatization," 95.

46. "Generative phenomenology . . . is the most concrete dimension of phenomenology; it concerns intersubjective historical movement. (2) Genetic phenomenology treats generativity shorn of its historical/generational dimension. The movement . . . here would be from generational temporalization or historicity to individual self-temporalization or facticity. (3) Finally, generativity can be addressed statically through yet another level of abstraction, shorn of all temporal becoming." Steinbock, *Home and Beyond*, 266–67.

47. Think, most notably, of Leibniz's conception of the series of possible worlds existing in God's mind from before creation. See Gilles Deleuze, *Bergsonism*, trans. Hugh Tomlinson and Barbara Habberjam (New York: Zone Books, 1988), 20.

48. Again, this is similar to a function in calculus, which can be defined only as a relationship and can be given no positive value until at least one term in the relationship is given an actual position. Ibid., 97.

4. Making Sense of Experience:
The Transcendental Implications of Expressivity

1. See Karen M. Barad, *Meeting the Universe Halfway: Quantum Physics and the Entanglement of Matter and Meaning* (Durham, NC: Duke University Press, 2007), 333.

2. De Beistegui also raises this question. See *Immanence: Deleuze and Philosophy* (Edinburgh: Edinburgh University Press, 2010), ix.

3. Note that, in light of our discussion in previous chapters, we might instead say "an investigation into the sensings operative in our experience." The history of the concept of the transcendental in Western philosophy is discussed briefly in Sara Heinämaa, Mirja Hartimo, and Timo Miettinen, eds., *Phenomenology and the Transcendental* (New York: Routledge, 2014), 1–18, cited in text as MHC, and in more length in Part I of that book.

4. See Kant's definition of the transcendental as "all cognition which is occupied not so much with objects as with the mode of our cognition of objects in so far as this mode of cognition is to be possible *a priori*." *Critique of Pure Reason*, A11–12/B25.

5. This is not mere sophistry; as we will see in Chapter 5, it is essential to the entire phenomenological method that the transcendental conditions be (generative or actual) conditions of experience, and not conditions devoid of experience.

6. See *LI* I, 184 and Chapter 1.

7. The language of "virtuality" is prevalent in Deleuze, who defines it as such: "The characteristic of virtuality is to exist in such a way that it is actualized by being differenciated, and is forced to differenciate itself, to create its lines of differenciation in order to be actualized." *Bergsonism*, trans. Hugh Tomlinson and Barbara Habberjam (New York: Zone Books, 1988), 97. This notion of a self-differentiating movement of actualization obviously parallels the cogenerative force of expressive phenomenality discussed in the preceding chapter.

8. MHC, 8: "the transcendental and the empirical refer to two different aspects within the conscious life of the individual."

9. This is also crucial, we will see, to understanding subjectivity, since the relation and mutual necessity of the transcendental and the empirical is considered to be the very "paradox of subjectivity" by Husserl (Hua 6, 178). See also David Carr, *The Paradox of Subjectivity: The Self in the Transcendental Tradition* (New York: Oxford University Press, 1999).

10. Jacques Derrida, *Voice and Phenomenon: Introduction to the Problem of the Sign in Husserl's Phenomenology*, trans. Leonard Lawlor (Evanston, IL: Northwestern University Press, 2010), 11, cited in text as VP: "a difference in fact distinguishing nothing, a difference separating no state, no experience, no determined signification—but a difference which, without altering anything, changes all the signs." It is significant for the present discussion that Derrida then goes on to say that it is precisely in this difference "alone [that] the possibility of a transcendental question is contained."

11. For more on the distinction between the empirical and the transcendental accounts of language and writing, and their (possibly immense) significance for our understanding of the development of Derrida's thought, see Joshua Kates, *Essential History: Jacques Derrida and the Development of Deconstruction* (Evanston, IL: Northwestern University Press, 2005), chap. 3, "Derrida's 1962 Interpretation of Writing and Truth."

12. This complex relationship of "living in" and "living through" as it pertains to the empirical and transcendental not only confirms our earlier analysis of the "mutual asymmetry" of a phenomenological account of expressivity, but it also opens up the empirical and transcendental significance of tendencies, patterns, habits, and so on, that is, of the "passive syntheses" that Husserl discusses at length in Hua 11, but also in many of the unpublished manuscripts. On this, see MHC, 9–10, and Chapter 7.

13. Richard Dawkins, *The Selfish Gene* (New York: Oxford University Press, 1989).

14. This begins to show the difficulty of a simple "translation" from the logic of predication to a logic of events. It is too simple to equate the former with analytic philosophy and the latter with Continental philosophy. Nevertheless, I think it might be the case that a different understanding of sense is partially to explain for the relative difficulty in "crossing the divide" between analytic and Continental philosophy, especially when it comes to the transcendental elements of Continental thought.

15. In this regard, Kates's reading of IOG as a "sustained argument for the validity of Husserl's approach to history" that breaks "with the prevailing wisdom at the time" (Kates, *Essential History*, 54–55) provides a revelation of the deeply transcendental and phenomenological nature of Derrida's thought. Hence, Kates's title—*Essential History*—takes on a significant double meaning: not only is an understanding of the history of Derrida's thought "essential" to a proper understanding of the development of deconstruction, but what such an understanding reveals is also a particular understanding of the essential nature of history itself, in the transcendental fashion we are currently discussing.

16. Hence, the claim of Heinämaa, Hartimo, and Miettinen that the transcendental "must be straightforwardly given in experience" (MHC, 7) must be nuanced here: while we agree that the transcendental is given in experience (which, it should be noted, is the main emphasis of their claim), it seems that its mode of givenness is not "straightforward," at least in the sense that it is not

given "objectively" or as the direct object of an experience—it is not given as a phenomenon.

17. See Thomas Nail, *Being and Motion* (New York: Oxford University Press, 2019), 58, for more on the relationship between fields and waves.

18. On the significance of such "peripheral" experiences, see Cressida J. Heyes's use of "liminal experiences" in *Anaesthetics of Existence: Essays on Experience at the Edge* (Durham, NC: Duke University Press, 2020).

19. A point Deleuze deals with extensively in *Logic of Sense* in terms of the nonsense of sense that "signifies the operation of sense itself"; see de Beistegui, *Immanence*, 90. This is captured, for example, in Lewis Carroll's figure of "the Snark," of which Deleuze says: "sense is the Snark" (LS, 20).

20. See Gilles Deleuze, *The Logic of Sense*. trans. Mark Lester and Charles Stivale (New York: Columbia University Press, 1990), 73, though this point is equally at home in Merleau-Ponty, Husserl, and various other phenomenological thinkers, as we will see.

21. For more on the notion of levels or layers in Husserlian phenomenology, see Peter R. Costello, *Layers in Husserl's Phenomenology: On Meaning and Intersubjectivity* (Toronto: University of Toronto Press, 2012).

22. This problem marks Husserl's attempts to articulate the most basic phenomenological level at least since his work on time-consciousness. In that work, it is solved by his notion of double intentionality, in which the same act is both horizontally and transversely intentional. See Toine Kortooms, *Phenomenology of Time: Edmund Husserl's Analysis of Time-Consciousness* (Dordrecht: Kluwer Academic, 2002); and Neal DeRoo, *Futurity in Phenomenology: Promise and Method in Husserl, Levinas, and Derrida* (New York: Fordham University Press, 2013), chap. 1.

23. Eugen Fink, *Sixth Cartesian Meditation: The Idea of a Transcendental Theory of Method*, trans. R. Bruzina (Bloomington: Indiana University Press, 1995), 92–93.

24. See Renaud Barbaras, *The Being of the Phenomenon: Merleau-Ponty's Ontology*, trans. Leonard Lawlor and Ted Toadvine (Bloomington: Indiana University Press, 2004), 68. I try to do this vis-à-vis Merleau-Ponty's account of expression in "Merleau-Ponty and Ab/Normal Phenomenology: The Husserlian Roots of Merleau-Ponty's Account of Expression," in *Normality, Abnormality, and Pathology in Merleau-Ponty*, ed. Talia Walsh and Susan Bredlau (Albany: State University of New York Press, 2022).

25. See Gilles Deleuze and Felix Guattari, *What Is Philosophy?*, trans. Hugh Tomlinson and Graham Burchell III (New York: Columbia University Press, 1991).

26. The point is that it is not restricted merely to descriptive statements, nor to understanding "description" as predications concerning my immediate first-person perspective; see MHC, 8.

27. Mariana Ortega, "Hometactics," in *50 Concepts for a Critical Phenomenology*, ed. Gayle Weiss, Gayle Salamon, and Ann V. Murphy (Evanston, IL: Northwestern University Press, 2020), 169–73.

28. Hanne Jacobs, "Phenomenology as a Way of Life? Husserl on Phenomenological Reflection and Self-Transformation," *Continental Philosophy Review* 46 (2013): 349–69; see also Husserl, Hua 34, where this theme is discussed at length.

29. In this regard, they function in a way similar to the conceptual or metaphysical schemas in Johanna Oksala, *Feminist Experiences: Foucauldian and Phenomenological Investigations* (Evanston, IL: Northwestern University Press, 2016). See 34.

30. See also Dan Zahavi, "Transcendental Subjectivity and Metaphysics," *Human Studies* 25 (2002): 103–16.

31. Linda Martín Alcoff, "Sexual Violations and the Question of Experience," *New Literary History* 45, no. 3 (2014): 445–62, at 457.

32. George Yancy, *Black Bodies, White Gazes: The Continuing Significance of Race* (Lanham, MD: Rowman & Littlefield, 2008), 228. The example from which the "elevator effect" draws its name is discussed in chapter 1 of that work.

33. Following Merleau-Ponty's use of "operative intentionality" in *Phenomenology of Perception*, I am here using "operative concept" as a kind of shorthand for the passive syntheses—habits, tendencies, associations, and so forth—that shape our preobjective engagement with the world, and which are the result of our sensings of the world, as filtered through our spiritually and culturally constituted horizons of expectation (as discussed in Chapter 3). As preobjective, these things require a judgment in order to be objectified (e.g., into a concept, in the strong sense), but they themselves function as the basis for such objective judgments. To use another Merleau-Pontian word he adapted from Husserl, this is a matter of the "style" of our engagement with the world; see Hua 6 and Merleau-Ponty, *Eye and Mind*.

34. Yancy, *Black Bodies, White Gazes*, chap. 7.

35. See Gilles Deleuze, *Difference and Repetition*, trans. Paul Patton (London: Athlone Press, 1994), 56. Later, in *Difference and Repetition* (86–87), this transcendental empiricism is connected explicitly to the Husserlian notion of passive synthesis; see also Joe Hughes, *Deleuze and the Genesis of Representation* (London: Continuum, 2008), 10–19. This is significant, given the connection we made earlier between the "transcendental empiricals" and Husserl's notion of passive synthesis.

36. See Michael Kelly's analysis of such "meta-phenomenological" concerns in *Phenomenology and the Problem of Time* (London: Palgrave Macmillan, 2016).

37. See also VI, 46–47; MHC, 10–11; and Fink, *Sixth Cartesian Meditation*, 77–84.

38. Steinbock, *Home and Beyond*, 260.

39. Lisa Guenther, "Critical Phenomenology," in *50 Concepts for a Critical Phenomenology*, ed. Gayle Weiss, Gayle Salamon, and Ann V. Murphy (Evanston, IL: Northwestern University Press, 2020), 11–16, at 14.

40. Ibid., 15; see also Frantz Fanon, *Black Skin, White Masks*, trans. Charles Lam Markmann (New York: Grove Press, 1967), 82.

41. Ortega, "Hometactics," 170.

42. Ibid., 171.

43. This point is, of course, a part of the phenomenological tradition at least since Heidegger, whose *Destruktion* of metaphysics constituted perhaps the first attempt within phenomenology to articulate the empirical nature of what had previously been taken to be a transcendental claim.

5. The Subject, Reduction, and Uses of Phenomenology: The Methodological Implications of Expressivity

1. Dan Zahavi, at least, seems to suggest the answer to this question is no. Zahavi, "Applied Phenomenology: Why It Is Safe to Ignore the Epoché," *Continental Philosophy Review* (2019): 1–15.

2. I have tried to avoid doing this too much earlier in the book, but the method of doing such a "reading" has perhaps now been justified by the arguments of the previous chapter, and so I am open to use it more legitimately here.

3. See Remigius Kwant, *Phenomenology of Expression*, trans. Henry J. Koren (Pittsburgh, PA: Duquesne University Press, 1969), 60–61, cited in text as PE. Kwant goes on to show how this idea is not unique to Merleau-Ponty but is found in several other phenomenological contemporaries, notably Sartre and Levinas (PE 61–63).

4. It also necessarily opens onto visibility, language, and the other sensings; see VI, 134.

5. In the quote, it is visibility and not tangibility that is at issue. However, the text is clear that the tangible and the visible are not just similar in this regard, but are also themselves intertwined. Ibid.

6. See Gilles Deleuze, *The Fold: Leibniz and the Baroque*, trans. Tom Conley (Minneapolis: University of Minnesota Press, 1993), e.g., 64; *The Logic of Sense*, trans. Mark Lester and Charles Stivale (New York: Columbia University Press, 1990), e.g., 109; and various of his seminars on Leibniz. Deleuze's reading of Leibniz is thematized quite clearly in Daniel Smith, "Deleuze on Leibniz: Difference, Continuity and the Calculus," in *Current Continental Theory and Modern Philosophy* (Chicago: Northwestern University Press, 2006), 127–47.

7. See Merleau-Ponty's description of the visible as "borne by a wave of Being" (VI, 136).

8. See *Phenomenology of Perception*, trans. Colin Smith (New York: Humanities Press, 1974), but also, in a way, all of Merleau-Ponty's work; see Donald A. Landes, *Merleau-Ponty and the Paradoxes of Expression* (London: Bloomsbury Academic, 2013), for a compelling account of how the notion of expression and expressive embodiment runs throughout the whole of Merleau-Ponty's corpus.

9. Though he is sometimes uncomfortable with it; see, for example, VI, 137–38.

10. For more on the development of this relation in Merleau-Ponty's work, especially as it pertains to expression, see *The Sensible World and the World of Expression: Course Notes from the Collège de France, 1953*, trans. Bryan Smyth (Evanston, IL: Northwestern University Press, 2020).

11. There is an obvious reference here, both to Heidegger and, perhaps more notably in the French context, to Levinas and his early work on the emergence or "escape" of consciousness from the anonymity of the *il y a*; see Emmanuel Levinas, *Existence and Existents*, trans. Alphonsus Lingis (Pittsburgh, PA: Duquesne University Press, 1978), and *On Escape*, trans. Bettina Bergo (Stanford, CA: Stanford University Press, 2003). In that context, it is significant that Merleau-Ponty here seems to ascribe a will to the *il y a*, which is therefore prepersonal and not simply anonymous. This seems to steer Merleau-Ponty closer to Husserl's spiritual analysis than to Levinas.

12. Since this "will of the *there is*" is simply "the realization of an invisible that is exactly the reverse [or other side] of the visible, the power of the visible" (VI, 145), we can recognize here an account of the transcendental operation of subjectivity as a field, as an unfolding of flesh.

13. The quote adds: "as well as a relationship with the other." We will take up the inherent relation to the other, and to sociality more broadly, in Chapter 6.

14. Perhaps most famously in French philosophical phenomenology, there is Janicaud's critique of "theological" phenomenology in France. Dominique Janicaud, "The Theological Turn of French Phenomenology," in *Phenomenology and the Theological Turn: The French Debate*, ed. Dominique Janicaud et al., trans. Bernard G. Prusak (New York: Fordham University Press, 2000), 16–103. However, there are also several debates in the application of phenomenology to various fields: e.g., Linda Finlay, "Debating Phenomenological Research Methods," *Phenomenology & Practice* 3 (2009): 6–25; Amedeo Giorgi, "Concerning Variations in the Application of the Phenomenological Method," *The Humanistic Psychologist* 34, no. 4 (2006): 305–19; Annelise Norlyk and Ingegerd Harder, "What Makes a Phenomenological Study Phenomenological? An Analysis of Peer-Reviewed Empirical Nursing Studies," *Qualitative Health Research* 20, no. 3 (March 2010): 420–31.

15. This element is especially crucial to the use of phenomenology across a range of social and natural scientific disciplines. In these contexts, "phenomenology" often seems to denote little more than qualitative data presented on the basis of first-person accounts.

16. "The West" here names a particular *Stiftung* and not a geographic or historical identity. We will return to this issue of *Stiftungen* in the last part of this chapter.

17. See Heidegger's discussion of various meanings of "phenomenon" and "appearing" in §7 of *Being and Time*.

18. Michel Henry discusses this understanding of science at length in *Barbarism*, trans. Scott Davidson (London: Continuum, 2013).

19. It must be said that some theorists seem to try to use phenomenology, especially the *epoché*, as a means of diminishing the value of subjective experience insofar as they seek to "bracket" all of our theoretical presuppositions so as to approach the object of investigation unsullied by presuppositions, with an

"open mind," in a "neutral" posture, and so on. See, for example, Linda Finlay, "A Dance Between the Reduction and Reflexivity: Explicating the 'Phenomeno-logical Psychological Attitude,'" *Journal of Phenomenological Psychology* 39 (2008): 1–32. Such an account would remain broadly "empiricist" in orientation, despite its use of phenomenological terminology.

20. In this regard, I find Zahavi's brief discussion of "Husserl's correlationism" quite surprising (Zahavi, "Applied Phenomenology," 10), especially in light of speculative realism's critique of phenomenology as a type of correlationism; for one example of this critique, see Quentin Meillassoux, *After Finitude: An Essay on the Necessity of Contingency* (New York: Continuum, 2010). I prefer to speak, instead, of mutually delimiting, expressive generation rather than simply correlation.

21. For more on the apparent tension at work in the "principle of principles" and how it opens the need to understanding a relationship of "tension" between two poles (a relation we now recognize as expression), see Neal DeRoo, *Futurity in Phenomenology: Promise and Method in Husserl, Levinas, and Derrida* (New York: Fordham University Press, 2013), 141; and John Panteleimo Manoussakis, *God after Metaphysics: A Theological Aesthetic* (Bloomington: Indiana University Press, 2007), 14–19.

22. See Husserl's words in the *Crisis*: "What must be shown in particular and above all is that through the epoché a new way of experiencing, of thinking, of theorizing, is opened to the philosopher" (Hua 6, 152).

23. This is true even of those physical reductionists (like Richard Dawkins, for example) who think that the "set" of mental or spiritual objects is simply empty. Nonetheless, their very understanding of the physical world and how it operates tends to be continuous with Descartes's understanding of the *res extensa*, and in that regard they remain defined by the Cartesian dualism.

24. Husserl makes this point explicitly in §14 of *Cartesian Meditations*, but also, albeit with slightly different terminology, in §108 of *Ideas I*.

25. This is not to equate flesh with sensings, spirit, and/or *Stiftungen*; rather, those name the primary means by which we access (and are accessed by) flesh.

26. This very helpful "philosophical v. nonphilosophical uses of phenom-enology" distinction comes from Zahavi, "Applied Phenomenology."

27. Ibid., 9.

28. Max van Manen, *Phenomenology of Practice* (New York: Routledge, 2014); Max van Manen and Catherine Adams, "Phenomenological Pedagogy," in *Encyclopedia of Educational Theory and Philosophy*, ed. D. C. Phillips (Thousand Oaks, CA: Sage, 2014), 607–10; Max van Manen, "Phenomenology in Its Original Sense," *Qualitative Health Research* 27 (2017): 810–25.

29. This could include people like Max Van Manen or Clarence Joldersma in education theory; Jonathan Smith, James Morley, or Amedeo Giorgi in psychology; Kristiaan Martiny in nursing studies; and so on.

30. Zahavi, at least, seems to have reservations about how well we can ask people without formal training in philosophy to do this kind of philosophical,

methodological work; see "Applied Phenomenology," 10; and Dan Zahavi, "Getting It Quite Wrong: Van Manen and Smith on Phenomenology," *Qualitative Health Research* 29, no. 6 (2018): 900–907.

31. Zahavi, "Applied Phenomenology," 10; Amedeo Giorgi, "The Descriptive Phenomenological Psychological Method," *Journal of Phenomenological Psychology* 43 (2012): 3–12; James Morley, "It's Always about the Epoché," *Les Collectifs du Cirp* 1 (2010): 223–32.

32. Zahavi, "Applied Phenomenology," 9.

33. Another possibility would be to add philosophical phenomenologists to teams doing (inter)disciplinary research in phenomenology. Such philosophical phenomenologists would likely be more effective if they had some training in the applied field of study, however, and therefore might end up being something like the methodological scholars described earlier.

34. See Morley, "It's Always about the Epoché," 223–24, on how we risk sliding back into a naturalistic paradigm if we aren't purposeful in avoiding it. Zahavi discusses this claim on "Applied Phenomenology," 9, where his criticism seems to be directed against the notion that only the transcendental reduction, in its Husserlian sense, can help us avoid this risk, rather than against the claim that such a risk must be avoided.

35. My hope is that the current book will prove especially helpful to scholars, like Johanna Oksala and Cressida Heyes, who are trying to do this methodological work in critical discourses like feminism, race theory, queer theory, disability studies, and so on.

36. Herman Dooyeweerd makes this case in much more detail in *A New Critique of Theoretical Thought*, trans. David H. Freeman and William S. Young (Philadelphia: Presbyterian and Reformed Publishing Company, 1953). The details of his argument differ from mine in some respects, but the overall claim of his argument—that theoretical thought is not presuppositionless but inherently presumes certain supratheoretical commitments—is consistent with my own.

6. Toward a Phenomenological Politics: The Political Implications of Expressivity

1. Most notably, Searle, Foucault, and Habermas make variations of this argument. See John Searle, "Social Ontology: Some Basic Principles," *Anthropological Theory* 6 (2006): 12–29; Michel Foucault, "Truth and Power," in *The Foucault Reader*, ed. Paul Rabinow, 51–75 (New York: Pantheon Books, 1984); Jürgen Habermas, *On the Pragmatics of Social Interaction: Preliminary Studies in the Theory of Communicative Action*, trans. B. Fultner (Cambridge, MA: MIT Press, 2001).

2. Timo Miettinen, "Transcendental Social Ontology," in *Phenomenology and the Transcendental*, ed. Sara Heinämaa, Mirja Hartimo, and Timo Miettinen (New York: Routledge, 2014), 147–71, at 150, cited in text as TSO.

3. For more on the notion of empathy in Husserl, and in phenomenology more broadly, see Thomas Szanto and Dermot Moran, "Introduction: Intersubjectivity and Empathy," *Phenomenology and the Cognitive Sciences* 11, no. 2 (2012): 125–33; Dan Zahavi, "Empathy and Other-Directed Intentionality," *Topoi* 33 (2014): 129–42.

4. Robert Pfaller, *Die Illusionen der anderen: Über das Lustprinzip in der Kultur* (Frankfurt am Main: Suhrkamp, 2002).

5. This theme of a pre-primordial relationship with the Other that is constitutive of my own experience as a subject is a major phenomenological theme in Levinas. See Emmanuel Levinas, *Otherwise Than Being, or, Beyond Essence* (Pittsburgh, PA: Duquesne University Press, 1998). For more on the phenomenological resonances of Levinas's work, see John Drabinski, *Sensibility and Singularity: The Problem of Phenomenology in Levinas* (Albany: State University of New York Press, 2001); and Neal DeRoo, *Futurity in Phenomenology: Promise and Method in Husserl, Levinas, and Derrida* (New York: Fordham University Press, 2013), chaps. 4–6.

6. Via our earlier analyses of spirit (e.g., in Chapter 2) we have already come to see something of this duality, insofar as spirit is both a necessary factor in any and all intuition of the world and is expressed in concrete spiritual products like houses, bridges, works of art, theorems, and so on.

7. This theme is expanded upon in Ichiro Yamaguchi, *Passive Synthesis und Intersubjektivität bei Edmund Husserl* (The Hague: Martinus Nijhoff, 1982), 19, and Anthony Steinbock, *Home and Beyond: Generative Phenomenology after Husserl* (Evanston, IL: Northwestern University Press, 1995), 104–5

8. The issue of "style" is also a key theme of Merleau-Ponty's philosophy. See EM, 10n27; "Indirect Language and the Voices of Silence," in *Signs*, trans. Richard McCleary (Evanston, IL: Northwestern University Press), esp. 53–54; "The Body as Expression, and Speech," PhP. See also Andrew Inkpin, "Merleau-Ponty and the Significance of Style," *European Journal of Philosophy* 27, no. 2 (2019): 468–83; Meirav Almog, "Merleau-Ponty's Ontology of Style—Thought, Expression, and Art," *Pli: The Warwick Journal of Philosophy* 29, no. 1 (2018): 1–24.

9. John Searle, "Social Ontology and Political Power," in *Socializing Metaphysics: The Nature of Social Reality*, ed. Frederick Schmitt (Lanham, MD: Rowman & Littlefield, 2003), 195–210.

10. See also Yamaguchi, *Passive Synthesis*, 103; TSO, 154; Dan Zahavi, *Self-Awareness and Alterity: A Phenomenological Investigation* (Evanston, IL: Northwestern University Press, 1999), 73.

11. And, of course, granted that intentionality is not inherently purposive, as we made clear in our clarification of intentionality in Chapter 5. In this regard, one should be clear that the difference between phenomenology and social ontologies like Searle's is not so much about the adjective that proceeds intentionality (individual vs. collective), but about the understanding of intentionality itself: Searle is adamant that intentionality needs to be purposive,

willed, or "active" ("consciously shared behavior" as he states on page 198 of "Social Ontology and Political Power"), while phenomenology is willing to speak of "passive intentionality," "operative intentionality" (PhP, xx), and so on.

12. This, it seems, opens the door to rethinking intentionality (as our relation with the world) through the lens of a certain account of protention (as the "striving" or directed character of subjectivity), one that opens us also onto the infinity of the Other (who is not simply one other among others, but the very alterity of others), and a certain "counter-intentionality" directed from the Other toward us. This would be in line with Levinas's invocation of the reversal of *Sinngebung*. See, e.g., Emmanuel Levinas, *Discovering Existence with Husserl*, ed. and trans. Richard A. Cohen and Michael B. Smith (Evanston, IL: Northwestern University Press, 1998). See Derrida's discussion of intentionality in his *Introduction to Husserl's Origin of Geometry*, and the work on futurity in DeRoo, *Futurity in Phenomenology*.

13. I borrow this concept from TSO. See also Thomas Szanto and Dermot Moran, eds., *Phenomenology of Sociality: Discovering the We* (New York: Routledge, Taylor & Francis Group, 2016).

14. See Raimo Tuomela and Kaarlo Miller, "We-Intentions," *Philosophical Studies* 53 (1988): 115–37; Wilfrid Sellars, *Essays in Philosophy and Its History* (Dordrecht: Reidel, 1974).

15. Wilfrid Sellars, *Science and Metaphysics* (London: Routledge and Kegan Paul, 1968), 203.

16. See John Searle, *The Construction of Social Reality* (New York: Free Press, 1995), 23–27; David P. Schweikard and Hans Bernhard Schmid, "Collective Intentionality," *The Stanford Encyclopedia of Philosophy*, Summer 2013 Edition, ed. Edward N. Zalta (https://plato.stanford.edu/archives/sum2013/entries /collective-intentionality/); see also Max Weber, *Gesammelte Aufsätze zur Wissenschaftslehre*, ed. Marianne Weber (Tübingen: J. C. B. Mohr, 1922).

17. Wilfrid Sellars, "On Reasoning about Values," *American Philosophical Quarterly* 17, no. 2 (1980): 98. This position seems to be consistent with Searle's claim that collective intentionality can be had by envatted brains, insofar as it ignores all the preobjective connection between subjectivity and world that comes, we saw in Chapter 2, by understanding the subject as the embodiment of the world. John Searle, "Collective Intentions and Actions," in *Intentions in Communication*, ed. P. Cohen, J. Morgan, and M. E. Pollack (Cambridge, MA: MIT Press, 1990), 401–15, at 406.

18. See Searle, *The Construction of Social Reality*, 46; Raimo Tuomela, "Collective Intentionality and Group Reasons," in *Concepts of Sharedness*, ed. Hans Bernhard Schmid, Katinka Schulte-Ostermann, and Nikos Psarros (Frankfurt: Ontos Verlag, 2008), 3.

19. Recall our definition of "political" in the Introduction as that which constitutes a social body in the dual sense of that which is constitutive for that body (what makes a particular community what it is) and that which is constituting that body (as a transcendental constituting force).

20. It is for this reason that phenomenology would differ from the assumptions of "collective intentionality," not so much on the "individual ownership thesis" (i.e., that each person has his or her own mind), but rather on the claim that intentionality is about minds. Rather, intentionality, phenomenology would argue, is a matter of subjectivity (as a process), not subjects or minds (as distinct things). While minds may be individual, and individually "owned," this is orthogonal to the question of intentionality, which pertains primarily to subjectivity's engagement with the world and only secondarily (or tertiarily) to individual mind's thoughts about the world.

21. Miettinen discusses it at length in section 4 of TSO.

22. See David Carr, *Interpreting Husserl: Critical and Comparative Studies* (Dordrecht: Martinus Nijhoff, 1987), 268. Schütz certainly read Husserl this way, though Ricoeur did not. Alfred Schütz, *Collected Papers III: Studies in Phenomenological Philosophy* (The Hague: Martinus Nijhoff, 1975), 39; Paul Ricoeur, *From Text to Action: Essays in Hermeneutics* II, trans. Kathleen Blamey and John B. Thompson (Evanston, IL: Northwestern University Press, 1991), 244.

23. One might say that the movement of Western "politics" that I am suggesting here, the movement from being about the generative constitution of subjects to the interaction of constituted substances, is contained *in nuce* in Cicero's translation of Plato's *Politeia* (constitution) into Latin as *Res Publica*, the public "thing" or substance.

24. This is obviously a simplification of the *Stiftung* of "modern" social and political thought—but it is not inaccurate or unhelpful for that reason alone. It could be the case that something like the autonomous subject (or the related notion of the subject as sovereign) is the instituting principle inaugurating this "new" *Stiftung*, even if this *Stiftung* nevertheless grows out of earlier ones. Derrida's late work, especially *Rogues*, can be read as supporting something like this thesis.

25. Derrida recognizes this point in his notion of the Democracy-to-Come and, more broadly, in his distinction between Undeconstructibles and their deconstructible expressions; Jacques Derrida, *Specters of Marx: The State of the Debt, the Work of Mourning, and the New International* (New York: Routledge, 1994).

26. One of these generative conditions would likely be the transcendental process of racialization sometimes called "whiteness." Whiteness has long been tied to universality, perhaps because of the ways it grows out of Christianity and its "comprehensive vision." See, for example, Lewis R. Gordon, "Fanon, Philosophy, Racism," in *Racism and Philosophy*, ed. Susan E. Babbitt and Sue Campbell (Ithaca, NY: Cornell University Press, 1999), 32–49, at 34; Willie James Jennings, "Overcoming Racial Faith," *Divinity* (Spring 2015): 5–9, at 7. So the urge to articulate "universal" human rights—and the failure to see how this might simply be the elevation of a particular (white) understanding of subjectivity to the level of the generic or universal "human" understanding— may itself be a result of whiteness as a particular "ongoing and unfinished

history, which orientates bodies in specific directions, affecting how they 'take up' space." See Sara Ahmed, "A Phenomenology of Whiteness," *Feminist Theory* 8, no. 2 (2007): 149–68, at 150.

27. To be clear, this is not the stated goal in, for example, the Declaration of Independence or the *Universal* Declaration of Human Rights adopted by the UN. In both those documents, the universal nature of human rights is assumed to hold for all people (or at least all men, in the Declaration of Independence), even if they are not yet realized for all people.

28. See, for example, Ilan Kapoor, *The Postcolonial Politics of Development* (New York: Routledge; 2008); Ramon Grosfoguel, "Decolonizing Post-Colonial Studies and Paradigms of Political Economy: Transmodernity, Decolonial Thinking, and Global Coloniality," *Transmodernity: Journal of Peripheral Cultural Production of the Luso-Hispanic World* 1, no. 1 (2011): 1–34.

29. Even here we would have to distinguish between the transcendental dimension of a community (as a process of sense-bestowing or sense-constitution) and the empirical dimensions of a community, such as demographic details and the like. A *Stiftung* is not immediately equivalent to a demographic community, even if the "content" of the two (i.e., the actual people who make up the community) does not differ.

30. For example, if the colonized justify the colonization within the lifeworld of the colonized, but do so *qua* colonized, then it is debatable whether it is still the lifeworld of the (colonized) culture any longer, or whether it hasn't already become part of the lifeworld of the colonizing lifeworld.

31. See George Yancy, *Black Bodies, White Gazes: The Continuing Significance of Race* (Lanham, MD: Rowman & Littlefield, 2008); Ahmed, "A Phenomenology of Whiteness"; Sara Heinämaa, *Toward a Phenomenology of Sexual Difference: Husserl, Merleau-Ponty, Beauvoir* (Lanham, MD: Rowman & Littlefield, 2003); Alia Al-Saji, "Bodies and Sensings: On the Uses of Husserlian Phenomenology for Feminist Theory," *Continental Philosophy Review* 43, no. 1 (2010): 13–37; Sara Ahmed, *Queer Phenomenology: Orientations, Objects, Others* (Durham, NC: Duke University Press, 2006).

32. In this latter case, it seems likely to be a conjunctive case ("and") and not a disjunctive one ("or").

33. We can consider geometry a community, then, only when we are looking at how the *Stiftung* of geometry produces geometers, and how the function of those geometers is necessary for geometry. This is something we *could* look at when we study geometry, but we could also look only at the theorems produced, at the collection of insights and their communication in language, or at the continuity of certain moments in contemporary geometry with various moments in geometry's "essential history" without focusing on the subjects producing (or reanimating) the insights, or the subjects who are communicating, and so on.

34. See Cressida Heyes, *Self-Transformations: Foucault, Ethics, and Normalized Bodies* (Oxford: Oxford University Press, 2007).

35. For more on Husserl's understanding of culture, see also Ernst Wolfgang Orth, "*Kulturphilosophie* und Kulturanthropologie als Transzendentalphänomenologie," *Husserl Studies* 4 (1987): 103–41, and James Hart, "The Rationality of Culture and the Culture of Rationality," *Philosophy East and West* 42, no. 4 (1992): 643–64.

36. G. W. F. Hegel, *The Philosophy of History*, trans. J. Sibree, rev. ed. (New York: The Colonial Press, 1899), 30.

37. John Dewey, *The Later Works of John Dewey 1925–1953*, vol. 5 in *Collected Works of John Dewey (1925–1953 Essays)* (Carbondale: Southern University of Illinois Press, 1984), 35.

38. This last quote is from an earlier version of TSO, available online (https://www.academia.edu/12338041/Transcendental_Social_Ontology). It does not appear in the published version.

39. Fredric Jameson. *The Political Unconscious: Narrative as a Socially Symbolic Act* (New York: Routledge, 1983).

40. On whiteness as a "habit world" or "orientation," see Ahmed, "A Phenomenology of Whiteness."

41. So, while altering the social conditions may begin to alter that spiritual situation, if we do not attend more carefully to the transcendental (empirical) processes of constitution at work, such social change will, perhaps inevitably, lead to backlash. See George Yancy, *Backlash: What Happens When We Talk Honestly about Racism in America* (Lanham, MD: Rowman & Littlefield, 2018).

42. Judith Butler, *The Force of Non-Violence: An Ethico-Political Bind* (New York: Verso, 2020), cited in text as FNV.

43. Butler is here quoting from Lisa Guenther, *Solitary Confinement: Social Death and Its Afterlives* (Minneapolis: University of Minnesota Press, 2013).

44. See Judith Butler, *Frames of War: When Is Life Grievable?* (New York: Verso, 2009).

45. For example, while Butler "moves between a psychoanalytic and a social understanding of interdependency" (FNV, 48), I wonder whether phenomenology, and more specifically the kind of phenomenological politics under discussion in this chapter, might offer a better account of interdependency with which to undergird the type of "social imaginary"—or transcendental processes of generation—that Butler seeks.

Conclusion: The Logic of Phenomenality

1. It is not yet clear whether a subjective act of, say, perception is an expression of the subject and of visibility and of tactility and so forth, or whether it simply expresses the subject who, *qua* expression of subjectivity, is necessarily already in touch with visibility, tactility, and the like. If all the various sensings are already interimplicated in each other, is this mutual implication already an expression, such that subjectivity, in expressing flesh, also expresses all the qualities of flesh?

2. *Stiftungen* are not, strictly speaking, simply cultural nor simply communal, but a kind of boundary between them, simultaneously shaping subjects within a community and being a product of that community. As *Stiftungen*, they are a kind of "promissory phenomenon," inherently taking up a particular project in a particular way, in and as their very 'essence.' In this regard, it is probably more accurate to distinguish between *Stiftungen* and concrete phenomena, not as two distinct things, but as distinct types of phenomenality, that is, as yet another expressive level by which concrete phenomena express a particular *Stiftung*, which itself expresses a particular spiritual community, and so on. We have already gestured in this direction with our distinction between empirical, transcendental empirical, and transcendental levels of analysis.

3. For reasons that will become apparent in time, I cannot speak here simply of "living," in a broad sense; rather, I refer specifically to the biotic type of living characteristic of *bios* and studied in biology.

4. This way of formulating the "logic of sense" seems more appropriate, in light of the results of the present study. Whether it is also more appropriate to Gilles Deleuze's intentions in *The Logic of Sense* is a question we will not tackle here.

5. See Martin Heidegger, *Being and Time*, trans. Joan Stambaugh (Albany: State University of New York Press, 1996), §7.

6. Though we do not have time to discuss it here, this duality is central, not just to sensing, but to its logic, as it manifests the juncture—the folding together—of the tasks of transcendental and formal logic. See Gilles Deleuze, *The Logic of Sense*, trans. Mark Lester and Charles Stivale (New York: Columbia University Press, 1990), 97. This point is central to Husserl's "logical" works (*Logical Investigations*, *Formal and Transcendental Logic*, and *Experience and Judgment*), and so is central, I think, to understanding the (phenomeno) logic of phenomenology.

7. Johanna Oksala makes this point in a *Stiftung* that is much broader than simply that of phenomenology: "After the linguistic turn, the question of language in metaphysics cannot be bypassed" (FE, 29).

8. One sees Merleau-Ponty's initial attempts to make sense of this connection in *The Sensible World and the World of Expression: Course Notes from the Collège de France, 1953*, trans. Bryan Smyth (Evanston, IL: Northwestern University Press, 2020).

9. I mean "adequate" here in the traditional sense, by which a meaning is considered "adequate" if it causes people to think of things the way they actually are. It should be clear that, even as a guiding principle or Kantian ideal, such a theory of adequation does not align well with an expressive logic.

10. This example of (potential) sexual harassment therefore reveals that sexual harassment is not a matter of taking "innocent" comments and "reading into them" some nefarious or political motives. Rather, the issue of sexual harassment has brought to light—unfortunately through the negative experiences of countless individuals, most of whom were not fully "at home" in the dominant

sexual milieu (women, queer folk, transgender people, etc.)—that there always *were* political constitutions at play in such comments. The work of critical theorists of gender or sexuality did not make these experiences "political"; they simply helped us see the politics already at work in our experiences.

11. A point that had become increasingly clear throughout the twentieth century, as the connection between sense and the language community was explored in great detail. One could cite Derrida or Foucault here, but also Speech Act Theory, or Habermas's "Communicative Rationality" or Quine's "post-analytic" philosophy or Rorty or Brandom's pragmatism. All of these, in various ways, have highlighted the nonneutrality of language vis-à-vis sense, and the relation between language use and the communities or contexts in which that language is used or generated. See Jacques Derrida, *Of Grammatology*, trans. Gayatri Chakravorty Spivak (Baltimore: Johns Hopkins University Press, 1998), and *Limited Inc.*, trans. Samuel Weber (Evanston, IL: Northwestern University Press, 1988); Michel Foucault, *The Order of Things: An Archaeology of the Human Sciences* (New York: Vintage Books, 1994); Jürgen Habermas, *The Theory of Communicative Action* (Boston: Beacon Press, 1984), vols. 1 and 2; Willard Van Orman Quine, *Word and Object* (Cambridge, MA: MIT Press, 1960); Richard Rorty, *Philosophy and the Mirror of Nature* (Princeton, NJ: Princeton University Press, 1979; Robert Brandom, *Making It Explicit* (Cambridge, MA: Harvard University Press, 1998), and *Articulating Reasons* (Cambridge, MA: Harvard University Press, 2000).

12. Albeit in a different context, Nietzsche seems to have foreseen this point when he said: "I am afraid we are not rid of God because we still have faith in grammar." Friedrich W. Nietzsche, *Twilight of the Idols, Or, How to Philosophize with the Hammer* (Indianapolis: Hackett, 1997), 21. At the very least, such claims would seem to violate "common sense"; at most, they may be taken as an attack against "good sense" (i.e., the will to truth). For more on the Deleuzian distinction between common sense and good sense, and the attempt to bypass both through the logic of sense; see Jack Reynolds and Jon Roffe, "Deleuze and Merleau-Ponty: Immanence, Univocity and Phenomenology," *Journal of the British Society for Phenomenology* 37, no. 3 (2006): 228–51.

13. Deleuze, *Logic of Sense*, 21.

14. This is at least one way of understanding phenomenologically some of what is at stake in Audre Lorde's infamous "The Master's Tools Will Never Dismantle the Master's House," in *Sister Outsider: Essays and Speeches* (Berkeley, CA: Crossing Press, 2007), 110–14.

15. As with Deleuze's use of Lewis Carroll in *The Logic of Sense*.

16. Bertrand Russell speaking of Heidegger in *Wisdom of the West, : A Historical Survey of Western Philosophy in Its Social and Political Setting* (London: Bloomsbury Books, 1989), 303.

17. This is a quote from the infamous "Cambridge Affair," in which many leading analytic philosophers wrote to *The Times* (London) in criticism of

Derrida's possibly being awarded an honorary doctorate of letters from Cambridge. Barry Smith, "Letter to the Editor," *The Times* (London), May 9, 1992.

18. Ibid. Smith's letter also says that Derrida's "works employ a written style that defies comprehension," mainly consisting of "translating into the academic sphere tricks and gimmicks similar to those of the Dadaists or of the concrete poets."

19. Sanja Dejanovic, "The Sense of the Transcendental Field: Deleuze, Sartre, and Husserl," *Journal of Speculative Philosophy* 28, no. 2 (2014): 191.

20. This, perhaps, is another way of understanding Foucault's use of "genealogy" in a way that does not pit it against phenomenology, but helps transform phenomenology's self-understanding; see AE, chap. 1; FE, chap. 3.

21. Clarifying this point further would require a clarification of Deleuze's notion of expression and its relation to Leibniz's account of the calculus. Daniel Smith begins this work in "Deleuze on Leibniz: Difference, Continuity and the Calculus," *Current Continental Theory and Modern Philosophy*, (Chicago: Northwestern University Press, 2006), 127–47; and "Mathematics and the Theory of Multiplicities: Deleuze and Badiou Revisited," in *Essays on Deleuze*, (Edinburgh: Edinburgh University Press, 2012), 287–311.

22. Deleuze, *Expressionism in Philosophy: Spinoza*, trans. Martin Joughin (New York: Zone Books, 1992), 321.

23. Ibid.

24. As Merleau-Ponty says, tactility is part of visibility, etc. (VI, 134).

25. See Levinas, "Substitution," in *Otherwise Than Being*, trans. Alphonso Lingis (Pittsburgh, PA: Duquesne University Press, 1969), 99–131.

26. Derrida makes this point clear in his reflections on the transcendental necessity of language as arche-writing and "originary supplement." See *Voice and Phenomenon: Introduction to the Problem of the Sign in Husserl's Phenomenology*, trans. Leonard Lawlor (Evanston, IL: Northwestern University Press, 2010), 88–107; and *Of Grammatology*.

27. This does not necessarily rule out the possibility of an "object-oriented ontology," at least as a methodological choice. It simply opens the necessity of a justification for pursuing one. If an object-oriented ontology is not more "real" or more "actual" than a phenomenological orientation, then we must ask: What is the methodological benefit of beginning from an object-oriented ontology? How can one account for the primacy of the expressive logic of phenomenality within (and so be able to theoretically ground) an object-oriented ontology?

28. See Dooyeweerd's notion of the "subject" function and the "object" function. Herman Dooyeweed, *A New Critique of Theoretical Thought*, trans. David H. Freeman and William S. Young (Philadelphia: Presbyterian and Reformed Publishing Company, 1953), vols. 1 and 2.

29. The logic of phenomenality necessarily calls for some type of excess. Whether this excess must take the form of the excess posed by Marion is incidental to our broader purposes here, though it is a question that any rigorous examination of phenomenology itself must answer. See Jean-Luc

Marion, *In Excess: Studies of Saturated Phenomena*, trans. Robyn Horner and Vincent Berraud (New York: Fordham University Press, 2002).

30. No one has done more in the history of phenomenology to bring this relation to light than Michel Henry, who lays out the need for phenomenology to understand the rooting of consciousness, subjectivity, and the appearing of things *to* a subject in a relation of affectivity that necessarily precedes consciousness, subjectivity, and "hetero-manifestation" or "hetero-affectivity."

Works Cited

Abram, David. "In the Depths of a Breathing Planet: Gaia and the Transformation of Experience." In *Gaia in Turmoil: Climate Change, Biodepletion, and Earth Ethics in an Age of Crisis*, edited by Eileen Crist and H. Bruce Rinker, 221–42. Cambridge, MA: MIT Press, 2010.

Ahmed, Sara. "A Phenomenology of Whiteness." *Feminist Theory* 8, no. 2 (August 2007): 149–68.

———. *Queer Phenomenology: Orientations, Objects, Others*. Durham, NC: Duke University Press, 2006.

Alcoff, Linda Martín. "Dangerous Pleasures: Foucault and the Politics of Pedophilia." In *Feminist Interpretations of Michel Foucault,* edited by Susan J. Hekman, 99–135. University Park: Pennsylvania State University Press, 1996.

———. "Sexual Violations and the Question of Experience." *New Literary History* 45, no. 3 (2014): 445–62.

———. "Towards a Phenomenology of Racial Embodiment." *Radical Philosophy* 95 (1999): 15–26.

Almog, Meirav. "Merleau-Ponty's Ontology of Style—Thought, Expression, and Art." *Pli: The Warwick Journal of Philosophy* 29, no. 1 (2018): 1–24.

Al-Saji, Alia. "Bodies and Sensings: On the Uses of Husserlian Phenomenology for Feminist Theory." *Continental Philosophy Review* 43, no. 1 (2010): 13–37.

Aquila, Richard E. "Husserl and Frege on Meaning." *Journal of the History of Philosophy* 12, no. 3 (1974): 377–83.

Badiou, Alain. *Deleuze: The Clamor of Being*. Translated by Louise Burchill. Minneapolis: University of Minnesota Press, 2000.

Barad, Karen M. *Meeting the Universe Halfway: Quantum Physics and the Entanglement of Matter and Meaning.* Durham, NC: Duke University Press, 2007.

Barbaras, Renaud. *The Being of the Phenomenon: Merleau-Ponty's Ontology.* Translated by Leonard Lawlor and Ted Toadvine. Bloomington: Indiana University Press, 2004.

Beaulieu, Alain. "Edmund Husserl." In *Deleuze's Philosophical Lineage*, edited by Graham Jones and Jon Roffe, 261–81. Edinburgh: Edinburgh University Press, 2009.

———. *Gilles Deleuze et la phénoménologie.* Paris: Vrin, 2004.

Bowden, Sean. "The Intensive Expression of the Virtual: Revisiting the Relation of Expression in Difference and Repetition." *Deleuze Studies* 11, no. 2 (2017): 216–39.

Brandom, Robert. *Articulating Reasons.* Cambridge, MA: Harvard University Press, 2000.

———. *Making it Explicit.* Cambridge, MA: Harvard University Press, 1998.

Butler, Judith. "Endangered/Endangering: Schematic Racism and White Paranoia." In *Reading Rodney King, Reading Urban Uprising*, edited by Robert Gooding-Williams, 15–22. New York: Routledge, 1993.

———. *The Force of Non-Violence: An Ethico-Political Bind.* New York: Verso, 2020.

———. *Frames of War: When Is Life Grievable?* New York: Verso, 2009.

———. *Precarious Life: The Powers of Mourning and Violence.* New York: Verso, 2006.

Carr, David. *Interpreting Husserl: Critical and Comparative Studies.* Dordrecht: Martinus Nijhoff, 1987.

———. *The Paradox of Subjectivity: The Self in the Transcendental Tradition.* New York: Oxford University Press, 1999.

Casey, Edward. "Taking a Glance at the Environment: Preliminary Thoughts on a Promising Topic." In *Eco-Phenomenology: Back to the Earth Itself*, edited by Charles S. Brown and Ted Toadvine, 187–210. Albany: State University of New York Press, 2003.

Cisney, Vernon W. *Derrida's Voice and Phenomenon.* Edinburgh: Edinburgh University Press, 2014.

Costello, Peter R. *Layers in Husserl's Phenomenology: On Meaning and Intersubjectivity.* Toronto: University of Toronto Press, 2012.

Crowell, Steven. "Transcendental Phenomenology and the Seductions of Naturalism: Subjectivity, Consciousness, and Meaning." In *The Oxford Handbook of Contemporary Phenomenology*, edited by Dan Zahavi, 25–47. Oxford: Oxford University Press, 2012.

Dawkins, Richard. *The Selfish Gene.* New York: Oxford University Press, 1989.

De Beauvoir, Simone. *The Second Sex.* Translated and edited by H. M. Parshley. Harmondsworth: Penguin, 1953.

De Beistegui, Miguel. *Immanence: Deleuze and Philosophy.* Edinburgh: Edinburgh University Press, 2010.

————. *Truth and Genesis: Philosophy as Differential Ontology*. Bloomington: Indiana University Press, 2004.

Dejanovic, Sanja. "The Sense of the Transcendental Field: Deleuze, Sartre, and Husserl." *Journal of Speculative Philosophy* 28, no. 2 (2014): 190–212.

Deleuze, Gilles. *Bergsonism*. Translated by Hugh Tomlinson and Barbara Habberjam. New York: Zone Books, 1988.

————. *Difference and Repetition*. Translated by Paul Patton. London: Athlone Press, 1994.

————. *Expressionism in Philosophy: Spinoza*. Translated by Martin Joughin. New York: Zone Books, 1992.

————. *The Fold: Leibniz and the Baroque*. Translated by Tom Conley. Minneapolis: University of Minnesota Press, 1993.

————. *The Logic of Sense*. Translated by Mark Lester and Charles Stivale. New York: Columbia University Press, 1990.

————. "The Method of Dramatization." *Bulletin de la Société Française de Philosophie* 62 (1967): 89–118.

Deleuze, Gilles, and Felix Guattari. *What Is Philosophy?* Translated by Hugh Tomlinson and Graham Burchell III. New York: Columbia University Press, 1991.

DeRoo, Neal. "A Positive Account of Protention and Its Implications for Internal Time-Consciousness." In *Epistemology, Archaeology, Ethics: Current Investigations of Husserl's Corpus*, edited by Pol Vandevelde and Sebastian Luft, 102–19. London: Continuum, 2010.

————. *Futurity in Phenomenology: Promise and Method in Husserl, Levinas, and Derrida*. New York: Fordham University Press, 2013.

————. "Meaning, Being and Time: The Phenomenological Significance of Dooyeweerd's Thought." In *Phenomenology for the Twenty-First Century*, edited by J. Aaron Simmons and James E. Hackett, 77–96. London: Palgrave MacMillan, 2016.

————. "Merleau-Ponty and Ab/Normal Phenomenology: The Husserlian Roots of Merleau-Ponty's Account of Expression." In *Normality, Abnormality, and Pathology in Merleau-Ponty*, edited by Talia Walsh and Susan Bredlau, 63–78. Albany: State University of New York Press, 2022.

————. "Spiritual Expression and the Promise of Phenomenology." In *The Subject(s) of Phenomenology: Rereading Husserl*, edited by Iulian Apostelescu, Verdran Grahovac, and Patrick Flack, 245–69. New York: Springer, 2020.

————. "Spiritual Life and Cultural Discernment: Renewing Spirituality through Henry." In *The Practical Philosophy of Michel Henry*, edited by Brian Harding and Michael R. Kelly, 45–65. New York: Bloomsbury Press, 2022.

Derrida, Jacques. *Edmund Husserl's* Origin of Geometry: *An Introduction*. Translated by John P. Leavey. Lincoln: University of Nebraska Press, 1989.

————. *Limited Inc*. Translated by Samuel Weber. Evanston, IL: Northwestern University Press, 1988.

———. *Of Grammatology*. Translated by Gayatri Chakravorty Spivak. Baltimore, MD: Johns Hopkins University Press, 1998.

———. *Of Spirit: Heidegger and the Question*. Translated by Geoffrey Bennington and Rachel Bowlby. Chicago: University of Chicago Press, 1989.

———. *The Problem of Genesis in Husserl's Philosophy*. Translated by Marian Hobson. Chicago: University of Chicago Press, 2003.

———. *Specters of Marx: The State of the Debt, the Work of Mourning, and the New International*. New York: Routledge, 1994.

———. *Voice and Phenomenon: Introduction to the Problem of the Sign in Husserl's Phenomenology*. Translated by Leonard Lawlor. Evanston, IL: Northwestern University Press, 2010.

Dewey, John. *The Later Works of John Dewey 1925–1953*. In *Collected Works of John Dewey (1925–1953 Essays)*, vol. 5. Carbondale: Southern Illinois University Press, 1984.

Donohoe, Janet. *Husserl on Ethics and Intersubjectivity: From Static and Genetic Phenomenology*. New York: Humanity Books, 2004.

Dooyeweerd, Herman. *A New Critique of Theoretical Thought*. Translated by David H. Freeman and William S. Young. Philadelphia: Presbyterian and Reformed Publishing Company, 1953.

Drabinski, John. *Sensibility and Singularity: The Problem of Phenomenology in Levinas*. Albany: State University of New York Press, 2001.

Du Bois, W. E. B. "The Souls of White Folk." In *W. E. B. Du Bois: A Reader*, edited by David Levering Lewis, 453–65. New York: Henry Holt, 1995.

Edelglass, William, James Hatley, and Christian Diehm. *Facing Nature: Levinas and Environmental Thought*. Pittsburgh, PA: Duquesne University Press, 2012.

Falque, Emmanuelle. "The Discarnate Madman." Translated by Sarah Horton. *Journal for Continental Philosophy of Religion* 1, no. 1 (2019): 90–117.

Fanon, Frantz. *Black Skin, White Masks*. Translated by Charles Lam Markmann. New York: Grove Press, 1967.

Ferrari, Martina. "Poietic Transpatiality: Merleau-Ponty and the Sense of Nature." *Chiasmi International* 20 (2018): 385–401.

Fink, Eugen. *Sixth Cartesian Meditation: The Idea of a Transcendental Theory of Method*. Translated by R. Bruzina. Bloomington: Indiana University Press, 1995.

Finlay, Linda. "A Dance Between the Reduction and Reflexivity: Explicating the 'Phenomenological Psychological Attitude.'" *Journal of Phenomenological Psychology* 39 (2008): 1–32.

———. "Debating Phenomenological Research Methods." *Phenomenology & Practice* 3, no. 1 (2009): 6–25.

Fóti, Véronique. *Tracing Expression in Merleau-Ponty*. Evanston, IL: Northwestern University Press, 2013.

Foucault, Michel. *The Order of Things: An Archaeology of the Human Sciences*. New York: Vintage Books, 1994.

———. "Truth and Power." In *The Foucault Reader*, edited by Paul Rabinow, 51–75. New York: Pantheon Books, 1984.

Frege, Gottlob. *The Foundations of Arithmetic: A Logico-Mathematical Enquiry into the Concept of Number*. Translated by J. L. Austin. Evanston, IL: Northwestern University Press, 1960.

———. "Sense and Reference." *The Philosophical Review* 57, no. 3 (1948): 209–30.

Giorgi, Amedeo. "Concerning Variations in the Application of the Phenomenological Method." *The Humanistic Psychologist* 34, no. 4 (2006): 305–19.

———. "The Descriptive Phenomenological Psychological Method." *Journal of Phenomenological Psychology* 43 (2012): 3–12.

Gordon, Lewis R. *Bad Faith and Antiblack Racism*. Atlantic Highlands, NJ: Humanities Press, 1995.

———. "Fanon, Philosophy, Racism." In *Racism and Philosophy*, edited by Susan E. Babbitt and Sue Campbell, 32–49. Ithaca, NY: Cornell University Press, 1999.

Grosfoguel, Ramon. "Decolonizing Post-Colonial Studies and Paradigms of Political Economy: Transmodernity, Decolonial Thinking, and Global Coloniality." *Transmodernity: Journal of Peripheral Cultural Production of the Luso-Hispanic World* 1, no. 1 (2011) 1–34.

Guenther, Lisa. "Critical Phenomenology." In *50 Concepts for a Critical Phenomenology*, edited by Gayle Weiss, Gayle Salamon, and Ann V. Murphy, 11–16. Evanston, IL: Northwestern University Press, 2020.

———. *Solitary Confinement: Social Death and Its Afterlives*. Minneapolis: University of Minnesota Press, 2013.

Günzel, Stephan. "Deleuze and Phenomenology." *Metodo: International Studies in Phenomenology and Philosophy* 2, no. 3 (2014): 31–45.

Habermas, Jürgen. *On the Pragmatics of Social Interaction: Preliminary Studies in the Theory of Communicative Action*. Translated by B. Fultner. Cambridge, MA: MIT Press, 2001.

———. *The Theory of Communicative Action*. Boston: Beacon Press, 1984.

Hart, Hendrik. "Dooyeweerd's Gegenstand Theory of Theory." In *The Legacy of Herman Dooyeweerd: Reflections on Critical Philosophy in the Christian Tradition*, edited by C. T. McIntire, 143–66. Lanham, MD: University Press of America, 1985.

Hart, James. "The Rationality of Culture and the Culture of Rationality." *Philosophy East and West* 42 no. 4 (1992): 643–64.

Hegel, G. W. F. *The Philosophy of History*. Rev. ed. Translated by J. Sibree. New York: Colonial Press, 1899.

Heidegger, Martin. *Being and Time*. Translated by Joan Stambaugh. Albany: State University of New York Press, 1996.

———. *Introduction to Metaphysics*. Translated by Ralph Manheim. New York: Doubleday, 1961.

Heinämaa, Sara. "Embodiment and Expressivity in Husserl's Phenomenology: From *Logical Investigations* to *Cartesian Meditations*." *SATS: Northern European Journal of Philosophy* 11 (2010): 1–15.

———. "On the Transcendental Undercurrents of Phenomenology: The Case of the Living Body." *Continental Philosophy Review* 54, no. 2 (2021): 237–57.

———. *Toward a Phenomenology of Sexual Difference: Husserl, Merleau-Ponty, Beauvoir*. Lanham, MD: Rowman & Littlefield, 2003.

Heinämaa, Sara, Mirja Hartimo, and Timo Miettinen, eds.. *Phenomenology and the Transcendental*. New York: Routledge, 2014.

Henry, Michel. *Barbarism*. Translated by Scott Davidson. London: Continuum, 2013.

———. *The Essence of Manifestation*. Translated by G. Etzkorn. Dordrecht: Springer, 1973.

———. *Incarnation: A Philosophy of Flesh*. Translated by Karl Kefty. Evanston, IL: Northwestern University Press, 2015.

———. *Words of Christ*. Translated by Christina Gschwandtner. Grand Rapids, MI: Eerdmans, 2012.

Heyes, Cressida J. *Anaesthetics of Existence: Essays on Experience at the Edge*. Durham, NC: Duke University Press, 2020.

———. *Self-Transformations: Foucault, Ethics, and Normalized Bodies*. Oxford: Oxford University Press, 2007.

Hughes, Joe. *Deleuze and the Genesis of Representation*. London: Continuum, 2008.

Husserl, Edmund. *Analyses Concerning Active and Passive Synthesis: Lectures on Transcendental Logic*. Dordrecht: Kluwer Academic, 2001.

———. *Aufsätze und Vorträge: 1922–1937*. Edited by T. Nenon and H. R. Sepp. The Hague: Kluwer Academic, 1998.

———. *Cartesian Meditations: An Introduction to Phenomenology*. Translated by Dorion Cairns. Dordrecht: Kluwer Academic, 1999.

———. *The Crisis of European Sciences and Transcendental Phenomenology*. Translated by David Carr. Evanston, IL: Northwestern University Press, 1970.

———. *Die Krisis der europaischen Wissenschaften und die transzendentale Phänomenologie*. Edited by Reinhold N. Smid. The Hague: Kluwer Academic, 1992.

———. *Die Lebenswelt: Auslegungen der vorgegebenen Welt und ihrer Konstitution*. Edited by Sowa Rochus. Dordrecht: Springer, 2008.

———. *Einleitung in die Ethik: Vorlesung en Sommersemester 1920 und 1924*. Edited by Henning Peucker. Dordrecht: Kluwer Academic, 2004.

———. *Erste Philosophie: Zweiter Teil—Theorie der phänomenologischen Reduktion*. The Hague: Martinus Nijhoff, 1959.

———. *Experience and Judgement: Investigations in a Genealogy of Logic*. Translated by James Churchill and Karl Ameriks. Evanston, IL: Northwestern University Press, 1973.

———. *Formal and Transcendental Logic*. Translated by Dorion Cairns. The Hague: Martinus Nijhoff, 1969.

―――. "Fundamental Investigations on the Phenomenological Origin of the Spatiality of Nature." In *Shorter Works*, translated by Fred Kersten, edited by Peter McCormick and Frederick A. Elleston, 222–33. South Bend, IN: University of Notre Dame Press, 1981.

―――. *Ideas Pertaining to a Pure Phenomenology and to a Phenomenological Philosophy, Book 1: General Introduction to a Pure Phenomenology*. Translated by F. Kersten. The Hague: Martinus Nijhoff, 1983.

―――. *Ideas Pertaining to a Pure Phenomenology and to a Phenomenological Philosophy, Book 2: Studies in the Phenomenology of Constitution*. Translated by Richard Rojcewicz and André Schuwer. Dordrecht: Kluwer Academic, 1989.

―――. *Logical Investigations*. Translated by J. N. Findlay. London and New York: Routledge, 2000.

―――. *On the Phenomenology of the Consciousness of Internal Time*. Translated by John Barnett Brough. Dordrecht: Kluwer Academic, 1991.

―――. "Origin of Geometry." In *The Crisis of European Sciences and Transcendental Phenomenology*, 353–78. Translated by David Carr. Evanston, IL: Northwestern University Press, 1970.

―――. *Phänomenologische Psychologie: Vorlesungen Sommersemester 1925*. The Hague: Martinus Nijhoff, 1962.

―――. *Zur Phänomenologie der Intersubjektivität: Texte aus dem Nachlass. Zweiter Teil: 1921–28*. Edited by Iso Kern. The Hague: Martinus Nijhoff, 1973.

―――. *Zur Phänomenologie der Intersubjektivität: Texte aus dem Nachlass. Dritter Teil: 1929–35*. Edited by Iso Kern. The Hague: Martinus Nijhoff, 1973.

―――. *Zur Phänomenologischen Reduktion: Texte aus dem Nachlass (1926–1935)*. Edited by Sebastian Luft. Dordrecht: Kluwer, 2002.

Inkpin, Andrew. "Merleau-Ponty and the Significance of Style." *European Journal of Philosophy* 27, no. 2 (2019): 468–83.

Irigaray, Luce. *An Ethics of Sexual Difference*. Translated by Carolyn Burke and Gillian Gill. Ithaca, NY: Cornell University Press: 1993.

Jacobs, Hanne. "Phenomenology as a Way of Life? Husserl on Phenomenological Reflection and Self-Transformation." *Continental Philosophy Review* 46 (2013): 349–69.

Jameson, Fredric. *The Political Unconscious: Narrative as a Socially Symbolic Act*. New York: Routledge, 1983.

Janicaud, Dominique. "The Theological Turn of French Phenomenology." In Dominique Janicaud et al., *Phenomenology and the Theological Turn: The French Debate*, translated by Bernard G. Prusaki, 16–103. New York: Fordham University Press, 2000.

Jennings, Willie James. "Overcoming Racial Faith." *Divinity* 14, no. 2 (2015): 5–9.

Jones, Meredith. *Skintight: An Anatomy of Cosmetic Surgery*. Oxford: Berg, 2008.

Kant, Immanuel. *Critique of Pure Reason*. Boston: Bedford, 1929.

Kapoor, Ilan. *The Postcolonial Politics of Development*. New York: Routledge, 2008.

Kates, Joshua. *Essential History: Jacques Derrida and the Development of Deconstruction*. Evanston, IL: Northwestern University Press, 2005.

Kelly, Michael R. *Phenomenology and the Problem of Time*. London: Palgrave Macmillan, 2016.

Kortooms, Toine. *Phenomenology of Time: Edmund Husserl's Analysis of Time-Consciousness*. Dordrecht: Kluwer Academic, 2002.

Kwant, Remigius. *Phenomenology of Expression*. Translated by Henry J. Koren. Pittsburgh, PA: Duquesne University Press, 1969.

Landes, Donald A. *Merleau-Ponty and the Paradoxes of Expression*. London: Bloomsbury Academic, 2013.

Lawlor, Leonard. "The End of Phenomenology: Expressionism in Deleuze and Merleau-Ponty." *Continental Philosophy Review* 31 (1998): 15–34.

———. *Thinking through French Philosophy: The Being of the Question*. Bloomington: Indiana University Press, 2003.

Levinas, Emmanuel. *Discovering Existence with Husserl*. Edited and translated by Richard A. Cohen and Michael B. Smith. Evanston, IL: Northwestern University Press, 1998.

———. *Existence and Existents*. Translated by Alphonsus Lingis. Pittsburgh, PA: Duquesne University Press, 1978.

———. *On Escape*. Translated by Bettina Bergo. Stanford, CA: Stanford University Press, 2003.

———. *Otherwise Than Being, or, Beyond Essence*. Translated by Alphonso Lingis. Pittsburgh, PA: Duquesne University Press, 1998.

———. *Totality and Infinity: An Essay on Exteriority*. Translated by Alphonso Lingis. Pittsburgh, PA: Duquesne University Press, 1969.

Lloyd, Genevieve. *The Man of Reason: "Male" and "Female" in Western Philosophy*. 2nd ed. New York: Routledge, 1993.

Lorde, Audre. "The Master's Tools Will Never Dismantle the Master's House." In *Sister Outsider: Essays and Speeches*. Berkeley, CA: Crossing Press, 2007.

Lyre, Holger. "Handedness, Self-Models and Embodied Cognitive Content." *Phenomenology and the Cognitive Sciences* 7 (2008): 529–38.

Macey, David. "Fanon, Phenomenology, Race." *Radical Philosophy* 95 (1999): 8–14.

Manoussakis, John Panteleimon. *God after Metaphysics: A Theological Aesthetic*. Bloomington: Indiana University Press, 2007.

Marion, Jean-Luc. *The Idol and Distance: Five Studies*. Translated by Thomas A. Carlson. New York: Fordham University Press, 2001.

———. *In Excess: Studies of Saturated Phenomena*. Translated by Robyn Horner and Vincent Berraud. New York: Fordham University Press, 2002.

———. *Reduction and Givenness: Investigations of Husserl, Heidegger, and Phenomenology*. Evanston, IL: Northwestern University Press, 1998.

Meillassoux, Quentin. *After Finitude: An Essay on the Necessity of Contingency*. New York: Continuum, 2010.

Merleau-Ponty, Maurice. "Eye and Mind." In *The Primacy of Perception*, translated by Carleton Dallery, edited by James M. Edie, 159–90. Evanston, IL: Northwestern University Press, 1964.

———. "Indirect Language and the Voices of Silence." In *Signs*, translated by Richard McCleary, 39–83. Evanston, IL: Northwestern University Press, 1964.

———. *Institution and Passivity: Course Notes from the Collège de France (1954–1955)*. Translated by Leonard Lawlor and Heath Massey. Evanston, IL: Northwestern University Press, 2010.

———. *L'institution / La passivité: Notes de cours au Collège de France (1954–1955)*. Paris: Editions Belin, 2003.

———. *Phenomenology of Perception*. Translated by Colin Smith. New York: Humanities Press, 1974.

———. "The Philosopher and His Shadow." In *Signs*, translated by Richard McCleary, 159–81. Evanston, IL: Northwestern University Press, 1964.

———. *The Sensible World and the World of Expression: Course Notes from the Collège de France, 1953*. Translated by Bryan Smyth. Evanston, IL: Northwestern University Press, 2020.

———. *The Structure of Behavior*. Translated by Alden L. Fisher. London: Beacon Press, 1963.

———. "Themes from the Lectures at the College de France, 1952–1960." In *Praise of Philosophy and Other Essays*. Translated by John O'Neill. Evanston, IL: Northwestern University Press, 1988.

———. *The Visible and the Invisible*. Translated by Alphonso Lingis. Evanston, IL: Northwestern University Press, 1968.

Miettinen, Timo. "Transcendental Social Ontology." In *Phenomenology and the Transcendental*, edited by Sara Heinämaa, Mirja Hartimo, and Timo Miettinen, 147–71. New York: Routledge, 2014.

Morley, James. "It's Always about the Epoché." *Les Collectifs du Cirp* 1 (2010): 223–32.

Morris, David. "The Chirality of Being: Exploring a Merleau-Pontian Ontology of Sense." *Chiasmi International* 12 (2011): 165–82.

Nail, Thomas. *Being and Motion*. New York: Oxford University Press, 2019.

———. "Expression, Immanence and Constructivism: 'Spinozism' and Gilles Deleuze." *Deleuze Studies* 2, no. 2 (2008): 201–19.

Nerlich, Graham. "Hands, Knees, and Absolute Space." *Journal of Philosophy* 70 (1973): 337–51.

Nietzsche, Friedrich. *Twilight of the Idols, Or, How to Philosophize with the Hammer*. Indianapolis: Hackett, 1997.

Norlyk, Annelise, and Ingegerd Harder. "What Makes a Phenomenological Study Phenomenological? An Analysis of Peer-Reviewed Empirical Nursing Studies." *Qualitative Health Research* 20, no. 3 (2010): 420–31.

Oksala, Johana. *Feminist Experiences: Foucauldian and Phenomenological Investigations*. Evanston, IL: Northwestern University Press, 2016.

Online Etymology Dictionary. "Em-." Douglas Harper. https://www.etymonline.com/word/em-.

———. "En-." Douglas Harper. https://www.etymonline.com/word/en-.

Ortega, Mariana. "Hometactics." In *50 Concepts for a Critical Phenomenology*, edited by edited by Gayle Weiss, Gayle Salamon, and Ann V. Murphy, 169–73. Evanston, IL: Northwestern University Press, 2020.

Orth, Ernst Wolfgang. *"Kulturphilosophie* und Kulturanthropologie als Transzendental Phänomenologie." *Husserl Studies* 4 (1987): 103–41.

Pfaller, Robert. *Die Illusionen der anderen: Über das Lustprinzip in der Kultur.* Frankfurt am Main: Suhrkamp, 2002.

Polkinghorne, Donald. *Practice and the Human Sciences: The Case for a Judgment-Based Practice of Care.* New York: State University of New York Press, 2004.

Pulkkinnen, Simo. "Lifeworld as an Embodiment of Spiritual Meaning: The Constitutive Dynamics of Activity and Passivity in Husserl." *The Phenomenology of Embodied Subjectivity*, edited by R. T. Jensen and Dermot Moran, 121–41. Cham, Switzerland: Springer, 2013.

Quine, Willard Van Orman. *Word and Object.* Cambridge, MA: MIT Press, 1960.

Reynolds, Jack, and Jon Roffe. "Deleuze and Merleau-Ponty: Immanence, Univocity and Phenomenology." *Journal of the British Society for Phenomenology* 37, no. 3 (2006): 228–51.

Ricoeur, Paul. *From Text to Action: Essays in Hermeneutics II.* Translated by Kathleen Blamey and John B. Thompson. Evanston, IL: Northwestern University Press, 1991.

Rorty, Richard. *Philosophy and the Mirror of Nature.* Princeton, NJ: Princeton University Press, 1979.

Russell, Bertrand. *Wisdom of the West: A Historical Survey of Western Philosophy in Its Social and Political Setting.* London: Bloomsbury Books, 1989.

Salomon, Gayle. *Assuming a Body: Transgender and Rhetorics of Materiality.* New York: Columbia University Press, 2010.

———. "'The Place Where Life Hides Away': Merleau-Ponty, Fanon, and the Location of Bodily Being." *Differences* 17, no. 2 (2006): 96–112.

Schües, Christina. "Conflicting Apprehensions and the Question of Sensations." In *Alterity and Facticity*, edited by Natalie Depraz and Dan Zahavi, 139–62. Dordrecht: Kluwer, 1998.

Schütz, Alfred. *Collected Papers III: Studies in Phenomenological Philosophy.* The Hague: Martinus Nijhoff, 1975.

Schweikard, David P., and Hans Bernhard Schmid. "Collective Intentionality." In *The Stanford Encyclopedia of Philosophy*, Summer 2013 Edition, edited by Edward N. Zalta. https://plato.stanford.edu/archives/sum2013/entries/collective-intentionality/.

Scott, Joan W. "The Evidence of Experience." *Critical Inquiry* 17, no. 4 (1991): 773–97.

Searle, John. "Collective Intentions and Actions." In *Intentions in Communication*, edited by P. Cohen, J. Morgan, and M. E. Pollack, 401–15. Cambridge, MA: MIT Press, 1990.

———. *The Construction of Social Reality.* New York: Free Press, 1995.

———. "Social Ontology: Some Basic Principles." *Anthropological Theory* 6 (2006): 12–29.

———. "Social Ontology and Political Power." In *Socializing Metaphysics: The Nature of Social Reality*, edited by Frederick Schmitt, 195–210. Lanham, MD: Rowman & Littlefield, 2003.

Sellars, Wilfrid. *Essays in Philosophy and Its History*. Dordrecht: Reidel, 1974.

———. "On Reasoning about Values." *American Philosophical Quarterly* 17, no. 2 (1980): 81–101.

———. *Science and Metaphysics*. London: Routledge and Kegan Paul, 1968.

Smith, Barry. "Letter to the Editor." *The Times* (London), May 9, 1992. http://ontology.buffalo.edu/smith/varia/Derrida_Letter.htm.

Smith, Daniel. "Deleuze on Leibniz: Difference, Continuity and the Calculus." *Current Continental Theory and Modern Philosophy*, edited by Stephen H. Daniel, 127–47. Evanston, IL: Northwestern University Press, 2006.

———. *Essays on Deleuze*. Edinburgh: Edinburgh University Press, 2012.

Steinbock, Anthony. *Home and Beyond: Generative Phenomenology after Husserl*. Evanston, IL: Northwestern University Press, 1995.

———. "Husserl's Static and Genetic Phenomenology: Translator's Introduction to Two Essays." *Continental Philosophy Review* 31, no. 2 (1998): 127–34.

Szanto, Thomas, and Dermot Moran. "Introduction: Intersubjectivity and Empathy." *Phenomenology and the Cognitive Sciences* 11, no. 2 (2012): 125–33.

———. *Phenomenology of Sociality: Discovering the We*. New York: Routledge, Taylor & Francis Group, 2016.

Taylor, Charles. *A Secular Age*. Cambridge, MA: Harvard University Press, 2007.

Tuomela, Raimo. "Collective Intentionality and Group Reasons." In *Concepts of Sharedness*, edited by Hans Bernhard Schmid, Katinka Schulte-Ostermann, and Nikos Psarros, 3–20. Frankfurt: Ontos Verlag, 2008.

Tuomela, Raimo, and Kaarlo Miller. "We-Intentions." *Philosophical Studies* 53 (1988): 115–37.

Vallier, Robert. "Institution: The Significance of Merleau-Ponty's 1954 Course at the Collège de France." *Chiasmi International* 7 (2005): 281–302.

Van Cleve, James, and Robert E. Frederick. *The Philosophy of Right and Left: Incongruent Counterparts and the Nature of Space*. Dordrecht: Springer, 1991.

Van Manen, Max. "Phenomenology in its Original Sense." *Qualitative Health Research* 27 (2017): 810–25.

———. *Phenomenology of Practice*. New York: Routledge, 2014.

Van Manen, Max, and Catherine Adams. "Phenomenological Pedagogy." In *Encyclopedia of Educational Theory and Philosophy*, edited by D. C. Phillips, 607–10. Thousand Oaks, CA: Sage Publications, 2014.

Waldenfels, Bernhard. "Experience of the Alien in Husserl's Phenomenology." Translated by Anthony J. Steinbock. *Research in Phenomenology* 20 (1990): 19–33.

Wasser, Audrey. "Deleuze's Expressionism." *Angelaki: Journal of Theoretical Humanities* 12, no. 2 (2007): 49–66.

Weber, Max. *Gesammelte Aufsätze zur Wissenschaftslehre.* Edited by Marianne Weber. Tübingen: J. C. B. Mohr, 1922.

West, Cornel, and David Ritz. *Brother West, Living and Loving out Loud: A Memoir.* New York: Smiley Books, 2009.

Whitmoyer, Keith. "Sens/Sense." In *50 Concepts for a Critical Phenomenology,* edited by Gayle Weiss, Gayle Salamon, and Ann V. Murphy, 303–7. Evanston, IL: Northwestern University Press, 2020.

Yamaguchi, Ichiro. *Passive Synthesis und Intersubjektivität bei Edmund Husserl.* The Hague: Martinus Nijhoff, 1982.

Yancy, George. *Backlash: What Happens When We Talk Honestly about Racism in America.* Lanham, MD: Rowman & Littlefield, 2018.

———. *Black Bodies, White Gazes: The Continuing Significance of Race.* Lanham, MD: Rowman & Littlefield, 2008.

———. "Confiscated Bodies." In *50 Concepts for a Critical Phenomenology,* edited by Gayle Weiss, Gayle Salamon, and Ann V. Murphy, 69–75. Evanston, IL: Northwestern University Press, 2020.

Zahavi, Dan. "Applied Phenomenology: Why It Is Safe to Ignore the Epoché." *Continental Philosophy Review* (2019): 1–15.

———. "Empathy and Other-Directed Intentionality." *Topoi* 33 (2014): 129–42.

———. "Getting It Quite Wrong: Van Manen and Smith on Phenomenology." *Qualitative Health Research* 29, no. 6 (2018): 900–907.

———. *Self-Awareness and Alterity: A Phenomenological Investigation.* Evanston, IL: Northwestern University Press, 1999.

———. "Transcendental Subjectivity and Metaphysics." *Human Studies* 25 (2002): 103–16.

Zavota, Gina. "A Feminist Approach to *The Visible and the Invisible* through Karen Barad's Agential Realism." *Acta Structuralica* Special Issue 2 (2018): 147–69.

Index

actualization 84–86, 89, 91, 98–99, 105, 115–17, 120, 142–43, 146, 139, 158, 162, 171–72, 176, 204n7; self- 115, 117

affectivity 5, 12, 25, 39, 58, 60, 62, 65, 68, 79, 94, 106, 151, 162–63, 165–66, 176–77, 196n30, 220n30

agency 82–83, 203n40

Ahmed, Sara 2, 64–65

Al-Saji, Alia 2, 57, 63, 195nn21,22, 197n43

Alcoff, Linda Martín 6, 16

alien 41–43, 110–11, 152; alienworld 10

alienation 64

anthropocentrism 55

anthropology 65, 129–30

applied phenomenology 14–15, 23, 130–31, 185nn23,24, 209n14

art 55, 76, 78, 125, 155, 203n34, 212n6

asymmetry 4, 13, 21–22, 27, 29, 32–34, 42–45, 53, 69, 104, 123, 152, 162, 177, 183n3, 189n15, 190n17, 199n4, 205n12; mutual 22, 32–33, 42–43, 45, 53, 69, 104, 123, 205n12

audibility 71

autogeneration 77

autopoiesis 11, 23, 78, 82, 85, 94, 99, 104, 114, 129, 145, 147–48, 151–52, 159–62, 172–74, 176, 179

autoproduction 34, 75, 77, 98, 190n18

background 29, 33–34, 57, 73, 85, 90. *See also* field of sensings

Barad, Karen 22, 81–83, 198n1, 203n40

Barbaras, Renaud 32, 72, 189n13

becoming 11, 17, 37, 42, 53, 106, 157, 203n46

Begriffsschrift 71

being 3, 11–12, 14, 22–23, 35, 39–40, 42, 44–46, 56–57, 61–62, 64, 66, 68, 72–75, 81–83, 100–1, 103, 106, 116–17, 121, 126, 138, 144, 157–59, 172–75, 177–78, 189–90n15, 190n16, 199n7, 200n13, 208n7; being-in-the-world 17; being-sense relation 33–35, 43–45, 56, 66, 68, 72–73, 75, 77–78, 85, 122, 172–73, 190nn16,17; of beings 101–2; differentiation of 76–78, 85; human 50–51, 73, 174, 176; as interrogation 34, 74–75; non-being 200n12; as process 45, 68, 72–78, 82, 85, 101, 116, 176; spiritual 50, 55, 66

Black Lives Matter 151

Blackness 107, 110, 149, 150

bodies 49–52 55, 57–58, 60–61, 64, 66, 69, 72, 80, 116, 119, 164, 195n19, 197n36, 198n45, 199n4, 214–15n26; animal 80; Black 64, 106–7; constitution of 10, 18, 178, 213n19; earth as 59–60, 70, 72–74, 196n27; expressive 48, 50–51, 60, 63, 116–17, 119, 195n19; feminine 80, 106; living 48, 50, 55–59, 60, 62–66, 74, 80, 117, 119, 129, 184n10, 193n4, 195nn19,21, 196nn27,35, 197n41, 198n48; men's 198n48; "my" body 50, 58, 62–65, 73–74, 118, 195nn19,22; objective 57–59, 62, 66, 129, 195n19; political 9; sensuous-spiritual 52, 55–56, 57, 63–64, 116; social 9–10, 18, 141, 178, 213n19; subjective 57, 62; tactile 63, 195n21, 197n41, 199n4; women's 198n48. *See also* body-person relation; *Leib*; soul-body relation; subject-body relation

body-person relation 51, 56, 193n3

body-soul relation 50–51

"both siderism" 151–52

Bowden, Sean 36

bracketing 39, 65, 115, 121, 125–26, 199n5, 209n19

Butler, Judith 64–65, 157–58, 201n23

Christianity 4, 214n26

co-delimitation 43, 72, 90, 110

cognition 7, 22–23, 83, 89, 95, 115, 120–22, 138, 204n4

colonialism 42, 147–49, 152, 215n30

community 5, 9–10, 12, 53, 55, 65, 135–60, 165, 213n19, 215n29, 217n2; cultural 17, 105, 154–55, 158, 169, 184n10, 194n14; historical 17, 105; political 1–2, 10, 18, 48, 84, 144, 151, 166, 178, 217n2; sense- 18; spiritual 139–43, 145, 148, 155–56, 158, 164–66, 170, 179, 193n8, 197n38, 217n2

conditions 11–12, 15, 37–38, 57, 62, 69, 70–75, 77–79, 86–91, 98, 101, 107–10, 126, 138, 146–50, 157–58, 165–69, 172, 175, 178–79, 204n5, 214n26; of appearing 166; constitutive 17; economic 81, 83–84; empirical 7, 11–12, 17, 23–24, 86, 88, 99, 104–11, 113, 150, 154, 160, 179; historical 6, 56; material 56, 139; phenomenal 8, 23, 33–35, 44, 57, 61, 65, 71–72, 83, 95, 104, 112–13, 173, 196n32; political 25, 81, 84, 114; of possibility 88–90, 95, 117, 157; practical 6; pre- 60; social 6, 81, 146, 216n4; spiritual 64, 125, 139; transcendental 2, 17, 23–24, 60, 63, 87–90, 92, 96–99, 105, 108–11, 113, 123, 128–89, 150, 160, 204n5

consciousness 6, 14, 24, 29, 33, 48, 58–60, 69, 73–74, 79, 91, 98, 116–17, 121–26, 139, 143, 177, 184n10, 193–94n9, 195n22, 200nn12,18, 209n11, 220n30; time-consciousness 206n22

constitution 2, 4, 6, 9, 11, 13, 21, 41–42, 51, 53, 64, 71, 76, 96, 101–2, 107, 114, 133, 140, 145, 149–51, 153–56, 170, 173–74, 184n16, 216n41; co- 4, 8, 13, 22–24, 42–43, 53, 72, 85; of experience 2, 8, 11, 14, 16, 21, 54, 67, 87, 107; expressivity and 5, 59; meaning- 55, 106; of phenomenal unity 29–31, 33, 36; phenomenological 21, 23; political 10, 18, 23–24, 48, 65, 89, 105, 137, 141, 144–45, 151, 154, 179, 213n19, 214n23, 217–18n10; pre- 55; sense- 67, 83–84, 94, 100, 215n29; social 10, 18, 66, 142, 178, 216n41; and the subject 6, 21, 36, 40, 43–44, 47–49, 56, 64, 66, 82, 110, 136, 140–45, 153, 156, 214n23; of subjectivity 22, 24, 43, 55, 63, 87, 89, 145, 153, 155, 179, 198n51; transcendental 17, 24, 88–89, 108, 178

Continental philosophy 14, 185n25, 205n14

core of experience 10–16, 21, 40, 68, 72, 77, 149, 158–59, 173–74, 176

institution 9–10, 35, 77, 130, 144, 149, 154, 179, 184n16, 190n20, 200n18
intentionality 24, 29–30, 44, 48, 51, 54, 69, 80, 90, 120–21, 125, 129, 131, 136, 138–41, 143, 156, 165, 170, 194n10, 202n33, 212–13n11, 214n20; act- 22, 30, 40; collective 140–41, 156, 212–13n11, 214n20; double 193–94n9, 206n22; meaning-intention 28, 30; operative 207n33, 212–13n11; perceptual intention 30; we-intention 141
interiority 35, 116
internal 9–10, 34, 38, 43, 50, 55, 93, 99, 108, 125, 136, 142, 163, 173–74, 184n16; arrangement 9, 32; force 43, 77; logic 34
interrogation 34–35, 45, 74–75, 82, 109, 192n29
intersectionality 18
intersubjectivity 2, 10, 17, 41, 66, 84, 135, 137, 140–43, 203n46; ontology- 24
intertwining 20, 23, 33, 40, 47, 64, 72–73, 78, 91, 94–95, 116, 119, 160, 166, 169, 172, 208n5; of expression 20, 119; phenomenal 33, 76, 78, 133, 144, 179; of sense and being 33, 44–45, 47, 72, 76, 172
intrasubjectivity 22, 67, 92, 156
intuition 14, 16, 30, 49–51, 54, 60, 66, 68, 91, 95, 98, 107, 120, 124, 138, 193–94n9; clarifying 54, 68, 193–94n9; confirming 54, 193–94n9, 194n10

Jacobs, Hanne 104

Kant, Immanuel 11, 53, 89, 90, 117, 121, 172, 193n6, 204n4, 217n9
knowing-being-doing 3, 12, 23, 40, 44, 68, 78, 83, 116, 126, 144, 159, 172–78
Körper 58–59, 195n19
Kwant, Remy 32

Landes, Donald 5, 32, 190n22, 192n28
language 4, 15, 20, 40, 44, 61, 85, 91, 92–93, 96, 99, 104, 107, 114, 118, 161,

167, 170, 172, 205n11, 215n33, 217n7, 218n11, 219n26; experience and 8, 97–98, 179; expression and 20–21, 36–37, 39–40, 96, 170–71; phenom-enology and 8, 14, 100, 131, 157, 170; philosophy of 5, 30; sense and 67, 71, 170, 208n4, 218n11
langue 85–86, 90, 92, 99–100, 105
langue-parole distinction 85
laws 9, 14, 144, 154, 179; governing 9; political 144–47; social 10
Lebenswelt 35, 52, 56,
Leib 48, 58–59, 62, 64, 195n19, 195n21, 196n35; *Leibkorper* 50, 193n4
Leibniz, Gottfried Wilhelm 117, 158, 188n1, 191n26, 193n5, 204n47, 208n6, 219n21
Levinas, Emmanuel 15, 59, 173, 195n18, 197n38, 208n3, 209n11, 212n5, 213n12
lifeworld 12, 35, 55, 129, 131, 139–40, 148–49, 215n30
linguisticality 71, 96, 99–100, 108, 118–19, 127–28, 165, 167, 175, 200–1n19
linguistics 5, 7, 17, 20, 71, 75, 78, 85, 93, 96–100, 102, 105–8, 110, 118–19, 128, 161–62, 167–78, 200–1n19; linguistic turn 7, 217n7; Saussurean 85, 92–93
little subjectivities 116–17, 127
"live in"–"live through" relationship 21–22, 29, 32–33, 35, 45, 51, 56–57, 69, 78, 92, 152, 199n4
localization (of sense) 58, 69, 117, 142–43, 175, 195n21
logic of predication 25, 94, 99, 161, 165, 167–68, 170–73, 205n14
logic of sensing 25, 161, 165–66, 170–73
logos 8, 128, 187n41

Macey, David 16
male gaze 80
Marion, Jean-Luc 101, 183n3, 219n29
masculinity 110
material 4, 18, 52–53, 56, 66, 77, 80, 83, 110, 125, 157, 194n11; immaterial 59; phenomena 82–83; physico- 52

17, 20, 23–24, 89, 111–12, 158; pre- 5,
118, 161; self- 88
reflexivity 63, 73, 118; self- 106
relata 22, 28, 36–40, 44, 53, 55, 59, 64,
82, 85, 101, 108, 151, 162, 171–72,
187n41
relativism 3, 81, 149, 151
relativization of subject/sense 25, 44, 47,
49, 61, 112, 159, 161, 173–76
religion 4, 12, 146
repetition 42, 91
res publica 10, 24, 144, 214n23
researchers 129–32, 149–50, 198n49;
mediating role of 131
reversibility 35, 59, 69–70, 77, 118, 152,
165
Russell, Bertrand 16, 185n22

Sache 50, 81
Sachen selbst 81, 121
Salomon, Gayle 64–65
scientific disciplines 209; inquiry in 31,
121, 131; knowledge of 90; methodology of 122; theorizing in 132–33, 155
Searle, John 140–41, 211nn1,11, 213n17
seeing 29, 69, 74, 117–20, 159, 163, 164,
172, 175–76, 187n41, 195n22, 200n16
seer 74, 118–19, 159, 172, 176
self 52, 57, 63, 65, 121–22, 132, 134, 138,
153, 157, 161, 173, 176–77, 191n24,
198n49, 199n5, 201n24, 203n46
self-affection 166
self-world relation 121–22, 125
Sellars, Wilfrid 141, 213n17
semantics 4, 82, 85, 90, 93, 99–100, 172
semiotics 4
sense 1, 6–13, 18, 20–28, 30–35, 39–41,
43–64, 66–89, 92–96, 99–101,
104–7, 112–16, 119, 122, 133, 139,
142, 158–59, 161, 167, 170–71, 174,
189nn6,7, 190nn15,16,17,18,
192nn29,31, 193n8, 199n2, 200n19,
201n26, 205n14, 206n19, 217n4,
218nn11,12; emergence 1, 11–12,
33–34, 60, 78; expression and 8, 20,
22, 28, 31–33, 35, 40, 43–45, 49,
71–72, 93–94, 99, 107, 167–72,
188n1, 189n7; making sense 6–8, 23,

41, 54, 71, 73–74, 76–77, 95, 99, 101,
107, 133, 160–63, 167, 177, 184n10,
193n8
sensibility 11, 57, 69, 74, 77–79, 165
sensuous-spiritual 50, 52–53, 56, 64,
67–72, 196n34
sex 64–65
sexism 87, 88, 156
sexual harassment 15, 217n10; objectification 80; violence 16; orientation 106
sexuality 23, 87, 111, 149–50, 217–18n10
sight 71, 118
sign(s) 4–5, 28
Sinngebung 8, 21, 48, 213n12
social context 7, 10, 70, 84, 168–69, 179
social ethics 17, 106, 155–56
social mores 9–10, 168–89
social relations 9–10, 141–42, 157, 169
social structures 17–18, 105–6, 110, 153,
156–57
sociality 71, 84, 142–43, 209n13
sociology 65, 129, 149
solitary mental life 32, 44, 53
sophistry 14, 171, 204n5
soul 50–51, 53, 55–56, 61
soul-body relation 56
spatializing 76, 78
speech 48–49, 118, 172–73; free 146
spiritual meaning 54–56, 79, 140, 155,
165
spiritual products 55, 79, 149, 155, 165,
212n6
spiritualism 49–50
static phenomenology 18, 84
Steinbock, Anthony 17, 27–28, 112, 152,
192nn30,31, 203n46
Stiftung 24, 34–35, 44–45, 75–78,
80–83, 87, 90, 92, 95, 99–115, 126,
129–33, 142, 144, 151, 160, 164, 167,
171–72, 176, 184n16, 188n1, 190n20,
192nn29,31, 193n8, 200nn14,19,
201n19, 209n16, 210n25, 214n24,
215nn29,33, 217nn2,7
style 106, 140, 142, 145, 154–57, 170
subject 1–2, 6–8, 10–13, 16–17, 20–25,
27–37, 40, 45, 47–52, 54–70, 74–80,
82–89, 95–98, 100, 105–6, 108, 110,
112–22, 124–27, 130, 132–33,

subject (*continued*)
135–77, 179, 192n31, 195nn21,22,
196n34, 197n39, 198n50, 199nn5,6,
200n19, 202n33, 212n5, 213n17,
214nn20,23,24, 215n33, 216n1,
217n2, 219n28; empirical 10, 105;
experiencing 105; expression and
32–33, 35–36, 40–45, 48, 66, 117,
119, 144, 158, 170, 188n1, 191n26;
and object 8, 13, 24, 44, 54, 58–64,
74, 76, 78–80, 82, 95–96, 119,
121–22, 124, 126, 136–37, 150, 161,
174–77, 195nn21,22, 197n39, 199n5,
199n6, 202n33, 219n28
subject-body relation 49, 61
subjective conceptions 7, 28, 44, 68–69,
79, 176
subjectivity 1, 2–7, 9–10, 16–17, 21–24,
28, 40–44, 48–49, 55, 63–65, 83–84,
87, 89, 91, 96, 100–3, 112, 114–49,
151 153–70, 173–79, 189n9, 195n21,
199n6, 200n18, 203n42, 204n9,
209n12, 213nn12,17, 214nn20,26,
216n1, 220n30; political 10, 17, 63,
65, 83–84, 135, 140, 142–49, 158,
160, 178; transcendental 100–3, 131,
138, 142, 160, 199n6, 209n12
substantialism 37, 40, 45, 72–73, 82, 124,
142–43, 162, 176–77
suprasubjective 62–63, 87, 135–36, 139

tactility 63, 71, 75, 78, 116–18, 120, 123,
127, 159, 164–65, 173, 195n21,
197n41, 216n1, 219n24. *See also* touch
Taylor, Charles 12
techne 83, 202n29
teleology 53
telos 77, 201n26
temporality 38, 60, 72, 76–78, 142,
193n9, 202n33, 203n46; spatio- 41,
91
thematization 55, 63, 123
things themselves, the 16, 24, 81, 98, 101,
105, 120, 122, 126, 133, 161, 173
third-person perspective 62–63, 197n39
threefold notion of expressivity 36–39,
45

thrownness 12
touch 21, 57, 60–61, 69–71, 116–18,
122, 159, 163–65, 195n19; co- 57;
primal 57
touched-touching relation 5, 57–59,
69–70, 74, 116, 118, 159, 165, 172,
195nn19,22, 197n43, 199nn4,5
tradition 14–15, 18, 35, 41, 75, 77, 92,
111–12, 171, 184n16, 190n20;
Anglo-American 14; of Christianity 4;
of phenomenology 5–6, 16–18, 47,
102–3, 114, 130–31, 161, 171,
208n43; of philosophy 102–3, 161;
religious 4
transcendental 1–2, 9, 10–12, 15–17,
21, 23–25, 60, 63, 84–91, 94–115,
128–34, 136–46, 148, 153–55,
157–60, 166, 171–72, 178–79,
186, 193n8, 199n6, 201n22,
204nn3,4,5, 205nn10,12,15,16,
208n43, 209n12, 213n19, 214n26,
215n29, 216n45, 217n6, 219n26;
guides 8, 11; historicity 84; intersubjectivity 24; materiality 84; "pure"
102–4, 106; reduction 211n34;
sociality 84; we 141–43, 148–49, 151,
158
transcendental-empirical relation 3,
10–14, 16–17, 21, 23–24, 84–92,
94–100, 102–13, 123, 126–28, 131,
133, 136, 139, 142, 144–51, 154–55,
158–61, 166, 175, 179, 192n31,
200n17, 204nn8,9, 207n35, 208n43,
215n29, 216n41, 217n2
transcendental phenomenology 2–3,
13–15, 17, 18, 24, 89, 98–101, 106,
108, 110–12, 131, 133, 161,
185nn22,24, 188n1
transcendentality 46, 88–89
transcendentalizing 20

ultratranscendental 20, 76, 99–100, 103,
128, 193n8, 201n21
unfolding 11, 17, 41–43, 68, 73, 75–78,
82, 85–86, 89, 91, 93, 101, 123,
144–45, 147–48, 151–53, 156, 159,
161, 163, 169, 172, 174, 178–79,

200n19, 209n12; auto- 98; self- 11, 18,
43, 45, 84–85, 129, 162–63; of
tradition 102–3, 115
unity of identity 13, 43, 162
unity of judgement 28
unity of substance 29, 123
universal human rights 146–48, 214n26,
215n27
universality 16–17, 34, 64, 126, 139,
147–48, 214n26

Van Manen, Max 130, 210n29
Verflechtung 20, 47, 91, 95, 166. *See also*
intertwining
violence 16, 152, 157
visibility 49, 70, 71, 75, 78, 116–20,
122–23, 125, 127, 138–39, 163–65,
173, 175, 179, 208nn4,5,7, 209n12,
216n1, 219n24
vision 60, 70, 118, 165, 172, 214–15n26

West, Cornel 64–65
whiteness 64, 106–7, 110, 214n26,
216n40; white gaze 64
women 16, 81, 149, 153, 198n48. *See also*
bodies
writing 48, 85, 92, 155, 205n11; arche-
219n26; transcendental 108

Yancy, George 2, 64–65, 106–7

Zahavi, Dan 131, 185n24, 186n28,
208n1, 210nn20,26,30, 211n34
Zavota, Gina 84

Neal DeRoo is Professor of Philosophy and Canada Research Chair in Phenomenology and Philosophy of Religion, at the King's University, Edmonton. He is the author of *Futurity in Phenomenology: Promise and Method in Husserl, Levinas, and Derrida*.

Perspectives in Continental Philosophy

John D. Caputo, series editor

Recent titles:

William S. Allen, *Aesthetics of Negativity: Blanchot, Adorno, and Autonomy*.

Jeremy Biles and Kent L. Brintnall, eds., *Georges Bataille and the Study of Religion*.

Tarek R. Dika and W. Chris Hackett, *Quiet Powers of the Possible: Interviews in Contemporary French Phenomenology*. Foreword by Richard Kearney.

Richard Kearney and Brian Treanor, eds., *Carnal Hermeneutics*.

A complete list of titles is available at www.fordhampress.com.

www.ingramcontent.com/pod-product-compliance
Lightning Source LLC
LaVergne TN
LVHW041705180225
804024LV00007B/182

* 9 7 8 1 5 3 1 5 0 0 0 5 4 *